The Secret of the Mantras

by Richard Blakely

This is for Nanou, and Benjamin, and Isabel, and Laurence.

On the long and winding road to getting this book published, many people have helped in many ways, usually by reading parts if not all of the manuscript, and getting back to me with comments. To all these people, my deepest thanks. To anyone I might have neglected to mention, my deepest apologies.

Marie-Christine Aquarone, Tina Blakely, Becky Chace, Candice Dahlstet, the Davies: Ari, Ben, Jaffa, and David, Adrienne Farb, Benjamin Felon, Lindsay French, Terry Gustafson, Joe Harley, Mika Keller, Chrissa Laporte, Nicholas Long, Larry Moll, Roberta Murtagh, Christine Puech, Carmel Rochet, Victoria Strauss, Pauline de Tholozany, Shari Underwood, Joy Veaudry, Annie Wiart, Maryse Wiart, Curtis Zimmermann.

With special thanks to Rosalyn Bonas.

Introduction

Everybody knows how memories become distorted over time, especially memories of memorable events. I'm sure the surviving members of my immediate family who underwent the events I describe in the early chapters of this book will not remember them as I do. I also realize some of them may be shocked or even offended by what my memory has chosen to remember, and for that I am sorry.

For events that took place after I left home to go to college, I had my trusty journals to fall back on, and did so massively, following the method I describe in Chapter 9.

In describing the very few events in this book where I was not an active participant or a wide-eyed witness, I have had recourse to accounts in print or on the web that I found to be trustworthy. It's always interesting for me to pick up another book about the Beatles or other notables who showed up at the Maharishi's ashram during that spring of '68 and read about the astonishing things that didn't happen there. Not that astonishing things didn't happen there. They just don't get talked about in most of those books.

But this is not another book about the Beatles. It's a personal story about my coming of age in the 'sixties. I started writing it in the mid-nineteen-seventies, when events were still fresh in my mind, and kept going back to it during sabbaticals and leaves of absence and in between jobs. I finished writing the first draft in February 2008, three days after the death of the Maharishi.

Except for those People whose identities it would be impossible to disguise, I have changed the names of almost everyone I mention in this book, out of respect for their privacy (and a healthy fear of litigation).

Table of Contents

Forward!

t all started with that MG. In a way that car took me to Paris, and then to India, back to Paris again, up to Sweden, back to California, and finally dropped me off here in New England, where I still dream about it forty years later.

It was a 1952 TD, the best looking of all the MGs. It had a shiny new coat of British racing green, black leather upholstery, and a mahogany dashboard. The hand-carved steering wheel was covered in soft brown leather so it wouldn't slip out of your grasp while taking sharp turns. The hood lifted open on each side, like two little wings. Beneath those wings, the engine gleamed. The conical chrome headlights were nestled between the dark green rise of the fenders and the vertical hood. While driving that car down the road that led to Half Moon Bay, I would lean out into the wind and watch the trees and sky and clouds swirl past in the polished chrome, and it felt like I was flying.

I first laid eyes on the car in Menlo Park when it pulled out in front of me on the Embarcadero. The top was up and taped to the inside of the plastic back window was a cardboard sign that said it was for sale. It turned into a gas station and I pulled in behind it. The driver was a young Chicano. I asked him how much he wanted for his car. He said he was asking $800. I said I couldn't afford more than five but I couldn't afford that. My checking account was almost below zero again and I hadn't yet bought any of the books for winter quarter.

The guy jotted down my number on a scrap of paper and said he might call, but I doubted he would. The car was easily worth what he was asking, and he could probably get a thousand, if he could wait.

Apparently he couldn't, because he called that night. In the gas station, I had noticed a young blonde sitting in the passenger seat. The whole time we were talking she never looked up. It occurred to me later they needed the money for an abortion. Those days the going rate down in Tijuana was $800.

He asked if I was still okay with $500 and if I could have the money ready by noon the next day and I said sure, no problem. I hung up wondering where I was going to get it.

It was my brother Tom who came through in the end. He was good that way. He wired the money up from LA the next morning, no questions asked. I figured I would pay him back as soon as I sold my '55 Chevy. It burned almost as much oil as gas, but it was a good looking car and I thought I could get three hundred for it as long as the buyer didn't look under the hood. The rest I could borrow from the Stanford Credit Union. As a TA I was considered a full-time employee, eligible for short-term loans.

The next day I had a cashier's check ready when the guy showed up with the MG. He arrived right at noon—his girlfriend following in another car—and pulled to a stop in front of the apartment I was renting in Palo Alto. The top was down on the car and he had given it one last polish. It looked brand new, sparkling in sunlight that was brighter still because of a storm that had blown through the night before, sweeping away the smog that tended to creep up from San Jose. I handed the guy the check and he gave me the keys.

"Take care of her, man. She's a bitchin' little car."

At certain moments in my life, for no apparent reason, I've been taken over by a feeling that I've come to associate with my earliest experience of pleasure outside the womb, a feeling that goes back to a time I can no longer consciously remember—probably back to when I was lying in a crib and watching the dust motes floating in the light around me, or being held in my mother's arms, warm and full and secure—as content as every newborn in this world deserves to be. At those moments the boundaries between myself and the world around me blur and I get the fleeting sensation, sometimes for only a few seconds, sometimes longer, that I am the *That* of the mystical "That thou art." Because it transcends the world we know, defining this sensation is impossible, but for me it has always been accompanied by a feeling of expansion, floating, and fullness. The feeling is in some way similar to very good sex, but less focused, more cosmic, not a physical sensation so much as an awareness—an "intimation of immortality." It seems to me that this is what Joyce is talking about when he describes Stephen Dedalus "almosting the something infinite" behind everything, or Proust, when trying to put into words the feeling that overwhelms Marcel when he takes into his mouth the spoonful of the madeleine dissolved in tea.

Climbing in behind the wheel of that MG, turning the key in the ignition, listening to the click-click-click of the electric fuel pump as it fed gas into the carburetor, pushing the little silver button that started the engine, that same feeling would often come over me, an impression that I was suddenly being lifted up, expanding, drawn towards something that was tantalizingly close, something that was profoundly important to me—that <u>was</u> me—familiar yet evanescent. At the same time I felt this deep, aching desire to know this something better, to one day merge with it for good.

The TDs were the last of the MGs with a chassis made of solid oak, which must have been why, while driving mine on the narrow roads above Palo Alto, I felt so much a part of the organic world around me. It had no gas gauge, but a dipstick that fit snugly along the top of the tank, behind the seat. The one-bladed windshield wiper worked sometimes, but usually not when it rained. The only flaw in the engine was a slow leak in the brake line. One afternoon in pouring rain I came down from Skyline Drive into San Francisco to discover that I had run out of both gas and brake fluid. I couldn't stop, I couldn't go, and I could hardly see. Like Moses crossing the Red Sea, I sailed through a red light on 19th Street during a miraculous break in traffic and pulled into a Chevron station a few blocks farther on, where the car came to a stop in front of a gas pump.

That's the way it was with that car. While driving it, I was lucky, and some of that luck has stayed with me all along, around all the bends and over all the ups and downs.

※ ※ ※

Four months after I bought that car, towards the end of spring quarter, I received the dreaded letter from the President, forwarded from my draft board in North Hollywood. The letter requested the pleasure of my company two weeks later at the U.S. Army Induction Center in Oakland.

As a student, I'd thought I was safe from the draft, but lately Johnson and McNamara had been calling for more troops to put an end to the war once and for all, and even middle-class white kids with student deferments like me were being called up.

I showed up for my physical with a letter from a doctor at UCSB, where I had been an undergraduate. The letter said I had "bronchial congenital asthma." It wasn't exactly a lie, but it wasn't the whole truth either. I had suffered a bit from asthma as a child, but it had gone away with puberty.

I was afraid the letter wouldn't work. Those days people who tried to dodge the draft were going straight to jail. But the doctor at UCSB had assured me it would do the trick and he was right. After the physical, when the army doctor handed it back, he said my new classification was going to be 1-Y.

"Does that mean I don't have to go to Vietnam?" I asked.

"Only after all the women and children," he replied.

I walked out of the Induction Center into a glorious morning. A breeze coming up off the Bay brought the scent of the open sea beyond the Golden Gate. Drifting out of a nearby bar came the voice of Louis Armstrong. "I see trees of green, red roses too…"

There was no more reason for me to stay in graduate school. A year of training for what the chair of my department liked to call "the business of scholarship" had taught me that getting a PhD in French had nothing to do with my love of literature and would probably kill it. And if this was what it was like as a graduate student, what would it be like when I was a tenured professor somewhere, browbeating graduate students of my own? Quoting my freshman English teacher, quoting Thoreau, "I did not wish to live what was not life."

So I decided to drop out and go to Paris. Ever since I'd spent some time there during my junior year abroad, I'd been wanting to go back for a longer stay. And besides, isn't Paris the place Americans dream of going when they're free?

The next day I put an ad in the paper to sell the MG. A week later it sold for $1,000, part of which I used to buy a one-way ticket to Paris.

But I never forgot how driving that car had helped me re-establish contact with the cosmos, and for years afterward it continued to remind me of where I was really headed, where I really wanted to go.

CHAPTER 1

Mantras by the millions

※ ※ ※

Instead of turning people on to meditation, the Maharishi's lecture in Paris in December of 1967 almost turned into a riot. It was held at the Paris Hilton, for one thing, a brand new glass and metal building that stood out like a sore American thumb right next to the Eiffel Tower, almost looking up its skirt. For another, when people arrived they discovered they had to pay admission, something that the ads had failed to mention. As if that were not enough, once everyone was seated inside the imitation Versailles ballroom that had been converted to a lecture hall, they had to wait almost an hour for the Maharishi to arrive. When he finally did appear at the back of the hall, draped in flowers and bathed in bright white light so that the camera crews could film his progress up the central aisle, he looked more like a superstar than a guru. Of course there was the talk of all the celebrities he had recently converted—including the Beatles, if such a thing could be believed—so maybe that was the reason for all the glitz and glare. But still.

What really set people off that night though was what the Maharishi said, or didn't say, about this "great new movement that is sweeping the world." Even for someone like myself, who had not been brought up in the rigorous French tradition, it was clear that the Maharishi's forty-minute introductory lecture was purposefully vague, intended more to spark curiosity about his new technique of meditation rather than answer anybody's questions about it. And the Q&A that followed was even worse. "But what exactly is a mantra?" someone would stand up to ask, once more, waiting for the question to be repeated in English by the translator who was sitting on the Maharishi's right, but slightly lower, on a folding chair.

Once more, using a flower that by now had lost most of its petals, the Maharishi would point to a poster set up on an easel to his left. The poster showed a vertical row of circles that got bigger and bigger as they rose, from a straight line at the bottom to a wavy line at the top. According to the Maharishi, this diagram depicted the normal process of thought, or "t'ot." Just like a bubble rising from the bottom of the sea, gradually expanding as it rose, a thought too began deep in the unconscious mind, then gradually, as it rose, got bigger and bigger, more and more "gross," until it finally burst on the surface of the conscious mind. During Transcendental Meditation one used this same, natural process, but in reverse, going from the surface level of everyday life in the relative world, with its constant ups and downs, down to the "wery source of t'ot," where one experienced an infusion of the absolute, gaining a brief foretaste of total, absolute bliss. Trying to describe what this was like to someone who had never experienced it before was like trying to describe the taste of an orange to an Eskimo who had never seen one. But soon, as one continued to meditate morning and evening for just twenty-thirty minutes, this daily infusion of the absolute would begin to permeate every level of one's life, until one attained permanent Cosmic Consciousness, true freedom and enlightenment, the goal of all religions, all civilizations everywhere throughout history. Today it was possible to achieve this ultimate goal not after a lifetime of sacrifice and denial, but now, within minutes, as soon as one closed the eyes and started using one's own special mantra according to the very simple instructions that could be imparted in a short time by a specially trained teacher of Tran-scen-den-tal Med-i-ta-tion!

The Maharishi had discarded his old flower and taken a new one. There were flowers everywhere. I hadn't seen so many flowers since my father's funeral. They lay in piles at the Maharishi's feet, hung in garlands around his neck, stood in vases all around the stage. As he pronounced the last two words of this long aside, he beat the flower gently, syllable-by-syllable, into the palm of his left hand. Everything he'd said that night came back to these two words, which he must have repeated a hundred times. When the translator had finished, the man who'd asked the question was still standing. The audience was growing restless. There were a few very audible sighs. The man said he understood the process, the Maharishi had already explained it many times, but could he perhaps give an example of a mantra, *"un exemple précis."*

The Maharishi thought for a moment and wobbled his head back and forth. But before he opened his mouth to answer someone said, in English, "How many are there?"

The question came from a hippie, sitting down in front. He had come in very late, even later than the Maharishi, and plopped down on the floor in front of him. The Maharishi looked down at him now and said, "Many."

"How many?" the hippie asked.

"Millions!" came the answer.

"Millions?"

The Maharishi nodded and looked back at the audience. "Mantras are names for God," he said quietly, "and God is everywhere." The translator repeated this in French. The man who was still standing shrugged and sat back down. The Maharishi continued. "The t'ing is, . . The t'ing is, . . ." He had a way of repeating certain words or phrases several times while plopping the fingertips of his right hand into the knuckles of his left, which he held in a loose fist, which invariably held a flower. It looked like he was searching for the right words, but maybe it was just a rhetorical trick the Maharishi used until he had recaptured the attention of his audience. "The t'ing is . . ." ploppety-plop. "The t'ing is . . ." ploppety-plop.

When the audience had quieted down again, the Maharishi went on to say that while the number of mantras was actually limitless—there are as many mantras as stars in the sky—it was very important that each person used a mantra that was specifically suited to his own personality. That was because during meditation, when one reached the subtle levels, the mantra became "wery, wery powerful." It was like an atom which, when split, could do untold damage, or untold good. Which was why it was so important that everybody's mantra be chosen specifically to match that person's individuality. For similar reasons, mantras should never be uttered aloud. Once learned, a person's mantra should always be kept private. Otherwise, the Mahahishi said, it would not be as "effectiu."

Mention of the atom brought the discussion around to the subject of world peace. Another man stood up and said that with the war raging in Vietnam and threatening every day to spill over into China, wasn't the Maharishi's insistence on meditation a little irrelevant? Once the question had been translated into English, the Maharishi wobbled his head back and forth, then announced that if only one percent of the world's population learned Trans-cen-den-tal Med-i-ta-tion, there would be peace throughout the world for a thousand years. The statement brought outcries of protest from several people in the audience. One woman, without waiting to be recognized, said that one percent of the population of the world was approximately fifty million people. How could the Maharishi seriously think he could ever reach so many people? Another woman, standing up and shouting to make her question heard, asked the Maharishi what his movement intended to do about the problem of world hunger. Wasn't it more important first to stamp out starvation, before trying to teach people how to meditate? Her question drew applause and cheers.

"What she wants to know?" The Maharishi's question to the translator was picked up by the mike in front of him. After the translator had repeated the woman's question in English the Maharishi smiled at the crowd, waited until it quieted down again, and said, "The hungry man who learns to meditate will soon become a happy hungry man."

It was at this point that things began to get seriously out of hand. Several people got up at once and started shouting. A chant, together with stamping feet and clapping hands, spread rapidly through the audience. "CHAR-LA-TAN! CHAR-LA-TAN! CHAR-LA-TAN!" By now most of the audience was on their feet. Some people were demanding their money back. Others were heading noisily for the door. The first two rows had been reserved for the Maharishi's followers, all of whom now were looking sheepishly around them, or down at the floor. As for the Maharishi, he didn't seem to notice, or perhaps to care. He sat there with his legs tucked up beneath him on the little sofa in the middle of the stage, picking the petals off another flower. Occasionally he would glance at the people still sitting in the two front rows and give a little laugh, or shrug, or sigh. He seemed apologetic, but it was as if he were apologizing not for what he had said, but for the way the people in the audience had reacted. "Forgive them, for they know not what they do."

Clearly, he did not understand what all the fuss was about.

"So whaddya say?" David said, as we made our way back to the end of the hall, stepping around and over chairs that had been pushed aside, or even toppled over. "You going to take the plunge into the cosmic mud?" It was David who had brought me there. He'd seen the ad in the *Herald Tribune* a couple of days before and suggested we check it out.

David was another dropout from the PhD program in French at Stanford, where we'd met. He too had been able to avoid the draft because of a letter from a doctor. His doctor was a psychiatrist friend of the family David called Sheldon Shrink. Sheldon's letter said David was a potentially schizophrenic manic depressive with severe hallucinatory tendencies. The letter was even more effective than mine, earning David an immediate 4-F. He didn't even have to show up for a physical.

David and I both arrived in Paris in June, 1966. We spent the whole summer and most of the fall exulting in our freedom. It was so good to be in country that was not being torn apart by war. It was so good not having to study and prepare for courses that we hated. It was so good being in Paris.

But then the weather took a turn for the worse, the way it always does in Paris in October—ushering in six months of cold and wet and gray they call *grisaille*—and both David and I started having problems with our health. For me it was asthma attacks, and bad ones. They would wake me up in the middle of the night and keep me sitting up in bed for hours, hunched over, fighting for air until dawn.

For David it was even worse. Some nights he didn't get any sleep at all, kept awake by the demons that came to hover over his bed as soon as he turned out the light. He was convinced they were astral creatures that were trying to tell him secrets about the cosmos. Which was how he'd heard about the Maharishi. In addition to starting analysis, to try to find out what was going on in his head, David had been doing a lot of reading, inspired by Jung, on all kinds of non-traditional therapies and Oriental mystical traditions.

David was not impressed with the Maharishi, however. On our way back out of the lecture hall he said he didn't think Transcendental Meditation was his "kind of racket." I said I was tempted to give it a try, just out of curiosity. True, nothing the Maharishi had said had been very informative, but I had to hand it to him for the way he sat there, imperturbably—maybe even, who knows? blissfully—throughout all those insults. I figured anyone who could just keep plucking petals off a flower while three hundred people, in unison, called him a liar, had to be some kind of wise man.

There was no way I was going to pay the fee though. One of the things that had set people off during the lecture was when the Maharishi had announced that anyone who wanted to learn his brand of meditation would have to make a contribution to his movement equivalent to one week's salary. He explained it as an adaptation of an Indian tradition, but as a middle-aged woman in the audience pointed out, compared to what one earned in India, one week's salary in the West was enormous.

Maybe for her it was.

When I first got to Paris I figured the money left over from selling the MG would last me three or four months at least. But by the end of July it was nearly gone and I realized if I was going to stay there I had to find a job. At the American embassy I got a short list of U.S. companies with branches in Paris. The next morning I put on my one and only suit and went out knocking on doors. By the end of the day I'd found a job at the Paris office of the New York Times.

In those days the New York Times was publishing its own international edition, in competition with the Paris Herald Tribune, and as luck would have it on the day I knocked on their door they happened to be looking for someone to fill a key position on their administrative staff. The title which I would assume, assuming I showed up for work the following Monday, was *Sous-chef des services intérieurs*, a.k.a. Assistant Office Boy. Not exactly what I had in mind, but I decided to take the job anyway, figuring it was a matter of months before something opened up at the associate editor level. In the meantime it would pay me more than any job I'd had before—almost 2,000 francs a month, about $400. In addition I would get a *prime de langue* of 300 francs tacked on to every paycheck, just because I happened to speak English.

To celebrate, and to fit in with all the other people I saw going to work every morning, I went out and bought myself a pair of shiny black Italian shoes with pointed toes. Within a few weeks after arriving in Paris I had realized that Hush Puppies pegged you immediately as an American. You'd be sitting across from a cute girl on the metro, her eyes would meet yours for a second or two, maybe longer, her gaze would fall to your shoes, the slightest smile would form on her lips, and then she'd go back to the book in her lap.

After a few months at the Times it began to dawn on me that a boring eight-to-five job in Paris was just as boring as an eight-to-five job anywhere, except that in Paris it was nine-to-six. By then I had been promoted to *Sous-chef des archives* and had a full-time secretary named Pauline who sat at her desk knitting baby clothes while I sat at mine reading all the news that was fit to print plus everything else that fit including all the ads and classifieds. Pauline was not married and didn't have any babies and whenever I asked her why she was knitting baby clothes she would give a little shrug and a make a little mou and and say, "*Oh monsieur Richard!*"

One day while reading the classifieds I came across an ad for "experienced teachers of English." As a T.A. at Stanford I'd gained a little experience teaching French so I called and made an appointment for an interview. The founder and president of the Institute for the Study of the English Language, *Société Anonyme*, was an affable Bostonian named Jack Donahue who said I could start working for him the following Monday. That was Thursday. On Friday I went to see my boss and told him an urgent problem had come up at home.

My boss, Monsieur Legrand, was a big man from Brittany with an MBA from Harvard and an uncanny ability to start swearing in French and switch to English without missing a beat. His fluency and range of obscenities in both languages were phenomenal. The fifty or sixty people who worked beneath Legrand at the Times either feared him or loathed him or both. I did neither, since I hadn't been there long enough. Also, Legrand seemed to have taken a kind of paternal interest in me, calling me "*mon petit Richard,*" whenever he called me into his office for a briefing, which usually took place every day and consisted of him telling me, between puffs on his cigar, that he had promoted me to the lofty position of *Sous-chef des archives* because he wanted me to keep the piles of old papers that were kept there "neat 'n tidy," puff puff, "neat 'n tidy."

Lately Legrand had been talking about getting me another full-time secretary and hinted that it was to be a special perk as part of my status of being his protégé. One day he took me out for an extended business lunch and taught me how to eat oysters. Another day he said he was going to invite me out to his farm in Brittany and kill a pig. There were no ulterior, sexual motives behind all this, I was sure. After all, another person he took out to lunch, and much more often than me, was Betty, his cute bilingual secretary, and whenever he left for lunch with Betty it was common knowledge they wouldn't be back for three or four hours, taking time out for a nap at a nearby hotel.

Rather, Legrand's interest in me, I gradually realized, was simply about power. For some reason he must have gotten it into his head that I was an up-and-coming member of the Paris edition of the *New York Times*, who some day might have a little power of his own, and when that happened he wanted me on his side and under his thumb.

Legrand might have been calculating and autocratic and vulgar but he was no fool. When I came into his office that Friday morning I had been rehearsing an elaborate story involving my least favorite brother Fred, which would require my flying back to California as soon as possible, like that afternoon. Before I'd delivered the first three lines, Legrand tilted his head to one side, squinted through the cigar smoke, and said, "Suicide?" He then took me further aback by leaning back in his chair, looking me straight in the eye and saying he didn't understand why I wanted to quit, but he wasn't going to stop me. He would however prevent me from ever getting another job at the Times or any other place in Paris where he had any influence, letting me know his influence was far reaching.

It all reminded me a little too clearly of what had happened when I told the chair of my department at Stanford that I'd decided to drop out of grad school. The decision had come as a little epiphany. I'd been on my way towards the credit union to pay another installment on my loan. It was the day after I had made the trip to Oakland and learned that I no longer had to remain a student to stay out of Vietnam. I was walking through an overgrown empty lot bordering a construction site where they were putting up another dorm. From off in the distance I heard the whine of a circular saw, followed within seconds by the shrill call of a meadowlark. And then it hit me. What was I doing there? I could sell the MG and go to Paris.

Instead of proceeding on to the credit union I walked straight to the Department of French and Italian. The secretary was a middle-aged emigrée from Switzerland who liked me. She said the chairman was in and could see me right away.

Unlike Jehane Legrand, Gaston Giron was dapper and suave. In fact the only thing the two men had in common was that both their desks were neat 'n tidy. Professor Giron had chosen himself as my thesis director. He had also chosen the topic of my thesis: The Influence of Cicero's Orations on Montaigne. He probably thought I'd come to see him with a bright idea for the first chapter. When instead I told him I wanted to drop out, the expression on his face, normally so handsome and composed, became a perfect illustration of the French word *déconfit*. His eyes, nose, mouth, ears… all of a sudden none of it fit together.

Recovering himself immediately, he picked up one of the five sharpened pencils on his otherwise empty desk, held the pencil horizontally between the index finger of each hand, and asked me if I was quite sure that's what

I wanted to do. I squirmed in my chair and told him yes. Giron shifted the pencil to his right hand, pointed it at me as if it were a pistol, and said that he'd do everything in his power to see that I'd never get back into Stanford, should I want someday to do so, nor into any other graduate program where his reputation as a scholar was known.

Jack Donahue was nothing like Jehanne Legrand, and even less like Gaston Giron, and working for the ISEL was nothing like working for the NYT. In ways it was a lot better; in other ways worse. Better because it was not an office job and I actually enjoyed teaching; worse because it paid a lot less, whenever it did pay. After getting out of the Navy, Jack Donahue decided to stay in France, where he'd been stationed, because it was a country where you could drink a whole bottle of Beaujolais over lunch, he said, and nobody would even notice. Although Donahue was a friendly guy with a lot of good stories to tell, his language school was a shoestring operation with a chronic problem of cash flow, meaning that the cash often didn't flow as far as the teachers. As a result, the night of the lecture at the Hilton I had less than fifty francs in my checking account and part of my next week's pay, if and when I got it, was going to pay back David what he'd loaned me so I could pay last month's rent.

Out in the lobby they had set up several tables where people could sign up for an appointment to learn meditation. They had obviously been expecting a larger crowd than the handful who now stood around in front of the tables. I went up to an empty one where a lone woman sat on the other side and told her about my financial troubles. "Just bring what you can afford," she said in English, with an English accent. Then she asked me when I had a free half-hour in the next three days.

That was Saturday night, December sixteenth. I made an appointment for the following Monday, the eighteenth, at 3:00 in the afternoon. Before I left, the woman gave me a slip of paper with the time and place of my appointment. I saw that it would take place not at the Hilton but at the Hotel Continental on the Place de la Concorde. I also noticed that in addition to my contribution, I was supposed to bring along "an offering of fruit and flowers, and a new, unused white handkerchief."

CHAPTER 2

Joyful morning

※ ※ ※

From the Hilton it was a short walk to the metro station at La Motte Piquet-Grenelle, and from there it was a straight short ride back to the apartment in the 16th *arrondissement* where I was renting a room. For David who lived on the Ile Saint Louis it was the same line but in the opposite direction. We left the Hilton together, walking down the Avenue de Suffren. It was a cold, raw night, threatening more rain or maybe wet snow, so we hunkered down into the wind and pulled our coats tighter around us. David came from a little town in Pennsylvania so he was used to the weather and had come equipped for it, with a heavy, hooded duffel coat. Born and raised in LA, I was not used to winters in Paris, or anywhere, and still had not bought anything to replace my lightweight, knee-length raincoat that was beginning to look a little ragged. I made up for it with two sweaters underneath and a long chocolate-colored scarf that dragged on the ground if I didn't loop it at least once around my neck. That night I'd looped it three times, which is why I didn't hear David's question.

"What do you make of the offering?" he said again.

"You mean the fruit and flowers? Yeah, weird." There had been no mention about any kind of ceremony, either during the lecture or afterwards, when I signed up for an appointment. "Maybe it's a gift for the Maharishi. But why a handkerchief? And a brand new one at that."

"Maybe to blow his nose."

We both laughed. The Maharishi did have a big nose.

"Yeah," I said, "and since he's an enlightened yogi he can only use brand new white ones."

"For all the cosmic conscious-snot."

It was good to see David in a cheerful mood. When we'd met at Stanford he was one of the most spontaneously funny people I'd ever known. Whenever we first-year grad students would get together to study for a seminar or cram for an exam we'd end up laughing instead, for hours, at David's nonstop word play and witty, off-the-cuff remarks. But since coming to Paris that playful sense of humor had been gradually eclipsed by whatever was going on in his head. It was as if David's sensitivity to the absurdity of life around him was no longer a reason for laughter, but a source of anguish. One minute he'd be lighthearted and jocular, his old self, and the next he'd become depressed and somber and it was no use trying to draw him out.

As we passed a café on the corner, turning left onto the Avenue de la Motte Piquet, I asked him if he wanted to go in and warm up over a cold beer, but he said he was anxious to get home. His demons had kept him awake most of the night before, he said, and he was hoping to get some sleep tonight.

Lately David had taken to drawing pictures of the strange creatures that he claimed came to visit him in the night, hovering over his bed. The pictures looked like crude Tibetan mandalas, drawn by a child with bright fluorescent markers. David drew them on big sheets of blank paper he would tear out of pads that he bought by the dozens. He had been doing these drawings only for a few months now but already there must have been hundreds of them. They lay scattered over the floor of his small apartment, or taped to the walls and the ceiling.

We continued down the street, now in the lee of the cold wind. David asked me again if I was really going to learn to meditate. He seemed mildly curious, maybe a little jealous. Of the two of us I had always been the more adventurous, the more willing to try something new on the spur of the moment. Perhaps the more foolhardy. I told him I wasn't sure. It would depend on how I felt when I got back to Paris Monday afternoon.

"That's the morning I teach at SNECMA," I said, "Remember?"

SNECMA, which David had nicknamed SMEGMA, was an acronym for Société Nationale de Something-or-other. It was a huge factory near Melun, about thirty miles southeast of Paris, where they made airplanes.

Early every Monday morning I would go to Denfert-Rochereau where I boarded a bus that would take me down there to teach English for three hours then have lunch with my three students in the company canteen. My three students were engineers who were collaborating with three engineers in England on drawing up plans for the Concorde. The money was good and the lunch was free but after a long, pre-dawn ride on a crowded bus, followed by three hours of intensive teaching, followed by "informal conversation" where my students were supposed to put into practice what they'd learned that morning, I was always exhausted, and could only think of going back home for a long nap. Now thinking back, I wondered why I had made an appointment for that afternoon. I also wondered why I'd made an appointment at all. Why start something new at this point in my life?

At the metro station at La Motte Picquet we gave our tickets to the *poinçonneuse*, who without a word returned them, punched with a stamp and a hole. David and I descended the stairs to the first landing then went our separate ways. As I reached the bottom of the stairs on my side the train came clanking into the station, letting off a burst of air as the brakes released, and bringing with it that particular metro smell that was always vaguely exciting, probably because it brought back the intensity of those first months in Paris, when the city was so full of the promise of adventure and romance. True, that was something I needed to be reminded of these days.

I cranked open the door of a second class car that was almost empty and sat down facing forward on a wooden bench polished to a luster by the *fesses* of millions of people who had sat there before me. On the publicity panel directly opposite and above me was a picture in black silhouette of a man hunched over a small round table that held a half empty bottle of wine. Standing in front of him on the other side of the table was a little boy, also in silhouette. A bubble above the little boy's head contained the caption, "*Papa, ne bois pas,*" to which someone had added, with a black felt marker, "*tout.*"

I glanced back over my shoulder and waved at David standing on the opposite quai. He was looking at me with his cigarette clenched between his teeth, still huddled against the cold.

The train picked up speed as it left the station and plunged into the tunnel, lit by an occasional bare bulb that darted past outside the window, lighting up my somber train of thought. After a year and a half in Paris I had to admit I was ready to throw in the towel and go back to California. The official reason I'd come to Paris in the first place, the reason I gave to my chairman at Stanford and my mother and anyone else who asked, was to "take a few courses and work on my French." But the real, underlying reason, which I hadn't shared with anyone except David and a few close friends back home, was to write.

At any one time there are between 40,000 and 50,000 Americans living in Paris as more or less permanent residents. It's a safe bet that a third of those people, perhaps as many as half, came to Paris to write. Maybe not to write the great American novel, but at least to soak up the atmosphere that had inspired the great expatriate writers who came before, and hope that sooner or later it would have the same effect on them.

Who knows? If you hung out long enough in the rue de l'Odéon or the Boulevard Montparnasse, maybe the ghost of Hemingway or Fitzgerald or Dos Passos would take possession of your soul and dictate works unwritten in their lifetime.

After a few months, meeting dozens of such people, it was humbling to realize I was one of them. By then I had written half a dozen stories, two of which I was fairly pleased with, the rest ashamed to re-read sober.

Within another two or three months it dawned on me that writing, or learning to write for those of us who weren't born writers, was a full-time job, and if you already had a full-time job trying to make ends meet in a place that turned out to be unimaginably expensive, Paris became just another city where you ground out a living every day and came home every night with the millions of other commuters to go to bed drunk on all the wine you drank with dinner to forget how exhausted and bored and frustrated you were.

When I was a junior in college I admitted to my favorite English professor that what I really wanted to do in life was write, to which he'd replied, "Well then, just write."

Yeah, right.

It's true that my current job did give me more free time than others. Or was supposed to. Teaching English an average of four to five hours a day left me in theory five or four hours to write. But to those hours teaching you had to add on unpaid travel time to the godawful factories in the god-forsaken suburbs where most of those courses were taught—*la Société Astra* in Asnières, *les usines Renault* in Boulogne-Billancourt, *La Smegma* in

Melun—so that by the time you got home you were just as worn out as a laborer working an eight-hour shift in one of those factories, and making just about the same money, just above minimum wage, but without all the benefits and the month-long vacations.

For me, another complicating factor, another reason I was tempted to throw in the towel and go back to the States, was the asthma. Why was I so sure that if I returned to California the asthma would disappear? But I knew as surely as I knew I had to breathe to live that this was true. That as soon as I was back there, right back where I started from—turning my back on whatever it was I had set out to find—the asthma would go away. Which was another humbling realization. How far had I come, anyway? How much had I grown and learned in the thirteen years since my father died?

The metro pulled into the station at Charles Michel. A handful of people got off, a handful got on, the doors banged shut, and the train continued on its way.

Another reason I'd left the States, and this one was no secret, was all those bumper stickers that told me to.

"AMERICA. LOVE IT OR LEAVE IT!"

So I finally left it, happy to leave behind me all the people who were more and more rabidly and blindly committed to the war, including and especially my mother. "Is it communism you believe in?" she'd asked me tearfully one day during one of my rare visits home from college. I was so dumbfounded I didn't know what to answer. It certainly wasn't any of her idols: Eisenhower, Nixon, J. Edgar Hoover, Goldwater, and now, unbelievably, Ronald Reagan.

The trouble with my mother started with the death of my father, at least for me. As Christian Scientists, my three older brothers and one younger sister had been brought up to believe that death did not exist, and we continued to believe that right up to, during, and even after the funeral. I was thirteen at the time. My brothers Simon, Tom, and Fred, twenty, nineteen and seventeen; my little sister Anne-Marie, four. During the funeral the five of us sat up front with mom, but in the wings, offstage, behind a black gauze curtain. It was as if we were watching a play we had all helped write.

Early that morning we'd had our last rehearsal. As soon as we had gotten up and gathered in the breakfast nook, mom passed around her leather-bound copy of *Science and Health, with Key to the Scriptures* and had each of us boys read various pre-selected passages, passages that my mother had been poring over for months now and knew by heart. All of the passages proved beyond a doubt that death was "error," an illusion created by mortal mind to prevent us from seeing the Truth.

Which was why I was so happy. All during the long drive in the limousine from our house in La Cañada, down to Pierce's Mortuary in Hollywood, and while we sat there in the alcove as the parlor filled with mourners, I couldn't keep from smiling. My brother Fred kept casting me stern looks. It wasn't that I didn't know what those looks meant. They meant I should at least put on a show of grief, for them, the ones who didn't know, who weren't in on the secret. But I couldn't have stopped smiling if I'd wanted to. It was all I could do to keep from laughing. Because it was all so funny, a big joke! Imagine all these people who had come to pay their last respects to my father, all the arrangements for the funeral, the grim-faced ushers standing around, the flowers everywhere, and he wasn't really dead! In *Science and Health* Mrs. Eddy said so, again and again. "There is no death." "Death [is] an illusion, the lie of life in matter; the unreal and untrue; the opposite of Life." And finally, the clincher that all Christian Scientists held at the ready to pull out at the first sign of adversity, the little seven-word mantra that worked when all else failed: "Man is not material. He is spiritual!"

In the center of the stage was a podium where various people came up to talk about what a good man my father was. Or is. On the other side of the stage, directly across from the alcove where we sat, was a long black chest. On top of the chest, at the far end, was a little pink cone turned upside down. Whenever my attention wandered I would focus on that little cone, or pyramid, or whatever it was. I figured it must have been some sort of Masonic symbol. In addition to being a Christian Scientist and a member of the Optimist Club, dad was also a Mason.

Whatever that symbol stood for, it seemed to mean a lot to everyone, not only Masons. When the service was over and people started filing across the stage in front of us, on the other side of the gauze curtain, many of them would stop and look at it for a while, then continue on, some visibly shaken. Louie Mingarouli, my father's favorite foreman, who had been painting for Blakely Brothers since before I was born, actually kneeled down in front of it and burst into tears, and then, to my amazement, crossed himself!

After everyone had filed past and the funeral was over, one of the ushers opened the curtain, inviting us too out onstage. As soon as I stood up I saw that the long black chest was actually my father's coffin, and the little pink pyramid was his nose.

But then it wasn't really, because whoever was in that coffin was not him. It was like a wax reproduction, dead matter, and we knew dad was not dead. It was Mom who said it for the rest of us. Or shouted it. I remember hearing the hysteria in her voice, and hoping no one else had. "Can't you see?" she cried out. "He's not here! That's not him!"

Seeing the simulacrum of my father laid out like that was clear proof of what Mary Baker Eddy said. That's why it was such a joyful morning.

A few years later, when I was fifteen or sixteen, I started having those dreams, dreams that I've continued to have ever since and that I know I'll continue having until it's my turn to die. In the dream people come to tell me that they've found my father and they are going to take me to him. Like Che, he's still alive, and waiting for the ransom to be paid. They take me to where he's hiding in the Hollywood Hills. When I finally see him again I'm so overcome that I start to cry. Although he was never a man to show emotion, I can see he too is on the verge of tears. He takes me in his arms and holds me, knowing that I finally know the Truth, the Truth that makes you free.

CHAPTER 3

We're on our way
to somewhere

After the station at Javel, the metro started its descent beneath the Seine, gradually picking up speed, each car jerking erratically back and forth. It was always a little scary how fast the train went as it crossed beneath the river, doubling, maybe tripling its speed, so that even if you were sitting you had to hold on or risk getting knocked to the floor. It made you wonder if the engineer knew something the rest of us didn't, stepping on the gas to get from one bank to the other before the tunnel caved in.

After the funeral my two older brothers went back to college. Fred, holding down two jobs and applying to college himself, was seldom home, so most of the time my mother and little sister and I were alone in that big house that had started out so full of light and promise and just got bigger and darker, and darker still.

For my father and mother it was a dreamhouse, literally the answer to their prayers. To help them find and buy it, they had engaged the services of a practitioner. A Christian Science practitioner was someone licensed by the Mother Church in Boston who in exchange for a fee would help you "do your work" and "know the Truth" during periods of seeming sickness or crisis. In practice, a practitioner was a kind of doctor but with no medical training. In a perfect world where there was no sickness and no death who needed medical training? Ours called himself Doctor Carberry.

Josiah C. Carberry had been doing work for our family since the birth of my brother Tom, who according to my mother had been born dead and was brought back to life by Dr. Carberry's praying. He went on to become such an important influence in my parents' life that I was named after him. Dr. Carberry was fond of his name and fond of me. Whenever he talked to me he always called me by my middle name, Josiah, and I think he managed to maintain the delusion, with the help of my mother, that a lot of other people called me that as well. Dr. Carberry was a big man with bushy gray hair and a perennial smile. He once sent me a photograph, taken in Australia, where he's holding two koala bear cubs. With Dr. Carberry's broad smile and his gray hair sticking up all over, a cub in each arm, it looks like a portrait of a proud father with newborn twins.

After dad died Dr. Carberry said I should consider him my earthly father, but it was impossible, unthinkable. In his presence I always felt uncomfortable. He was so big and jovial and smelled too much of a sweet cologne that was nothing like my dad's Old Spice.

In the fall before he died my father bought himself a 1956, two-tone Chevrolet Bel Air convertible, complete with a custom made tonneau cover that zipped shut all around when the top was down. When I first heard the word I thought it was a Tonto cover, and wondered for a long time what the Lone Ranger had to do with our snazzy new car. Later, and for an even longer time, I wondered why dad bought the car in the first place, just five months before he died. Despite all the work he was doing and the Truth he was knowing about this sore throat and cough, maybe he also knew that he was going to die, and buying the car was one last fling. Maybe it was like me and my MG; driving that car gave dad a foretaste of eternity.

Three years later I got a ticket for driving that car too fast. Since I was not yet sixteen and still had my learner's permit, I also got a summons to appear in court. For my mother, this was the beginning of my career as a juvenile delinquent, so she sent me off at once to see Dr. Carberry.

Sitting across from me at his big desk that was always neat and tidy— every item "in its rightful place" (Monsieur Legrand and Professor Giron would both have approved)—Dr. Carberry asked me why I had been driving fifty in a twenty-five mile zone. Instead of telling him the obvious, that that car was not meant to be driven slowly, especially in the flat and empty roads around the Rose Bowl, I said I'd been in a hurry. Why was I in a hurry? Because I was late for work. Why was I late for work? Because I'd been browsing in a bookstore in Pasadena, and had lost track of time. Dr. Carberry's smile got even wider. He leaned forward to push across the desk his big *Science and Health* bound in soft black pigskin. The book was already open to a passage he told me to read aloud. It was a paragraph where Mary Baker Eddy proved that time was nothing but an illusion created by mortal mind, incapable of conceiving of eternity. Like sin, disease and death, Mrs. Eddy explained, time was "error," her catchword for evil, or anything seemingly bad, the opposite of Truth.

"Are you telling me you lost track of error, Josiah?"

The waiting room outside Dr. Carberry's office was filled with clocks that he had brought back from his trips all over the world. There must have been fifty of them, all whirring and ticking away while you sat there reading the *Christian Science Journal*, or the *Sentinel*, or the *Herald*. When they all went off to sound the hour you knew that the person in his office was about to come out smiling and it was soon your turn to go inside.

To my dismay, instead of smiling or answering Dr. Carberry's question, I burst into tears. My brothers always said I was a crybaby. Here was proof. Dr. Carberry just leaned back in his leather chair and laughed, then he told me to come around the desk and had me sit in his lap while he hugged me and stroked my hair and talked to me about Love.

The metro slowed down, eased into the station at Eglise d'Auteuil, and pulled to a stop. I was the only passenger to get off. I emerged from the station at Place d'Auteuil and turned left on the Avenue Théophile Gautier. The only sign of life was a *clochard* wrapped in blankets and huddled in a doorway asleep. At least I hoped it was a sign of life. When the weather got this cold in Paris it took a daily toll on the people who lived in the streets. I put one more loop in the scarf around my neck, shoved my hands deeper into my pockets, and quickened my pace.

The house my parents ended up buying, with the help of Dr. Carberry's prayers, was at the north end of La Cañada, on Hillard Avenue, a straight street up a steep hill that ended in the foothills of the San Gabriel Mountains. As a general rule, the higher you got on Hillard, the fancier the houses were and the wealthier the people who lived in them. At 4901 we were a little over halfway up and a lot higher on the social ladder than we had been in our three-bedroom house in Cheviot Hills. Although the commute to the office was a lot longer and dad would have to get up an hour earlier to get to work on time, it would be worth it to live in what my parents called "God's Country."

We spent four years in God's Country before dad got sick. One early November morning in 1956 he offered to drop me off at school on his way to work. As he drove down the hill, and while we waited for the light at the bottom, I noticed he was coughing and clearing his throat more than usual. It had been going on a while now, at least six weeks or so, but of course seeing a doctor was out of the question. A few minutes later, when dad stopped the Chevy in front of La Cañada Junior High, he asked me to pray for him when I did my work in the morning. I opened the door and promised I would.

Six weeks later it was Christmas. We always opened our presents on Christmas Eve. It was an old Norwegian custom my mother's parents brought with them when they immigrated to Michigan. That Christmas Eve dad had started out sitting with the rest of us in the living room. By then he'd been bedridden for over a month, and a few days before he'd been moved to the front bedroom next to mine. That way, Dr. Carberry said, he could turn on the light and read his *Science & Health* and *Bible* in the middle of the night, and not bother mom and Anne-Marie in the master bedroom. They would also no longer be bothered by what had become his almost constant coughing.

But even before the first round of gifts that night dad's coughing got so bad he had to go back to bed. And even though the front bedroom was down the hall, around a corner and at the end of another long hallway, we could still hear him cry out now and then, as we continued unwrapping presents on the living room floor. Sometimes, when the cry was especially loud, we would interrupt the ritual of unwrapping gifts and repeat as fervently as we could, out loud and in unison, Mary Baker Eddy's formula to treat the illusion of pain: "There is NO sensation in matter!"

Dad's cries were so loud that night they even drowned out Gene Autry and Bing Crosby on the hi-fi. We didn't have any carols by Frank Sinatra because of his reputation as a heavy drinker and a womanizer, and mom said having a record of his would have been like inviting him into the house.

One night not long afterwards a doctor came to that house. Not a Christian Science practioner who called himself a doctor, but a real MD. This one was an obstetrician, the only real doctor my mother knew. Twenty years earlier he had been called to help deliver my brother Tom, who at the last minute looked like he might not make it despite all the work Dr. Carberry was doing.

Before the doctor arrived that night mom explained to all of us that even though this man practiced "materia medica," he was sympathetic to Scientists. Still, I couldn't believe we were inviting a doctor into the house. I'd always thought that doctors were the enemy, and this one even had a German name, Schoenhoff. For years after my father died I was sure the real reason for his death was that nocturnal injection of error into our household.

The doctor arrived after dinner, making the drive up to La Cañada after his regular hours, but I think this might also have been because my mother didn't want the neighbors to see. I remember we didn't turn on the floodlights when his car turned into the drive. His car was a big black Cadillac, but not particularly new. He parked in the circular driveway and walked up to the big front door in the dark. In his right hand he was carrying the black leather satchel doctors always carried in the movies.

As mom opened the big front door and invited him inside the four of us boys were lined up in the entrance hall. One by one he shook our hands, then followed mom down the dark hallway towards the front bedroom where dad was propped up in bed.

Half an hour later mom and the doctor came back through the hallway and went straight on outside to where his car was parked. They talked for a long time in the dark. I know because I watched them through the back porch window. Mom leaning down towards the driver's seat window, her pale face partially lit by the moon. I could tell she was crying. She was still crying when she came back into the house. She stood there in the entrance hall, tears streaming down her face, refusing to say the terrible secret word the doctor had told her out there in the dark, and which we read two weeks later in the obituary of the *La Cañada Valley Sun*.

Cancer.

Instead mom said that none of us, not even she herself, had been doing our work as well as we should have and that we'd all have to work harder from now on.

I turned left off the Rue de Rémusat to the Rue Félicien David, the only sound in the empty street coming from the leather heels of my Italian shoes echoing on the sidewalk. After a year and a half those shoes were still too tight. A nearby churchbell, probably coming from the Eglise d'Auteuil, started tolling eleven o'clock. Just a few more minutes until I got to the little dead-ended Rue Paul Dupuy, then I'd be back in my warm room slipping out of those too tight shoes and under the warm covers of my bed.

After the funeral, even though my two older brothers were living in their fraternities—Simon at Occidental and Tom at UCLA—they came home whenever they could to help out around the house and make things easier for mom, although their good intentions often backfired. In those days all three of my brothers were in various stages of post-adolescent rebellion, and without dad around to "box their ears" when they got out of line, they tended to get out of line a lot, and sometimes even fought among themselves.

Mom was unable to cope with any kind of adversity at this time, let alone open hostility among her children. For her, it was just one more thing she couldn't understand, another cruel blow that fate had dealt her.

One night Tom and Fred started arguing about whose turn it was to take out the garbage. They were standing on the oval carpet in the entrance hall, behind the big front door, right where mom had stood a few months earlier when she told us we had to pray harder. That night, immediately after dinner, mom had gone off to bed with four-year-old Anne-Marie. For months she hadn't been getting enough sleep, and sleep was her only solace, the only escape from a reality that had become unreal and unbearable.

Tom and Fred seemed to forget that she was in the house, or even to care. Soon their argument turned into a shouting match, and to my amazement they actually started to swear—something that was unheard of in a Christian Science household. I stood there watching, appalled. Where had they learned these words?

"You bastard!" Fred said.

"Son of a bitch!" Tom replied.

It was at this moment that mom came down the hall. She was wearing her pink robe over her light blue nightgown and she was crying, but she was always crying. From where I was standing, she stood silhouetted in the blue-green light of the big aquarium which separated the hallway from the living room. Between sobs, with bubbles coming up and tropical fish swimming around behind her, she told the boys that if they didn't stop fighting she was going to leave the house and never come back. Dangling from her right hand were her car keys. In her left was a wad of Kleenex.

Fred took advantage of the distraction to take a poke at Tom. Tom grabbed him by his T shirt and pushed him against the door of the closet where my father's overcoats and hats still hung. The door banged shut and a bunch of clothes fell down inside. From my mother's lips came a long, high wailing noise that I had never heard before, from any living being, much less from my mother.

She walked around us and into the kitchen where Simon was standing at the sink, finishing up the dinner dishes and listening to the radio. Mom went on by behind him, through the breakfast nook and into the back porch. I heard the back door open and slam shut. On the radio they were playing a song with Carmen Miranda and the Andrews Sisters.

> We gotta get goin', where're we goin',
> What are we gonna do?
> We're on our way to somewhere,
> The three of us and you…

Simon was the oldest. He'd know what to do. I told him mom was leaving, leaving for good. She was already out in the garage. She was probably backing her car out into the driveway. Without turning around, Si told me not to worry, she'd be back. He didn't even turn down the radio.

> We don't know where we're going,
> But we're gonna have a happy time.
> Cuanto le gusta, le gusta, le gusta,
> Le gusta, le gusta, le gusta,…

I ran to the back door and out into the breezeway. Yes. Mom was in the Olds, backing it up the driveway. I ran up and clung to the handle of the door, as if I could stop the car or pull it back down. Mom rolled down the window and put her hand on the top of the door. I covered it with my own and begged her to stay, to put the car back in the garage and come back into the house. The boys would stop fighting. Everything would be all right.

Mom said I was the only one who understood her now, the only one who loved her any more, or even cared. She took her foot off the brake and the car continued inching up the driveway. I stood there watching, helpless, not believing. The car backed off the concrete ramp and eased out onto the street. I ran to the end of the driveway and shouted, "They've stopped!"

Blowing her nose into a Kleenex with one hand, mom shifted into drive with the other and headed off down the road into the night. Lights were on in the house across the street. My fear of becoming an orphan outweighed that of being overheard by my friend Larry who lived there, or by my other friend Mike who lived in the next house down. I ran to the middle of the street and yelled at the top of my lungs, "Mom! Come back, mom!"

It was a quarter of a mile to the bottom of the hill. I watched until I couldn't see the taillights any longer. There was no way to tell if she'd turned right or left.

CHAPTER 4

Sex isn't everything

I slid the bigger of my two keys into the outer lock and let myself into the spacious, marble-lined foyer. I didn't much like living in the 16th, nor in this modern apartment building, but since I'd moved there two weeks ago my asthma seemed to be getting better, so I'd decided to stick it out at least until the spring.

I pressed the button next to the door that turned on the *minuterie*, skirted the elevator, and started up the stairs that wound around it. On the first landing I inserted the second key into the lock of the door on the right and turned it once all the way around, retracting the deadbolt—a welcome sign that Eugene was still out—then another quarter turn, releasing the latch.

Eugene Braun-Munk was the guy I rented a room from in this rather too fancy apartment that was too far from the center of town and smelled too much of the cologne Braun-Munk apparently took a bath in every morning—the reason I kept the door to my room closed and the window open.

Eugene was an effete, fastidious American who worked as some kind of editor at Hachette and who seemed intent on modeling his life on the life of Oscar Wilde—another reason for keeping the door shut.

I unwound my scarf, unbuttoned my raincoat, hung them on the rack behind the door, then opened the door off the hall into my room. The room was about twelve-by-twelve feet, with most of the space taken up by a large double bed and at its foot, to the right as you walked in, a large armoire. Squeezed in between the armoire and the outside wall was a small table on which I'd set up my little Slimline Olivetti typewriter, a gift from my mother when I went up to Stanford. Appropriately named, it was no more than four inches tall and fit snugly into its light blue leatherette case that zippered shut all around the bottom.

I pulled off my outer sweater, threw it on the bed, and went to the open window. The metal shutters on the outside were closed but cold air was coming in through the louvered openings. I closed both panes of the window and twisted the knob. It was chilly in the room, but the central heat seeping up from the floor would soon have it cozy warm, and soon after that too hot, so I'd have to open the window again before I went to bed. Good thing I didn't have to pay for all the heat that escaped out the window, which would have doubled my rent. At 300 francs a month the rent was cheap, especially for Paris. I figured if I cut back on movies and restaurants I'd soon be able to pay back David and actually start saving money for a change. On the other hand, this was Paris.

Another advantage of that apartment was that Eugene was hardly ever home, so I usually had the place to myself—the large *salon* with oriental carpets and a full-sized grand piano, a spacious, well-equipped kitchen where I could cook whenever I ate at home. Weekends too Eugene often went away, *"pour fuire Paris!"* usually to Cabourg or Deauville. He said he went there to drink in the charm of the empty casinos and the huge hotels, but I suspected it was also to add a Proustian polish to his Wildeian image.

So why had he been so anxious to rent me a room? It couldn't have been for the money. Given his salary at Hachette and what he spent on restaurants and hotels, my 300 a month could only have been a drop in the bucket. Maybe he just enjoyed the company on those rare occasions when he was home, and liked the idea of someone being there when he wasn't. Holding down the fort. Or maybe he liked me. Maybe he was in love with me. The idea was as ludicrous as it was unlikely.

Both physically and temperamentally Braun-Munk and I could not have been more different. At five-feet nine, I weighed less than 120 pounds. Braun-Munk was six feet tall and three feet wide. Around people I didn't know, and even those I did, I tended to be quiet and shy. Braun-Munk was gregarious and loud, and he took pleasure in shocking people by interjecting into his elegant witticisms the coarsest of vulgarities, in English or French.

Although he'd been born and raised in Kentucky, Braun-Munk claimed to be an heir to the Hungarian throne, hence the triple crown monogrammed on the pockets of all his shirts, shirts he changed every day. Me, I wore the same button-down Oxford, and the same pair of pants for five or six days in a row, and a tie only when I had to, when I had to teach.

I had met Eugene through Valentine, the mother of Jean-Pierre, who had been a fellow first-year graduate student with David and me at Stanford. When David and I decided to drop out at the end of the year Jean-Pierre longed do the same, since for him too it had been a year of disenchantment. And since he was French, he didn't have to worry about the draft. He did have to worry about his mother though, who was footing the bill for his studies.

Jean-Pierre's mother owned a perfume store, just off Place Vendôme, that she called "Valentine." According to David, who heard the story I don't know where, maybe from Valentine herself, in the early 'thirties Valentine had started working in a brothel. Gradually she worked her way up until she became the madame, a position she held for several years, which was how she'd eventually been able to save enough money to buy the *parfumerie*, as well as the luxurious fifth floor apartment she lived in, overlooking the circle of fountains on the Place Franklin Roosevelt.

According to David's same source of information, this also explained how Valentine and Jean-Pierre, born during the war, escaped being sent to a concentration camp, one of Valentine's regular customers during the occupation having been a member of the German general staff.

Another person who managed to survive that time was a tall, elderly gentleman who lived in Valentine's apartment, perhaps as her lover—it was never quite clear—whom Valentine introduced to us as Le Docteur Haas. Doc Haas, as David and I called him, called me Baby Limona because I reminded him of an American pilot he'd kept under cover during the war and treated for jaundice. Like me, the pilot looked a lot younger than his actual years. Doc Haas never told me if Baby Limona lived or died. From stories like this though David and I surmised that Doc Haas had been active in the Resistance, and was probably the physician-in-residence at the brothel as well.

In addition to the sprawling apartment at Franklin Roosevelt, Valentine also owned a one-bedroom apartment on the top floor, which she rented out to Eugene until he moved to the place in the 16th. In addition she owned a tiny studio in the same building, but on the second floor and with an entrance on the Rue Jean Mermoz. Valentine had bought the unit and set it up as a *garçonnière* for Jean-Pierre while he was studying at the Sorbonne, before he went to Stanford. This apartment was actually more like a short hallway, with just enough space along one wall for a desk and a twin bed, and to the left as you came in, a little *salle d'eau*, consisting of a toilet, a corner shower, and a bidet.

At the end of my first summer in Paris, after I'd been working at the *New York Times* for about a month, Valentine offered me the *garçonnière* rent-free, in exchange for licking stamps and sealing envelopes containing flyers for the *parfumerie*. A good deal, I thought, until I realized how many customers Valentine had and how often she sent out flyers. As the holiday season drew near the frequency of mailings increased until I was doing little else on nights and weekends besides stuffing envelopes and licking stamps, the Olivetti pushed to the back of the desk buried beneath brochures advertizing Chanel and Dior at special holiday prices. This was not the way I'd intended to spend my free time in Paris. Still, the rent was free and I was broke. I decided I'd give it another few months, postponing my writing career until I'd earned enough at the Times to afford some other place.

During those months Valentine treated David and me, but especially me, maybe since I lived under the same roof, with an almost motherly interest. In certain ways my own mother and Valentine were actually quite similar. Both were small, fine-boned, intelligent women, and in their gray sixties there was still a hint of the beauties they had been at thirty. But there the similarities stopped short. For one thing, Valentine was Jewish, while mom was anti-semitic. For another, Valentine was French in a way my mother would never have dreamed possible. As soon as Jean-Pierre's voice began to crack, Valentine had had him taken to a brothel in order to make sure he got off to a healthy start towards heterosexuality. When Jean-Pierre told me the story I laughed out loud. The thought of my own mother doing the same for me was simply unthinkable. If mom had ever allowed herself to have any doubts about my sexual orientation she would have known the Truth like crazy and sent me straight to Dr. Carberry, like a lamb to the slaughter, as it were.

The only time my mother ever brought up the subject of sex with me was during a brief conversation during the summer I came home from my first year in college. It was the same summer she asked me if I believed in communism. We were in the Oldsmobile on the way to Pasadena, crossing the Devil's Gate Dam. Mom was driving, and without taking her eyes off the road she suddenly said, "Richard, sex isn't all there is in life." Coming without any warning, I thought this might have been an introduction to some sort of confession she wanted to make about her own relationship with my father—something I did not want to hear. But when she followed it up with silence I realized she'd intended it as a kind of lecture on the topic, her personal, seven word discourse on the birds and the bees, which I guess she felt obligated to give me since dad was no longer around to talk to me man-to-man.

True, that summer I was in love with my first love who lived up in San Rafael and sex with her, or the painful lack thereof, was pretty much all I was capable of thinking about with any consistency. But still, my mother's off-the-cuff remark took me completely by surprise and, like her question about communism, left me uncharacteristically speechless.

As for sex and the painful lack thereof, that first year in Paris seemed designed to prove the truth of my mother's remark, both for myself and for David, who by the end of January was calling it "The Winter of Our Discuntent." Not that there weren't plenty of young women I found attractive. Paris was full of them. Too full. But they were always arm-in-arm with some creep who obviously didn't deserve them, or going in the opposite direction in the metro—the exquisite girl I'd been staring at through two panes of glass looking up to catch my stare, and stare back, just as her train started pulling away from mine.

David and I and everyone we hung out with in Paris those days spent a lot of time listening to the Beatles' latest album, *Rubber Soul*, and there was a song on it by John Lennon that summed up our feelings exactly. Not the bitterly ironic text, but the plaintive, yearning refrain. "Oh girrrrrlll! dit-dit-dit-dit-dit-dit-dit-dit, girrrrRRRlll!"

To get to the *garçonnière* (so cruelly named, as it turned out, but no more so than its English equivalent, "bachelor pad"), you first had to walk down a dark, narrow passage off the Rue Jean Mermoz. At the end of the passage was the lair of the concierge, an ill-shaven, puffy, Gollumesque, white toad of a man who obviously never saw the light of day and who sneered out at you from behind the tobacco-stained window of his *loge* whenever you walked past it at any hour of the day or night. Valentine and

Doc Haas said he'd gotten the job by having done certain favors for the *milieu*, the Marseille mafia, and that I should just ignore him, but that was hard to do since whenever I got mail I had to snatch it from his greasy palm and even add a little grease of my own now and then with a coin or two, to make sure I'd keep getting mail.

Once you got past the concierge you took the elevator up two flights to a brightly lit, long barren hallway with doors on either side. Judging by the distance between the doors, each of the units was the same size as mine, and had probably been built as servants' quarters for the people who lived in the luxury apartments over on the Franklin Roosevelt side. Walking down that hallway you had the feeling you were in a budget hotel, or maybe a *maison de passe*, which I began to think it actually was, at least for some of the people who lived there, at least for the woman who lived in the unit next to mine. The whole twelve months I lived there I never once set eyes on this woman, but I came to know her intimately all the same. I imagined her with shoulder-length dark hair, twenty-five to thirty, slim but well-built, 120 pounds, five foot two or three. I even gave her a name, Adele. Adele's bed was parallel to mine and as close as the wall was thin—a wall that contained no material to insulate sound, especially the sound of people making love. Judging by how often this happened and by the difference in register, tone and even accent of Adele's companions, I soon concluded that my next door neighbor was one of the classy prostitutes who frequented the ritzy cafes at that end of the Champs Elysees, and that her pimp was the slimy concierge.

At any rate, it was not a comforting sound. When it woke me up in the middle of the night I would lie there wide-eyed in the dark, plotting the outline of a story where Adele and I would meet while coming out of our rooms one day and she would fall in love with me and I would wrest her away from the clutches of the concierge and take her to California and introduce her to my mother and we would move to Big Sur and live happily ever after. But with Adele and her companion six inches away screwing their brains out it was impossible to turn on the light and get out of bed and start writing this down. Or even to stuff envelopes.

Gradually the tide of passion next door would ebb, giving place to the sound of pigeons cooing outside my window. The window looked out onto a solid cinderblock wall, just a few inches beyond my reach, decorated with pigeonshit and feathers. The pigeons would roost by the dozens on cracks and ledges in that wall and coo pretty much nonstop, night and day. My hatred of pigeons dates back to that time. It was as if their constant cooing and flapping of wings, with the occasional feather floating down, were meant as a reminder that sex wasn't everything.

Nevertheless, I managed to stick it out in that place until the following summer. By then my relationship with Valentine had degenerated from the semblance of surrogate son and substitute mother to the harsh reality of put-upon part-time employee versus hard-hearted boss and calculating landlady, for beneath that coy exterior of a charming, sentimental little lady, Valentine could be hard and unforgiving—another trait she had in common with my mother. But maybe she thought she had a reason to be unforgiving.

In early August, before leaving for a camping trip in Italy with David, I rang the doorbell of the apartment on the Franklin Roosevelt side and announced to Valentine that I'd be moving out of the little studio the end of the month, to move in with David to a place we'd decided to share. "*Ça m'arrange,*" was all she'd said, trilling her r the way she always did—the last vestige of her Eastern European accent. Then she'd given me a cold smile and shut the door in my face.

On the way down the elevator I wondered if she'd gotten wind of a moment of mutual *égarement* between Mary and me in the garçonnière one night a few weeks earlier. Mary was Jean-Pierre's American wife and she had come to visit her mother-in-law that summer while Jean-Pierre stayed behind at Stanford to work on his thesis. Mary was not fond of her mother-in-law, whom she found tyrannical and over-protective, constantly asking Mary where she was going and what she was going to do and with whom she was going to do it. Valentine would not allow Mary out on the streets of Paris after dark, unless she was accompanied by someone Valentine could trust. Me, for example.

The apartment David and I moved into on September first, a year and three months after we'd arrived in France, was typical of a lot of apartments in Paris. When you read the ad in the classifieds they sound great, but as soon as you pay the deposit on one and move in, you realize you've signed a lease on a dollhouse.

The incontrovertible good thing about this place was its location; right on the tip of the Ile Saint Louis, at 8 Rue Joachim du Bellay (a street named after a 16ᵗʰ century poet David and I had learned to loathe during a required seminar taught by Professor Giron). Unfortunately the apartment faced the courtyard so it didn't look out onto Notre Dame, but if it had it would have cost much more than 750 francs a month and we wouldn't have been able to afford it. Still, it was enough just coming out of the *porte cochère* onto the street every morning and catching sight of Notre Dame 200 yards away, as I started across the Pont St. Louis.

In those days I was doing a lot of my teaching in a studio apartment Donahue had converted to a classroom right near the Carrefour de l'Odéon, so my walk to work cut right through the enclosed garden and playground behind the cathedral. I would let myself in through the low wire gate, skirt the fountain until I had an unobstructed view, and sometimes, when I wasn't running late, just stand there among the flowers and the children and gawk.

How strange that something so lacy and light could be made out of rock. I decided the backside of Notre Dame was even more beautiful than her front, and on foggy mornings it was more beautiful still, because in the misty light the delicate sculptures and friezes and tapering fleches would fuse together into a towering, vibrating presence, both delicate and massive, intricate and collosal, evanescent and eternal. Sometimes while standing there I had the impression I could open my mouth and take it all in, this macro-microcosmic miracle, and that old feeling of union with the cosmos would come back to me in waves—not as strong as it did while driving the MG, but it was there all the same, a gentle reminder. During one of these little epiphanies it occurred to me that the real truth about man, about me, about us all, is that we are both spiritual *and* material.

The incontrovertible bad thing about that apartment on the Ile Saint Louis was that David and I were totally incompatible as roommates, especially in such tiny quarters—something we both found out within a few days. I don't know what it was I did, or didn't do, that got on David's nerves. Maybe just being there—stepping on his weird drawings, knocking over the stacks of notebooks in which he kept track of his dreams, breaking into his private thoughts—but the main reason he got on mine was that we didn't have the same notion of cleanliness. I didn't see why I had to keep cleaning the toilet all the time, and he didn't see why I had to keep cleaning the toilet all the time.

Although I was no longer in contact with Valentine I was still in touch with Eugene, with whom I spoke occasionally on the phone. On one of those occasions he said he was thinking of renting a room in his new apartment in the *seizieme*, and I told him I would be there the next day with all my worldly goods.

When I broke the news to David that night, coming home from an evening class I taught in a bank on the Champs Elysées, he got up from the chair he was reading in and took me in his arms and said I'd saved our friendship.

He could have been less gracious and simply said, "*ça m'arrange.*" For the past few months he'd been seeing a lot of an American girl named Audrey and lately Audrey had been making noises about moving in—yet another reason for my moving out.

After I finished washing my teeth, placing my toothbrush in the porcelain cup reserved for me, next to the one reserved for Eugene, next to a row of multi-colored jars of perfumes and ointments and god-knows-what, I went back to my room, turning out lights on the way and shutting the door behind me. I figured it would be another hour or two before Eugene got back and by that time I'd be fast asleep. I took off my watch and set it on the nightstand next to my alarm clock. 11:30. Too late to write a letter. I still hadn't written my mother telling her I'd moved, but that could wait another day.

On Sundays in Paris when everyone went out I loved to stay in. The next day I would get up early and put in a full day writing. The story I was working on and which was turning into more than just a story was about a graduate student at Stanford whose student deferment gets rescinded and who has to go to Oakland for a physical and when he finds out he doesn't have to go to Vietnam drops out and goes to Paris instead. Write about what you know. But did I know myself? After twenty-four years I was beginning to have doubts.

I undressed, draping my clothes over the back of the chair, pulled open the window, banged open the shutters and stood there naked in the cold night air. I took several deep breaths, filling my lungs then emptying them completely by pushing in my stomach. There was no wheeze, no whistle, not the slightest telltale tugging in my chest. So far, since moving into this place, I'd only had to take a pill two or three times before going to bed—one of the pills Doc Haas had given me—Tedral, or "Tederral," as he pronounced it, trilling his r's like Valentine. He'd also given me a prescription for suppositories that were much stronger than Tedral and worked much faster. The suppositories were called Theophylline. They looked like fat little purple bullets and they went off like bombs inside my chest as soon as they got there, somehow finding their way from my asshole up to my lungs. As a Christian Scientist I'd always been exempted from health and biology classes and still had only a vague notion of how my innards were connected, but I did know that as soon as I'd slid one of those waxy little bombs into the breech I had ten minutes before the explosion took place inside my lungs, clearing them out so I could breathe again but also speeding my breathing up so fast that I could hardly keep up with it, and then giving me an eight-hour case of the jitters.

I closed the shutters, wedged the windows open *à l'espagnolette*, turned out the light and slid beneath the covers. While waiting for my feet to get warm I thought again of the lecture that night at the Hilton, finding it a little strange that this was the first I'd thought of it since David and I separated at the metro. But now with my eyes closed I saw the Maharishi sitting on his dais surrounded by ruined flowers. In his right hand he was holding the stem of a dark red rose, which he was beating softly into the palm of his left, the petals floating to the floor. "The t'ing is,… the t'ing is,…"

CHAPTER 5

Siren song

The next day I spent the morning working in my room and working fairly well, cranking out four or five pages in longhand before I started typing them up on the Olivetti, revising as I typed away. I had typed up the first page and slid another behind the roller when there was a knock on the door.

"Entrez!" I said.

Eugene pushed the door open and stood in the doorway looking unhappy. He was wearing slippers and a terrycloth bathrobe but the bathrobe was open wide enough so I could see the monogrammed triple crown on the pocket of his silk pyjamas. He looked at me through his round, horn-rimmed glasses as if wondering who I was, and how I'd gotten there. Finally he said, "Blakelee, MUST you do that on a Sunday morning?"

I realized he meant the typing. It's true his room was right next door to mine. I told him I was sorry and I thought he was awake. It was past noon. He said when he stayed in town on Sundays he usually slept until two or three, something he'd been hoping to do that Sunday since he'd gotten home at four a.m.—he hoped I hadn't heard him—and now he had a splitting headache. I told him I would stop typing and he should go back to bed. He said he wouldn't be able to sleep anyway, and anyway he'd invited some friends over for brunch and did I want to join them? I said I was going to a movie with David.

Half an hour later I called David from a phone booth and asked him if he wanted to go to a movie. We met in the Latin Quarter and saw an old American flick at the Champollion with his current girlfriend Audrey and then went up to the *Centre Américain* on boulevard Raspail where we played a little ping pong and met a few more friends and went with them to a little restaurant called Chez Raton in the rue Guénégaud where we all drank too much wine, especially me, especially since it was Sunday night and I had to get up at five the next morning to go teach at Smegma. When I got back to the rue Paul Dupuy it was after midnight and all the lights were out and I figured Eugene must be in bed catching up on his sleep.

I went to bed immediately and woke up an hour later to the sound of sirens down in the street outside my window. PIN-PAN! PIN PAN! PIN PAN! Except there was no street outside my window. Then I realized the noise was coming from my chest.

I sat up, switched on the light, grabbed the plastic vial of Tedral from the nightstand, poured one into my palm and washed it down with a slug of Volvic from the bottle I kept on the floor beside my bed. Then I bunched up the pillows and the *traversin* behind me and leaned back.

I could tell right away it was a bad attack, maybe the worst yet, even since back when I was a kid. Now, sitting up, the noise coming from my lungs was louder. I was not breathing, I was braying. HEE HAW. HEEE HAWW.

It was so loud I was afraid I was going to wake Eugene.

I propped myself up on my knees, turned around so I was facing the wall, then leaned forward until I was sitting in a full fetal position, with my head resting on the pillow. Sometimes that helped. I remember my oldest brother Simon, whose asthma had been really bad when we were small, sitting like that for hours. I pulled the covers back up over me, tucked them in around my shoulders, and waited for it to pass.

It did not pass. Usually the Tedral began to take effect after thirty minutes. After forty-five the same strange noises were issuing from my lungs, strident, repetitious, mocking, and I still had to force the air in and back out again. Strange to have to make yourself do something you normally did without thinking. Strange and strangely humiliating.

I got out of bed and wrapped the bedspread around my shoulders and made my way through the dark apartment to the bathroom where I switched on the light and groped under the sink for my shaving kit. I had never taken a Theophyline on top of a Tedral before and I was sure it was not a good idea. But what could I do? My fingers were trembling so badly that I had to make a conscious effort to slowly open the foil wrapper and extract a suppository. It fell to the floor and rolled behind the bidet. I managed to retrieve it and then, still crouching, holding on to the rim of the bidet, shoved it in. When I stood back up I was hit by a wave of dizziness that almost knocked me over, and would have if the bathtub hadn't been there to grab onto. On the way back to my bedroom I held onto pieces of furniture and the wall. Back in my room I closed the door and collapsed onto the bed.

Now the wheezing was like singing. Sirens again, but this time the kind with human voices, luring you towards them. I let myself be lured. Was this what it was like to drown?

At some point I must have blacked out because the next thing I knew I was halfway in the bed and halfway out, all tangled up in the covers and sheets. The wheezing had stopped and instead of having to gasp for oxygen it was whistling through my lungs. My chest was a wind tunnel. With my fingers on my neck and my eyes on the second hand of my watch I counted the heartbeats: 130. Five minutes later, 135. Five minutes after that, 140. I stopped counting.

"Eugene," I called weakly, more air than voice.

No answer.

I mustered my strength to speak louder. "Eugene!"

Then on an outflow of breath, as loud as I could, "EUGENE!"

Hearing my own voice, I felt foolish. Luckily he still hadn't heard. There were no footsteps in the hall, no knocking at the door. Blakeleee? Maybe he wasn't even there. What could he do anyway? Take me to a hospital? He didn't have a car. Call a taxi? What could they do at a hospital? The second time I dropped acid with David in Palo Alto I had what people later told me was a bad trip, and which I didn't want to start thinking about now. But there was the same feeling of being totally out of control and wondering who was and not wanting to know.

First not enough air and now too much. What had I done to deserve this? But I knew what I had done and now it was coming back to me. Snatches of old prayers, old formulas, kept coming back. "There is no sensation in matter." "Man is not material, he is…" Oh god, oh god.

It was now 2:30. Only 2:30. At least another six hours of this. I slid down under the covers with my head propped up against the pillows and turned out the light.

At 5:00 I began to slumber. At ten past five my alarm went off. I was not shaking uncontrollably any more. I could get out of bed. I could move.

A little over an hour later I was standing on the curb at Denfert Rochereau, waiting for the Snecma bus, wishing I was somewhere else, anywhere else, preferably back in bed. At 6:30 in the morning it was still pitch black outside and the black was not going to start giving way to gray for another two hours. If ever. It was that kind of morning. As recently as two centuries ago the rue Denfert-Rochereau led to and from the catacombs and was called, simply, *la rue d'Enfer*, the road to hell, and that's exactly where I was.

In the middle of the *rond point* was a statue of a lion rising up on all fours. The lion didn't look happy, as if awakened from a nap by all these cars and trucks exhaling diesel fumes. Finally the Snecma bus appeared beneath it, peeled off from the circle of traffic and headed towards the corner where I was standing. The bus looked like a large, long shoebox painted dark green. It was probably an old army bus, since Snecma was owned by the government and made war planes as well as the Concorde. It pulled to a stop at the curb with a clank and a clatter. The driver cranked the door open and the people standing around me started to climb on board. There were forty or fifty of us. There was no line. It didn't matter who had gotten there first. This was France.

As I waited to climb on board I couldn't help thinking of the bus I'd boarded in Menlo Park to take me up to Oakland for my Army physical. Only then the people who'd boarded it with me were my age or younger, mostly younger. I'd been amazed that morning to see that some of them actually looked happy to be there, as if it were the beginning of a great adventure. Finally they were going somewhere. Suddenly their lives had a purpose. Killing gooks. For me it had been a nightmare—the nightmare I'd been having ever since I'd gotten that letter from my draft board. Variations on the theme of slogging through a rice paddy with a backback full of gear that was supposed to protect me but which just made me a bigger target and kept pulling me down and down. I would wake up in a cold sweat, hearing guns go off close by.

That morning in California too I'd been in terrible shape, hungover from too much wine and too little sleep, my throat raw from all the cigarettes I'd smoked in hopes that the wine and lack of sleep and cigarettes would bring on an asthma attack, a really good one, like I used to have as a kid. Because even though in my pocket I had that letter from the good doctor at UCSB, I was sure it wouldn't work, sure the army doctors would see through it and pack me off to Vietnam. Or to jail.

But it had worked. And here I was three years later the morning after a really good asthma attack, like I used to have as a kid, only worse. This time, without the pill and the suppository, I was pretty sure I wouldn't have made it.

"*Monsieur?... Ça va?*"

It was a woman. One of the people waiting to board the Snecma bus. She was about to climb on board and saw me standing there and was now inviting me to go ahead of her. I must have looked as bad as I felt. I shook my head to clear it and told her thanks, I was fine, and got on the bus.

I had been making that same Monday morning trip to Melun with the same group of people for three months now and this was the first time anyone had spoken to me. I knew this had to do with perceived class differences in France. As far as I could tell, all of my fellow travellers on the Snecma bus were "*ouvriers*," assembly line workers or other kinds of manual laborers who happened to live in Paris and whose unions had negotiated for free transportation to and from the factory. All of them wore casual clothes, which most would protect behind aprons as soon as they arrived at the factory, or exchange for "*bleus de chauf*," the heavy, royal blue overalls that are, ironically, the emblem of the working class in France.

Wearing a tie, even when it was hidden beneath coils of scarf, and shiny black Italian shoes with pointed toes, I was in their eyes immediately classified as "*cadre*," a member of the executive or managerial staff, to which they could never aspire to belong, because they had no university degrees for one thing, and for another, because their parents and grandparents and great grandparents had never belonged. And while they all must have wondered why a tie-clad cadre was taking a working class bus, no one would ever dream of broaching that or any other subject with me directly because the only time *ouvriers* communicated directly with *cadres* was while sitting opposite each other at a table prior to a threatened strike.

At first this bothered me. I would have liked to join in on their conversations about last year's vacation and next year's vacation and to tell them that I at heart was one of them, an *ouvrier* in *cadre* clothing, with an immigrant mother and a father who'd started out painting houses and eventually started his own company and ended up sending all his kids to college because that's the way it was in America where we had a classless society, unless of course you happened to be black, in which case you found employment with the army to go fight your country's stupid wars and then came home to go to jail.

But after a while I resigned myself to sitting alone and talking to no one, and now that someone had actually spoken to me, breaking through those class barriers to ask me if I was okay, I was physically incapable of responding.

I made my way to the back of the bus where I found an empty seat. No matter how crowded it got on that bus I always found an empty seat, as if it had been reserved for me, which it probably had and which always made me wonder if it was out of aversion or respect. But this morning I couldn't have cared less and collapsed into it, grateful that no one would dare or want to sit down next to me so I wouldn't have to talk about the shitty weather or next year's vacation or classless societies or racism in America or the Vietnam war or any damn thing.

Last night at the restaurant there'd been a lot of talk about Vietnam, all of it ominous and depressing. Chez Raton was a narrow vaulted cave, with a narrow table along each wall and benches where everybody sat all crammed in close together. Two of the people who'd come along with us from the American Center were the DaSouza sisters, Rose and Vivian, and I'd ended up sitting next to, very close to Rose. Rose or Rosela, as David called her, was the younger of the two sisters and pretty in a wan sort of way. She and Vivian lived with their parents in the 16th and now that we were neighbors I was hoping I might go there for a visit, or have Rose come and visit me some afternoon when Eugene was away. Rose and Vivian's mother tongue was Portuguese Brazilian, but they also spoke French as well as the French, and English with just the touch of an accent that I found very attractive, especially when Rose was doing the talking.

Rose and I had also talked about Transcendental Meditation, because she had read about it and was intrigued that I had made an appointment to learn it. She'd asked me to call her after my appointment to tell her what it was like. But now the very idea of going to the Continental that afternoon to learn a new technique of meditation that was sweeping the world seemed preposterous. Better to go straight home to bed for a long nap, and after that go to a travel agency to buy a cheap ticket back to California. Because if I was going to die I'd rather do it there. Where death did not exist.

From Paris to Melun it was a good hour and a half, when there was no traffic. Usually I used the time and the empty seat to get another hour's sleep but I knew that morning this was not an option. Taking one Tedral was like downing eight cups of expresso, one after another, and the side effects of Theophylline were even worse. I'd been vaguely hoping that the two together would cancel each other out but that was decidedly not the case. My breathing was thankfully clear but still very rapid, my heart was still thumping away and I felt shaky all over. How was I ever going to teach for three hours and then make intelligent conversation over lunch? Why hadn't I called Donahue at five a.m. and told him I couldn't do it? Because if I had no one else would have been able to do it either and the class would be cancelled and I would be out 150 francs and probably out of a job as well. That's why.

The bus rattled into gear, pulled away from the curb and merged back into the traffic wheeling around the angry lion. I slumped back against the vibrating wall of the bus and put my feet up on the seat next to me, resting them on the padded plastic cushion of the armrest. I knew it was an American thing to do, but I didn't give a shit. In fact I almost wished someone would call me on it. "*Vous faites ça chez vous?*" "*OUI, et qu'est-ce que ça peut vous foutre?*" But I knew nobody would. I was *cadre*.

The bus continued through the outskirts of Paris, heading southeast, as the air inside it filled with the acrid smoke of Gauloises. Because it was so cold outside, well below freezing, no one opened a window and the air got steamier and smokier until it began to burn my eyes. So I kept them closed, pretending to sleep and hoping I just might. Better to keep my eyes closed anyway. The outskirts of Paris in that area were mostly industrial; small factories with walls around them, warehouses and truck depots with now and then a sorry little village grouped around a soot-blackened 19th century Gothic church and bell tower, a café-tabac on a corner, dimly lit from inside where its first few *habitués* were slouching over the bar in front of their *café-calvas*. Here's the church with its ugly steeple, open the doors and see all the depressed, alcoholic, suicidal people.

But at least they could breathe.

Or could they? A pack or two of Gauloises every day for twenty years, that was a lot of Gauloises. Enough to start closing off the windpipes when you got to be thirty-five or forty. And for that there was no Tedral to the rescue.

When the bus was no longer stopping and starting up again at traffic lights and railroad crossings and was cruising along more or less smoothly on the three-lane highway that led to Melun I opened my eyes and sat back up. The level of chatter had died down and the smoking subsided. A lot of people were asleep, their heads thrown back or tilted sideways leaning against the shoulder of the person sitting next to them. A few were reading the paper they'd bought that morning before boarding the bus. Sitting across from me on the aisle seat one row back was the woman who had let me climb on board before her. She was not reading a paper but a book and she looked up when she felt me looking at her and nodded and smiled and I smiled and nodded back. Forty or forty-five, maybe younger. Black hair streaked with gray. A kind face but care-worn. Probably kids at home in Paris that she had just enough time to shop and cook for when she got back from the factory.

"*Monsieur!*" A forty-year-old woman calling me Sir! Usually it was "*jeune homme,*" if it was anything. Maybe that night, between midnight and five a.m., I'd aged ten years.

After the suburbs petered out the countryside between Paris and Melun consisted almost entirely of fields of sugar beets that got plowed under at the end of summer every year. It was an area that had been hotly disputed during the First World War, crisscrossed by trenches, bombed out, bombed under, bombed again, where after two years the number of people who had died on that land outnumbered those who were fighting for it. I wiped a clear spot in the condensation on the window and tried to peer through the darkness at the frozen mud outside that was anything but cosmic. I couldn't help wondering how many bones worked their way up through that mud back to the surface every spring, bones of young men who had died in the trenches at an even younger age than David and me and who had had no doctors' letters to get them out of their war.

※　※　※

"Peaches."

"Pishes."

"No. Peeeeches. And the whole sentence, remember?"

"Ah yes. Euh, I gaiv eem, euh, pishes. *Voilà.*"

"Yeah, right. Okay. Now you, Mr. Delaunay. Book."

Monsieur Delaunay thought for a few seconds then said, "I gaiv eem un bouc."

"Good," I said. "Excellent." Delaunay was the smartest of the three, the best in the class. "Now, Mr. Perrotin, dollar. A dollar." I threw in the article. Mr. Perrotin was the dumbest and the slowest. Nice, sweet in fact, but slow and dumb.

"Un dollahr."

"No. I gave him a . . . The whole thing, remember?"

"Ah yes, oh, excuse me. I euh gaiv eem euh a dollahr."

"Right. Good. Mary. Mr. Merle?" Mr. Merle looked at me funny, then he shrugged and said, "I gaiv eem Mary."

"No, no. I gave Mary a dollar."

"Ah yes! Oh! Ha ha!" He turned to the two others and translated into French what he'd just said. All three cracked up. I pretended it was not funny. Mr. Merle turned back to me, straightened up in his chair, and said the sentence correctly.

"Right," I said. "Now apple, Mr. Merle."

"Euh, me? Again? Abeul?"

"Yes you, Mr. Merle." It was a little punishment for speaking French. The rule was English only during class, and we were supposed to be hard-assed about it.

"I euh, *voyons*, gaiv euh Marie han abeul."

"Very good."

Mr. Merle formed his left hand as if he were holding an apple, and pointed at it with the right. "But um, euh, han abeul wiss un, euh, *comment dire*, vourm?"

"Ah, an apple with a worm, huh? Poor Mary."

"Yes. Ha ha. Pour Marie." He beamed and sat back in his chair.

Since I started working for the English Language Study Group I was constantly amazed at how you could take a small group of grown men or women, people twice or three times my age, at the height of their careers, sit them down in a row of student desks, pace up and down in front of them with an open book in your hand, and instantly they became the children they had been in school, thirty, forty years earlier. Monsieur Delaunay, the whiz kid who didn't have to study to stay at the top of the class but who tended to get bored and look out the window; Monsieur Merle the class wise guy, smart but a little lazy, prone to passing notes and shooting spit balls; Monsieur Perrotin a little dull but good-hearted, the butt of other people's jokes. All three men were chief engineers and they had to learn English in a hurry so they could communicate with their co-chief engineers in England, although I often wondered how their English colleagues were going to react to such communications as "I gaiv Marie un abeul," or "I gaiv my fahzair a bwed."

"No, Mr. Perrotin. Bread."

"Bwed."

"Just bread. Remember? In English it's a non-count noun, so no article. No ar-ti-cle."

"Are tickle? Ah, arTEEcle. Yes. No. Yes. Just bwed. Euh, um, I euh gaiv my fahzair... BWED!"

"Great, Mr. Perrotin. You got it. Good." The effort had caused sweat to break out on his forehead. He extracted a handkerchief from his pocket and wiped it off. I resisted the urge to reach forward and give his bald head a little pat. Instead I turned the page to an exciting new set of substitution drills based on the pattern sentence, "The lamp is on the table."

"Mr. Delaunay,…"

The book I was holding was full of such sentences. It was one of two books Donahue had given me when I came to work for him, one green, the other red, the *Bible* and *Science and Health* of the Audio-Lingual Method, invented by the authors of the two books, Professors Lado and Fries, and based on the Pavlovian principle that ceaseless repetition of a limited number of example sentences, or patterns, with a limited number of variations, will eventually turn you into a fluent speaker of the target language—unless it turns you into a dog.

David also taught occasionally for Donahue and together we'd fantasized about taking a group of beginning students and teaching them a completely bogus language, complete with pattern sentences and substitution drills.

"Woof bark, grrr sniff."

"Snap!"

"Woof bark, grrr snap!"

I glanced discreetly at my watch. Another half hour of this, but we'd almost made it. I was going to make it. Then lunch, then I'd be on my way back to Paris. One of the advantages for the teacher of the Audio Lingual Method was that it took virtually no preparation. You just opened the book where you'd left off last week and kept plugging away. Another advantage was that you could do the exercises more or less in your sleep, an advantage I'd taken full advantage of that morning.

After repeating the pattern sentence and correctly replacing the lamp with an apple, Mr. Delaunay stirred in his chair and stifled a yawn.

"We're almost there," I said. "And you've all worked well this morning. Everyone will get dessert." Everyone laughed.

Dessert for me that day was an apple I snatched up from my tray as I handed it to the tray-taker in the *cantine des cadres* of the Snecma cafeteria. After the taker took my tray I turned to say goodbye to my three students. We shook hands all around, Merry Christmas Happy New Year and all that. Since Christmas was the following Monday and New Year's the Monday after, we weren't scheduled to meet again for another three weeks, but as it turned out we would never meet again.

Like the morning's three-hour class, lunch had gone better than I had expected, in that I'd managed to stay awake all through it. My refusal to have any wine, even with the wedge of camembert I'd lifted from the dessert section along with the apple, prompted my students to conclude that I'd had too much wine the night before—not an inaccurate assumption as far as it went, but that in turn prompted me to give them an impromptu lesson on American words and phrases related to alcohol and the abuse thereof—drunk, plastered, blotto, crocked, loaded, looped, hammered, wasted, tipsy, trashed, tanked up, blasted, blitzed, bombed, drunk as a skunk, high as a kite, sails in the wind, pie-eyed, shit-faced, stinko, sloshed, soused, pickled, potted, hungover, hair of the dog, on the wagon, teetotaler, cold turkey, etc. By the time I'd finished the lesson, including an explanation of cultural referrents such as skunks, pickles, teetotalers and turkeys, lunch was over and it was time to catch my bus.

After leaving the company restaurant I went down a hallway and out into a central courtyard where I'd disembarked that morning with my fellow commuters from Paris. Now the courtyard was bleak and empty. The weather was still gray and cold but at least there was no freezing drizzle as there had been that morning at Denfert-Rochereau, and the puddles in the gutters did not have a coating of ice.

In many ways La Snecma resembled a prison, with a high wall enclosing the sprawling factory and grounds, three lines of barbed wire topping the wall, and security checkpoints at every entrance. I went out through the main front gate, waving my apple at the guard. I had been planning to eat the apple while waiting for the bus, but when I got to the street my bus was waiting for me with the engine running, so I stuffed the apple into my plastic briefcase, next to Lado and Fries, and climbed on board.

And it really was _my_ bus, waiting for _me_. When I'd agreed to take this job Donahue had said that transportation back to Paris would be in the 'company car' that left the factory every day at one and would drop me off at Place d'Italie. I thought he'd meant car and not _car_ and imagined a sleek black Citroen DS, but it turned out to be another bus (in French, "_car_"), sometimes the same as the one I'd ridden in that morning, sometimes different, but always painted the same dark green and freshly retired from the French army. The strange thing was that on the ride back to Paris there was never anyone else on that bus but the driver and me. All of the ten or twelve times I took it, I was the only passenger.

That day it was a different bus from the one in the morning and with a different driver, who nodded as I entered, "_Bonjour/Bonjour_," then closed the door and stepped on the gas, propelling me down the aisle. I caromed all the way down to the wayback, where I sprawled out on the long seat in the stern and went to sleep in about ten seconds.

When I awoke the sun was shining.

The Sun

Was Shining!

Outside the clouds had broken into huge cumulus clusters and between them there were patches of blue—more blue than black and gray—and through one of those patches the sun was beaming its beneficent, bright warm light.

"Monsieur!"

I pulled myself up to a sitting position and peered down at the driver at the other end of the bus. It was like looking the wrong way through a telescope. We were parked at Place d'Italie, and the engine was idling. This must have been the second or third time the driver had tried to rouse me. I had been having a dream and in that dream someone was saying "monsieur," and meaning me.

I got up and made my way back down the aisle, the driver, in the rearview mirror, eyeing me the whole way.

"_Désolé, je._"

He nodded. "*Bonne journée.*"

"*Bonne journée!*" I said, and descended the three steps onto the street. Lazarus emerging from a dark green shoebox of a tomb.

In French they call this abrupt change in the weather *une belle éclaircie*, and in the middle of winter it always comes as a sudden, unexpected illumination, raising your spirits and warming your insides and making you realize that all this dampness and gray would come to an end in April and then there would be blue skies and all the trees would be full of leaves and there'd be flowers everywhere, and Everything Would Be All Right.

On the corner in front of the bus, ten feet away, a woman was selling flowers from a cart. All the flowers suddenly made me think of the Maharishi, and my appointment with him that afternoon. In the pocket of my raincoat I found the slip of paper the woman had given me at the Hilton. The appointment was for 3:00. It was now 2:30. The metro ride from Place d'Italie to Place de la Concorde would take about half an hour, with only one change at Palais Royal. In the bottom of my briefcase was the apple I'd snatched off my tray at the Snecma cafeteria. I figured that could pass as an offering of fruit. The handkerchief in my back pocket was not exactly new, but it was relatively white and clean and freshly ironed. The woman at the cart was advertising *soucis*—the bright orange flowers with twisted light green stems that Van Gogh painted—two bunches for the price of one. I dug a silver five-franc piece out of my pocket, exchanged it for two bunches of *soucis* wrapped in a sheet of last night's France Soir, and made a dash for the metro.

CHAPTER 6

Piece of cake

※ ※ ※

The Continental is one of the oldest, swankiest, and most expensive hotels in Paris. Its twin, the Meurice, right next door, served as German military headquarters during the occupation. You know a place is really high class when you walk in wearing a shabby raincoat, carrying a plastic briefcase and a cheap bouquet and nobody looks at you. Nobody looked at me as I walked past the front desk and through the lobby. When I got to the elevator the man standing in front of it called me "*Monsieur*" (*décidément!*) and asked me "*quel étage?*"

I stepped off the elevator on the fourth floor and entered a cloud of smoke. The smoke was coming from incense burning somewhere and it got thicker as I continued down the hall. It looked like the whole floor had been taken over by the Maharishi and his followers. Several people were standing around in the hallway, or sitting on the floor with their backs against the wall. Almost all of them were holding flowers and all of them smiled as I went by, the smiles all so friendly and welcoming, and here in France, so fake.

Everyone seemed to be waiting, but waiting for what? Pairs of shoes were lined up on the floor outside many of the rooms. Flowers littered the hall as well, and there was even an occasional abandoned bouquet, propped up against the wall, as if marking the scene of a fatal accident.

I rounded the corner and continued down the next hall until I came to the room indicated on my slip of paper. The door was open, and the line of shoes outside it was especially long. Glad I'd put on socks that morning without holes, I added mine to the end of the row and went inside. Sitting at a desk was the English woman who had given me my appointment after the lecture at the Hilton. She looked up at me as I came in.

"Calendulas," she said. "How lovely!"

I assumed she was talking about my flowers. I said in French they were called "*soucis*," "worries."

"Giving our little worries to the Movement, are we? Quite appropriate, don't you think?"

Out of my wallet I took a wrinkled blue fifty-franc bill—about $10—and handed it over. In return the woman handed me a questionnaire, checked my name off a list, and told me to take a seat. "We're running a bit late," she added apologetically, "but it shouldn't be too long."

It was a double room, with the twin beds pushed against the walls, and other chairs and sofas that did not match brought in from other rooms nearby. About a dozen people were sitting around, trying to conceal their bare feet and offerings of fruit and flowers. All of the offerings were much more lavish than my own. Spiny pineapple leaves and other exotic greenery poked out of the tops of paper bags that bore the names of fancy stores. On the lap of an elderly woman was a gorgeous spray of gladiolas wrapped in cellophane that crinkled loudly every time she shifted position. She shifted position often, and apparently with some pain. Her hands and fingers were deformed with arthritis.

Sprawled on the floor in a corner was the black-haired hippie who had come in late the night of the lecture and sat down on the floor in front of the Maharishi. He was wearing the remains of an overcoat that looked like he had taken it off a dead *clochard*. But even his offerings, spread out on the floor beside him—some oranges and apples and a bouquet of anemones—looked better than my own.

I sat down on a gilded armchair next to the woman with the gladiolas. Using my briefcase as a desk, I started filling out the questionnaire. At the bottom was a question asking if I'd taken any drugs "within the last three days." Not knowing if Tedral and Theophylline were what they meant by drugs, I answered that question with a question mark. I got up and gave the form back to the woman sitting by the door. She took it with a smile and put it at the bottom of the pile next to the list of names in front of her. I returned to my seat, extracted the apple from my briefcase, and, while no one was looking, took the handkerchief from my back pocket. It definitely did not look new. It didn't even look unused.

There was no conversation in the room—people tended to avoid eye contact, preferring instead to look at their fruit or flowers, or down at their shoeless feet—but there was a detectable air of anxious anticipation, as if everyone kept asking themselves the same two questions: What were they doing there? What would happen if they got up and left? Everyone, that is, except the hippie, who seemed to be asleep. He jolted upright when a pretty young woman came in, took the top sheet from the stack of questionnaires in front of the woman at the door, and called his name. The young woman too was English. The hippie gathered up his offering and followed her out the door.

From then on, every ten minutes or so, someone would come into the room and call off the name of the person whose questionnaire was at the top of the pile, and then usher that person out of the room. In addition to the pretty young woman, there were also two men, one about my age, one about ten years older. All of them spoke with an English accent. I figured they were kind of like Maharishi's elves, whose job was to deliver each of us to the yogi, who would then give us our mantra and teach us how to meditate.

In addition to the English elves, the room was visited every now and then by a tall, dark-haired American who would come in, pace around in a circle, and make comments out loud, to no one in particular. "Piece of cake! Did it myself ten years ago. Changed my life. Best thing I ever did. Yep, best thing I ever did."

The man was around fifty and you could tell he was American not only because of his accent but because of the clothes he wore—a wrinkled Ivy League suit with a narrow tie, and heavy, black wing-tip Oxfords that he did not remove at the door. His comments were no doubt intended to make those of us remaining in the room feel comfortable about whatever we were about to undergo, but on me at least they had the opposite effect. Each time, before going back out of the room, the man would go up to the desk to check the list of names of people who were yet to be called, leaning far over the shoulder of the woman sitting there, whom he called Eileen. She called him Charles.

"How we doin, Eileen?"

"Just fine Charles."

"Yes sir. Piece of cake!"

Eileen was wearing a salmon-colored V neck sweater. The V didn't exactly plunge, but it did make a modest dive, revealing the beginnings of cleavage. Obviously the reason the American leaned so far over was to get a closer look, not at the list of names, but at Eileen's breasts, and for some reason I found this disturbing. Wouldn't someone who's been meditating for ten years be less in bondage to his lower chakras?

It was a question I'd be asking myself again.

I took another look at my watch. By then it was 4:30 and I was beginning to seriously consider walking out. The only reason I didn't was that I was afraid the big American would come in as I was going out and bully me back to my chair.

Finally the younger of the two male elves came in and called my name. Out in the hall, in a quiet voice, he told me his name was John and he was going to teach me how to meditate.

Ah. So I wasn't going to be taught by the Maharishi. John was about my size, with medium length light brown hair that matched his socks. We padded down the crowded hallway, stepping over bodies. John led me into a small anteroom with light green walls and we both sat down on two straight-backed chairs. John seemed a little ill at ease, as if he was embarrassed. He explained that the fruit and flowers were for a little ceremony he was going to perform, but first he wanted to ask me a few questions.

Aha. Now come the questions to find out exactly what kind of person I really am, so as to make sure I get the right mantra. Because there was certainly nothing in my questionnaire that would reveal who I really was, deep down, the real me. All John did though was read over the answers I had filled in, nodding now and then and saying "Hm, hm." When he got to the bottom of the form he looked up at me and said, "You don't know if you've taken any drugs within the last three days?"

I told him about the pill and the suppository and all he said was, "Ah yes, quite so. Hm." John made a little notation at the bottom of the form, set it on a table beside him, and asked me if I had any questions. Instead of asking him what we were doing there in our socks, or why he was going to teach me to meditate instead of the Maharishi, or how he knew exactly what mantra I was supposed to get, I said no, I didn't have any questions.

John nodded, cleared his throat, and said he was now going to take me into an adjoining room where he would perform a little ceremony. It was just a simple formality, he explained, a kind of homage to Maharishi's teacher. All I had to do was stand there and watch. After the ceremony was over, John was going to give me my mantra and tell me how to use it. At that point I was supposed to listen very carefully.

We both stood up. I was still holding my Snecma apple, my two bunches of *soucis*, and my obviously not brand new white handkerchief. In a low voice, I asked John if he wanted them now. Not yet, he whispered back.

John opened a door into a small, dark room which I immediately realized was the source of all the incense on the fourth floor. Here it was like a solid mass. There was also a lot of smoke from candles, the only source of light. The smoke hung in layers that separated as we moved into the room and then closed back in around us.

Directly in front of us, set up on a table that had been pushed against the wall, was a huge portrait of some kind of swami, sitting cross-legged on a low dais and wearing an orange robe. As my eyes got used to the dim light I could see that it was not the Maharishi. This man looked older and much sterner and he had a lot less hair. I figured it must have been the Maharishi's guru. Something that looked like peanut butter was smeared across his forehead. The table beneath the portrait was cluttered with a jumble of brass trays, bowls, incense and candle holders, and littered with flowers and pieces of fruit of all kinds and colors. John turned to take my handkerchief, apple, and flowers. He indicated I was to remain standing where I was, then he took three steps forward, cleared a spot on the table, and set down my offering.

Next he broke one of the flowers off its stem, dipped it into a bowl, and flipped it around. A drop of what I hoped was water landed on the bridge of my nose. As John began to move things around on the table he also began to mumble something in a low, droning voice, some kind of chant, in a language I didn't understand. Using both hands, he picked up a brass holder with an unlit candle, lit it with one that was already burning, and moved it in a wide circle in front of the swami's portrait, continuing to mumble all the time.

My mother had brought me up to believe that Catholics were superstitious idol worshippers. I wondered what she would say if she could see me now. The thought made me want to laugh. As I stood there watching John pick things up and push them around on the table, chanting all the time, the urge to laugh grew stronger. I also became distinctly aware of a drop of sweat that was running slowly down from my left armpit, inside my T shirt. The drop got to the first rib and stopped, then went on to the second and stopped, then on to the third, . . .

John picked up the apple and held it out as if showing it to the swami. See what a nice apple he's brought you from the Smegma cafeteria? He moved that too in a big circle in front of the portrait, then set it down at the swami's feet. He smudged something on my handkerchief then waved that too in a wide, slow circle. Why was my handkerchief supposed to be new if he was just going to smear it with something that also looked like peanut butter and maybe was?

Meanwhile the urge to laugh grew stronger still. By now I was biting my tongue and trying to think unfunny thoughts—Ronald Reagan, Nancy, napalm bombs, nuclear war—but nothing, nothing helped. Tears were beginning to trickle down my cheeks. I felt my whole body shaking. Within seconds I was going to burst out laughing. There was no way I could keep it inside any longer.

Just as I was about to clap both hands over my mouth to stifle the guffaw, the gusher, the roar that by now had reached my diaphragm, John went down on his knees. His head was bowed and between his joined hands he was holding one of my yellow flowers, a little bent souci. Still mumbling, his lips moving, he turned to look up at me over his shoulder. He wanted me to join him, to get down on my knees in front of that pagan altar. Why hadn't he warned me that I was supposed to kneel at the end of his silly ceremony? If I didn't what would they do? Would that annul the procedure? Would they refund my fifty francs? John looked up at me with beseeching eyes, his head tilted sideways.

My boss Jack Donahue had a big, smelly black poodle, named Jasmine. Whenever I went to Donahue's cluttered apartment on the Rue Richer to collect a check or attend a teachers meeting, Jasmine would come up to me wagging her tailless rump and bumping against me, trying to get me to pet her greasy unclipped curls. Sitting there on the floor looking up at me, John looked a lot like Jasmine. How could I just walk away, leaving this poor guy sitting there, dog-like? John was no longer mumbling some chant, but saying the same thing over and over again, the same two syllables, louder and louder. It was the sound that had been chosen just for me, my meaningless word, my mantra.

Keeping my back turned on my Protestant background, with generations of Quakers and Lutherans shaking their heads behind me, not to mention Mary Baker Eddy rolling over in her grave, I went down on my knees.

Three nights later I returned to the Continental for what they called a "checking session." Before leaving Paris, the Maharishi wanted to make sure everybody who had learned to meditate was off to a good start. I arrived at the hotel fifteen minutes late, walking over from a six o'clock class I taught at Morgan Guaranty Trust, on the Place Vendôme.

The checking session was being held in a reception room on the ground floor. I crossed through the lobby and started down the hallway indicated by a bellhop. Although the smell of incense was not nearly so prevalent as it had been up on the fourth floor the day of my initiation, it grew stronger as I neared the end of the hall. Beneath a sign proclaiming *L'Aiglon* in gold leaf letters was a set of high double doors, slightly ajar. I pushed one open a little wider and peeked inside.

Here the decor seemed more authentic than at the Hilton. The walls were decorated with ornate, gilded woodwork and mirrors that reached from the floor to the ceiling. Thick velvet curtains covered the twenty foot high windows, and from the richly illustrated ceiling hung two enormous chandeliers. Grouped around a small stage in the middle of the room were about fifty people, sitting with their eyes closed on sofas and chairs that had been pushed close together. On the stage, set up behind a microphone on a stand, was an empty blue sofa. I tiptoed into the center of the room, sat down on one of the empty chairs, and closed my eyes.

Once again, after repeating my mantra for a few minutes, it started happening. My hands, folded in my lap, felt like they were starting to grow, to expand, to become enormous. At the same time there was this fulness in my mouth, as if I just had to open it to take in the world. And I could have sworn I was starting to float. It felt as if I were weightless, rising.

It was just like driving the MG. Or almost. Since learning to meditate three days ago, that same old feeling, or mix of feelings, distant but familiar, would come over me while I was repeating the mantra, not for long, but faintly and intermittently, like a little light that would start to glow, then fade, then glow again. Tonight the feeling was back again and stronger than ever. If I did not think about it, and just continued repeating the mantra, it was there.

After a while the people around me started to stretch and stir. When I opened my eyes the Maharishi was sitting on the blue sofa up on the stage, looking around the room, smiling, raising his bushy eyebrows, nodding.

"It is easy, yes?" he asked, in his high, squeaky voice.

A few people answered "Yes. Oh yes!"

"*Qu'est-ce qu'il dit?*" asked the person sitting next to me. It was the elderly woman with the arthritic hands and the bouquet of gladiolas.

A translator was needed. The Maharishi asked for a volunteer and several hands went up, including my own. The Maharishi pointed at me and smiled. Someone brought forward a chair and placed it on the stage next to the Maharishi's sofa. It was the English woman, Eileen. In front of the chair, someone else placed another microphone—although with so few people, the microphones seemed unnecessary. I stepped up onto the dais and sat down. Since the chair was slightly higher than the sofa, my head, even when I slouched forward, was a few inches above the Maharishi's. He looked up at me and nodded again. "Wery good!"

"*Très bien!*" I said, into the mike. The Maharishi laughed and there were titters of laughter from the other meditators. In the audience I recognized some of the other people who had been waiting in the hotel room before initiation, including the hippie with the dirty overcoat. He wasn't wearing the overcoat now and his hair had been tied back, revealing dark eyes that gleamed.

The first thing the Maharishi wanted to discuss that night was the effects of meditation on our daily lives. Had anyone noticed any changes or felt differently since learning to meditate? While waiting for people to respond the Maharishi did something I had noticed him do during the introductory lecture. Holding his left hand in a loose fist, he drummed the fingertips of his right hand into the knuckles of his left, making a rhythmic plopping sound which this time was picked up by the mike a few inches away and made audible to everyone in the room. Ploppety-plop, ploppety-plop.

After a short while, perhaps lulled by the sound, people began to raise their hands in answer to the Maharishi's question. A few said they thought they felt calmer or had slept better, but a lot more people said they hadn't noticed anything special. In response to all these more neutral, and sometimes even negative comments the Maharishi nodded, then went on to reassure everyone that it was perfectly normal not to feel anything particular the first few weeks or even months. It was especially important for these people to continue meditating morning and evening every day for twenty to thirty minutes. The good effects would show up in good time.

After a short pause during which no more hands went up, I mentioned my own experience. First in English then in French, I described the asthma, how in the last year it had gradually gotten worse and worse until I had become more and more dependent on medication. I described the attack of the other night and how it had left me afterwards, worried that I would have another the following night, because during periods of crisis they usually occurred several nights in a row. But it hadn't happened, and somehow I knew it wasn't going to.

"Immediately after the initiation," I said, "while sitting there meditating in that chair, I felt my chest begin to relax. The tightness just went away, in seconds. And it hasn't come back since."

The Maharishi nodded emphatically and said, "<u>Dat</u> is right meditation!"

"*Ça c'est la vraie méditation!*" I said.

The rest of the checking session was mostly taken up by the Maharishi answering questions about the process of meditation and talking about it a bit more specifically than he had in his introductory lecture, this time preaching to the more or less converted.

A common complaint from those who still seemed skeptical was that the whole time they sat there repeating their mantras, or trying to, nothing seemed to be happening. In fact instead of meditating, whatever that was, many of these people said they were just sitting there, thinking of whatever happened to pop into their heads. This was not particularly unpleasant, most of them agreed, but it was boring and felt like a big waste of time. The Maharishi explained that all thoughts people had during meditation, no matter how seemingly irrelevant or banal, were an important part of the process.

"The t'ing is, . . . the t'ing is, . . ."

The little phrase turned out to be a lot more difficult to translate than I would have thought, along with other expressions the Maharishi used repeatedly, such as "We just take it easy," and "We just take it as it comes." To translate these phrases I found myself depending a lot on context, and coming up with several dubious variations. In this instance, the thing was that as soon as the meditator realized he had wandered from the mantra and was entertaining other thoughts, he was to put the mind "gently and naturally" back onto the mantra. This last phrase also gave me problems. Putting the mind gently and naturally onto anything did not seem to be something that could be done in French.

A few people said they were afraid they had forgotten their mantras or that they might have deformed them somehow, by repeating them over and over. The Maharishi said that immediately following tonight's meeting those people should see their initiators, who were all in attendance, and who would take them into a quiet room to have their mantras checked. Once again though, as he had done several times already, the Maharishi cautioned everyone against saying their mantras out loud, even to themselves in an empty room. "For mantra to be effectiu," he said. "*Pour que la mantra soit efficace, . . .*" it should only be repeated silently, "wid'out moving de tongue or de lips."

After people had no more questions the Maharishi began to talk about a three-month course he was going to be conducting in India, starting the end of January, to train additional teachers of Transcendental Meditation, and he asked if anyone in the room might be interested in attending.

Even before translating the question, I turned to him and said I would. I had recently finished reading Aurobindo's book on Pondichery, and the idea of packing up and going off to India for three months, especially in the middle of a Paris winter, was immensely attractive.

"You will leave your name and address after the meeting, yes?" the Maharishi said. I had already noticed his way of making a command sound like a question, but this was a command I was only too glad to obey.

As the Maharishi went on talking about the course though, my hopes of attending it quickly faded. To be able to go, first you had to fill out a three-page application, with names of references, that had to be in the London office by the end of the month, only ten days away. Most daunting of all, the course would cost $3,000, plus round-trip transportation. In answer to a question from the hippie, that brought laughter from the rest of the audience, the Maharishi said no, there were no scholarships.

When the meeting was breaking up and people were filing out of the huge room I decided to stick around anyway and leave my name and address, as the Maharishi had requested. A lot of other people wanted to see him too though, so I had to wait until the crowd thinned out. While waiting, I walked up to John, my initiator, who was standing off to one side with Eileen. By now Eileen seemed like an old friend. She smiled warmly as I approached. John congratulated me on getting rid of my asthma, but said he wasn't surprised. Eileen thanked me for translating and said how marvelous it would be if I got to go to India. I told her I was afraid I couldn't afford it. She suggested I save my money and apply next year. While we were talking we were joined by the tall American in the ivy league suit who had compared learning meditation to a piece of cake. Halfway through the meeting I had seen him come in and remain standing at the back of the group. "Did you feel it?" he asked me now.

"What?"

The man laughed as if I had cracked a private joke.

"Yes, Charles, what?" asked Eileen.

"The vibrations," he replied, turning to her. "They're the strongest I've ever felt. When you get that close it's like a magnetic field. You can't miss it. He knows what I'm talking about," he said, jerking a thumb in my direction. "He's a lucky man."

All three of them turned back to me. I glanced back at the Maharishi. The woman who'd been talking to him was bowing and backing away. In both hands she held the flower he had just given her. I excused myself and made a dash for the dais before someone else beat me to it. The Maharishi nodded again, warmly.

"You come to India?"

I told him there was nothing I would rather do, but there was no way I could afford it. He wobbled his head back and forth and asked a few questions—how old I was, where I was born, what I was doing in Paris. He wrote the answers in a little black notebook he brought out from underneath his shawl. I was struck by the way he did this—holding the pencil firmly in his short, stubby fingers, his hairy arm protruding out from under the shawl—and by the fact that he did it at all. Did gurus carry notebooks? Was the Maharishi what they called a guru? Did I now have a guru? While standing there I tried to detect some sort of vibrations or waves coming off of him. Something. Anything. But I felt nothing. Maybe that would come.

CHAPTER 7

Round trip

✳ ✳ ✳

"**B**lakelee, it's for you!"

Eugene's voice had woken me up. The luminous dial of the alarm clock said fifteen minutes past midnight. I switched on the lamp. My watch said the same thing.

"Blakeleeee?"

"Coming, coming."

I scrambled out of bed, wrapped myself in the bedspread, and opened the door. Eugene was standing in the hallway in his monogrammed silk pyjamas, holding the phone in one hand and the receiver in the other.

"Sorry Eugene."

He gave me the receiver, set the telephone back on the stand at the end of the hallway and returned to his room.

I figured it was my mother. I hadn't written her for a while but I had called her once and given her this number, telling her not to call after ten p.m., as Eugene had requested. Mom never seemed to understand that Paris was nine hours ahead of California. Whenever she called the first thing she asked was, "What time is it where you are?"

It was a woman's voice, but not my mother's. Whoever it was said she was calling from the London office of the SRM.

"The what?"

"The Spiritual Regeneration Movement. You remember."

I did not remember. What I did remember, as I continued to listen, was the face that started to match the voice. It was Eileen. The woman who, over a month ago, had given me my appointment to learn meditation, and who talked to me after I'd translated for the Maharishi at the Continental. She was talking about the Maharishi now, but what she said made no sense. Speaking louder and more slowly, she said it again. She had just had a call from the Maharishi in Los Angeles. He told her that he would be stopping over at Orly the following morning on his way to India, and he wanted me to meet him there, with my bags packed.

"You mean, to go to India?"

Eileen said she assumed that's what he had in mind, yes. I said there must have been some mistake. I had no money. I hadn't even sent in an application. And I had just taken a new job. At nine o'clock the next morning I was supposed to be teaching English at IBM. Eileen sounded surprised, maybe a little miffed, that I would even think of not doing something the Maharishi had requested. She said she hoped I would find a way to be there in any case, and I said I would try.

David was still awake when I phoned him a few minutes later. My call had interrupted him in the middle of another one of his mandalic paintings. In order to make extra money to help pay for his analysis, David too was teaching English at IBM. In fact it was David who had gotten me the job.

Working at IBM was not as congenial or as adventurous as working for Donahue at the Institute for the Study of the English Language, but the pay was better and the hours regular—8:30 to 12:30 every morning in their new headquarters in Vincennes, an easy commute from Place de l'Etoile on the new rubber-tired metro. And after classes there was free lunch in the company cafeteria. But best of all, after working there for one month I would be promoted to *cadre*, which meant that I would qualify for a renewable *carte de séjour*, a full month's vacation in August, health care, and all the rest of the good things you get when you work in a country that takes care of the people who work there. In a word, I would be legitimate, *en règle*, and my days of living in France as an illegal alien would be over. That afternoon, exactly thirty days after starting my new job, I had brought home the contract that I was to sign and return to IBM the following morning.

On the other hand, David and I agreed that a free trip to India was hard to pass up. If it was going to be free, that is. For all I knew the Maharishi was expecting me to pay my own way. Or, more likely, he'd gotten me mixed up with somebody else. I decided to show up at the airport the following morning anyway and see what happened. Just in case, I'd come with a suit-case packed for three months. What would you need for three months in India, I wondered. David didn't know. He said he'd tell our mutual boss at IBM that I had come down with a bad case of *la grippe*. If David didn't get a call from me the following night, he was to tell everyone the next day at work that I'd had to go back to California to attend to my dying grandmother.

※　※　※

The next morning the clerk at the Air India counter at Orly said he had no record of a reservation for me on their scheduled flight from Los Angeles to Bombay. The flight was running late. I dragged my suitcase to a row of seats and sat down to wait. On the seat beside me was an abandoned Herald Tribune, a paper I'd stopped reading because the news was always so bad. That day it was as bad as ever, if not worse. "ENEMY LOSES 382 MEN IN TWO FRONT OFFENSIVE . . . BODY COUNT NOT YET COMPLETE FOR AMERICAN TROOPS. JOHNSON FORMULA FOR PEACE PARLEY REFUSED BY HANOI. . . 302,000 MEN TO BE DRAFTED INTO THE ARMY DURING YEAR . . ."

On the back page, at the top of the People Column, was a picture of the Maharishi, sitting with Mia Farrow.

"Actress Mia Farrow plans to accompany Indian mystic Maharishi Mahesh Yogi to India this week, where she will try 'to be a better person.' Miss Farrow and the guru, spiritual advisor to the Beatles, held a press conference at which she appeared nervous and subdued. She answered only one question on why she was making the trip, and left. The guru was not so bashful and described Miss Farrow as a 'good person, intelligent, with good human qualities. . . who is seeking higher spiritual experience, just like so many young people today.'"

While I was reading the paper the Air India clerk came up and asked if he could see my passport. This time he was a lot more polite. I took my billfold out of my jacket pocket, extracted the passport, and handed it over. The clerk looked at the picture, then at me, then handed it back and asked me to follow him, saying I could leave my luggage behind the counter.

I followed the clerk up an escalator and into a waiting room for passengers in transit. The clerk pointed at some plastic benches and said I could wait there. Several other people were sprawled out on the benches trying to make themselves comfortable, in defiance of whoever had designed the benches. I sat down and did the same, trying to play the excitement of leaving against the disappointment of finding it was all a big mistake.

"Inja!" Eugene had said that morning when I gave him the news. "You'll have a wonderful time!" He'd made it sound as if I was going on some sort of safari. And for all I knew, maybe I was. Eugene had agreed to keep the few books and clothes I'd decided to leave behind, in exchange for a fee to be determined when I got back, which as I reminded him might well be that afternoon. That morning on the way to the airport I'd asked the taxi driver to stop at my bank where I all but emptied out my checking account. Luckily Donahue had paid me everything he'd owed me a few days before, and David said he would send my first and last check from IBM to wherever I ended up in India. If I ended up in India. An "if" that was growing bigger the longer I sat there.

I squirmed around on the bench to see if I could get comfortable enough to meditate. Ever since starting meditation five weeks earlier I'd continued doing it faithfully morning and evening, as the Maharishi had directed, sometimes adding another session at night before going to sleep. While nothing terribly exciting happened during those sessions—the mysterious feelings of floating and expansion had subsided after the first week—I still found it very relaxing and pleasurable. Best of all, there'd been no recurrence of the asthma, not the slightest trace.

While I was trying to get comfortable a double door burst open twenty yards away and through it came the Maharishi. He was accompanied by several people, including the Air India clerk who had asked to see my passport. All the people sitting around me turned out to be reporters. As soon as they saw the Maharishi, they grabbed their cameras or snatched up tape recorders and made a dash to be the first to get their question answered or their picture taken.

I got up and joined the fray, wedging myself forward as flashbulbs started going off like popcorn and everybody started shouting at once. "Is Miss Farrow on the flight with you?" "Did she break up with Frank

Sinatra?" "Is that why she's interested in meditation?" "Is it true the Beatles' manager committed suicide?"

The Maharishi stood there saying nothing, smiling happily. Over his shoulders was a tan shawl and around his neck a lei of orchids that looked like he'd been wearing it awhile. The Air India clerk raised both hands to calm the reporters, and then directed them towards a first class lounge where the Maharishi was to give a press conference. The reporters ran off in that direction, leaving me alone. The Maharishi smiled and raised a finger, beckoning me forward. When I was directly in front of him he said, "So, you are coming to India?" I told him I would love to but I couldn't afford it. I said I couldn't even pay the airfare. The Maharishi wrinkled his nose and waved a hand in front of his face, as if brushing away a fly. He turned to the woman standing next to him, a middle-aged woman with horn-rimmed glasses and straight brown hair down to her pointed chin and who also wore a faded lei around her neck. "Debbie," he said, "you will buy this boy a ticket so he can come with us, yes?"

Debbie looked at me, gave an almost imperceptible shrug, and said, "Whatever you say, Maharishi."

She took a checkbook out of her handbag and asked the Air India clerk how much it would cost. One way or round trip, he wanted to know. I held my breath until I heard her say, "Round trip."

CHAPTER 8

Flying over sand and water

❋ ❋ ❋

"Ladies and gentlemen, in a few minutes we will be landing at Bombay International Airport. The temperature outside is seventeen degrees centigrade. The local time is 7:20 a.m. We ask you to please fasten your seatbelts and extinguish all cigarettes. . ."

I pushed up the shade of my window and was dazzled by a bright orange stripe, the color of a ripe mango, painted across the horizon. The sun was rising over India.

It took me a while to remember where I was and what was happening. To me. It was not a dream. After Paris we had made stopovers in Frankfurt, Cairo, and Kuwait. After leaving Kuwait I had stared for a long time down at the darkened desert, gently rising and falling like an ocean of sand. It looked like the peaceful breathing of the world asleep. I wanted to sleep too, but couldn't, too keyed up by the events of the last twenty-four hours.

Finally, while we were flying over water, I leaned back in my seat and closed my eyes. I had thought I would try to meditate or sleep but I ended up doing neither, or both, or something entirely different. India was four and a half hours ahead of Paris, where it was now three o'clock in the morning. By now David would know I was not coming back to work and would have thought of something to tell everyone at IBM. I wondered what. Why not that I had gone to India to meditate for three months? Which was just as unbelievable as going back to California to attend to my dying grandmother. Especially since both my grandmothers were dead.

Shortly after we had taken off from Paris a tall guy about my age came down the aisle to the empty row where I was sitting. He had long black hair and around his shoulders he was wearing an Air India blanket. He joined his hands in front of him, introduced himself as Larry, and said something I didn't understand.

"Oh sorry," he said. "I thought you were a meditator."

I told him I *was* a meditator.

"And you're going to Rishikesh?"

I asked him if that was where the three month course was going to be and he said yes and I said yes.

"You're going to Rishikesh and you don't know what 'Jai Guru Dev' means?"

He sat down next to me to explain. "Jai Guru Dev" meant "Hail Holy Master," or something like that. Larry said it referred not to Maharishi but to his guru, Guru Dev, and to all the other gurus that had come before him. It was something meditators said to each other as a greeting, he said, especially when they greeted Maharishi. He reached down inside his shirt and pulled out a little medallion on a chain. On one side of the medallion was a picture of the Maharishi, on the other a picture of the stern old swami whose life-sized portrait I had stared at during my initiation. That, Larry said, was Guru Dev.

Larry seemed proud of his medallion. He said he'd picked it up at the SIMS office in New York, from a guy who'd gone on the Rishikesh course the year before and brought back thousands of them.

"The SIMS Office?"

Larry looked at me. "Man, you don't know anything, do you?" He said that SIMS stood for Students International Meditation Society. It was the younger of the two movements Maharishi had started to spread meditation. The first one was the Spiritual Regeneration Movement, or SRM, based in London, and it had been around since the early 'fifties, when Maharishi first left India and came to the west. SIMS, with its headquarters in L.A., had been started seven years ago, in an effort to attract younger people to the movement. Although SIMS had gotten off to a late start, it already had more members than the SRM, Larry said, and was now spreading like wildfire among people our age, especially in the States. I asked Larry if he thought that was because of the Beatles and Mia Farrow and he said yeah, no doubt, but not as much as people thought. Among the college crowd meditation had already started to take off before the celebrities began doing it, Larry said, probably because of drugs and the war in Vietnam. By now it was obvious that demonstrations wouldn't stop the war, so maybe meditation would. And as for drugs, how many could you take before you realized there had to be another way?

Larry asked if I knew Mia Farrow was on the plane with us, and I said I'd read something to that effect in this morning's paper. He said she was traveling up in first class with her sister and Maharishi, which was why the flight attendants were being so careful about keeping the curtain closed every time they went from one section of the aircraft to the other. Also up in first class was the wife of the head of SIMS, Larry said, who I realized was Debbie, the woman who had written the check for my ticket.

While we were talking, we were joined by a pretty young blonde whom Larry introduced as Rosalyn. I moved over to sit by the window, so she could sit between us. Like Larry, Rosalyn had joined the flight in New York, and was also a member of the SIMS center there, where they had met. With her hair cut short just above her ears, Rosalyn looked a little like Jean Seberg in *Breathless*. She also reminded me a lot of someone I had gone out with for three years in college, which was why I was glad to gather, as we talked, that she and Larry were just friends.

Rosalyn was a teacher in Brooklyn, whose school had granted her a three-month sabbatical so she could go to India and learn how to become a better teacher, she hoped, more in tune with her kids. Larry was a photographer who was hoping to learn how to take better pictures. Both of them had been afraid they wouldn't be allowed to come on the course because they hadn't been meditating long enough—Rosalyn, just over a year, Larry almost two.

"And you?" Rosalyn asked.

I thought for a moment. "One month and six days," I said.

They looked at each other, then Rosalyn looked at me. "You're kidding."

I told them about the asthma, about translating for Maharishi at the Continental, and about the phone call from London that I'd received the night before.

"Far out!" Larry said, when I had finished. Then he added that my karma must be "fucking unbelievable."

Rosalyn asked me what it had felt like to sit so close to Maharishi. I had to admit I hadn't felt anything, or didn't know it if I had. Rosalyn said that was one of the things she was looking forward to on the course—being so close to Maharishi all the time so she could absorb his vibrations. She had felt them once before, at a lecture in New York, from twenty feet away, and she said they had affected her meditations for days afterwards, making them a lot deeper. She was surprised she couldn't feel them now on the plane, but Larry said that was because of the vibrations from the engines, which were too gross and blocked out everything else.

After the stopover in Frankfurt the three of us continued sitting together while they passed out the meal that was going to serve as lunch and dinner—chicken curry for Larry and me, vegetable curry for Rosalyn. I asked her if she was vegetarian. She said no, but lately she'd been wanting to purify her system to get ready for the next three months.

Larry had advised her to take the chicken. "Your system will get pure fast enough up in Rishikesh, Roz. And you'll need the protein, believe me." He explained that Maharishi's ashram was in an area of India that was a kind of religious national park. There were animals everywhere, wild ones in the jungle, and cows and oxen in the towns, and eating meat of any kind, even fish, was strictly forbidden. "Eggs too," he added.

I imagined Yosemite, but with tigers and monkeys and cows, instead of bears and deer, and patrolled by Hindu priests instead of forest rangers. "What happens if somebody catches you poaching an egg?" I asked.

"Probably nothing. But the problem is you wouldn't find one."

As we ate, the conversation turned to the mystery of the mantras. Rosalyn wondered how many there were and how they were chosen. The three of us agreed that the questionnaire you filled out for initiation didn't seem like much of a tool for plumbing the depths of someone's inner self, and we wondered what the real criteria could be. Handwriting? Astrological signs? Physical characteristics? Rosalyn seemed to think it was a combination of all of these and probably some other things we'd learn about in India, like auras.

I said that at the lecture in Paris, when somebody asked how many mantras there were, the Maharishi had said "millions."

Rosalyn said she'd heard the same thing, but she'd also heard that of those millions a much smaller number were actually used for meditation, maybe a thousand or so. I remarked that a thousand new words in a foreign language would be a lot to learn, even in three months.

Larry didn't think it was all that complicated. He said the guy who took the course last year and brought back all the Guru Dev medallions was now initiating in New York and he was no genius, by any stretch. "You know him, Roz?"

Roz said she'd met him once or twice. Bill something. Or was it Steve? And Larry was right. "Nice, but a genius he isn't."

"Right," Larry said. "So if he could do it, why worry?"

Rosalyn started arranging empty plastic cups and dishes on her tray, so the stewardess could pick them up on her next pass.

"At any rate," she said, "three more months and we'll all be in on the secret. If we all pass, that is."

"You mean people flunk out?" I said.

Larry said he'd never heard of anyone actually failing the course. Everyone who made it to the end would probably pass, he thought, but there were a lot of dropouts on the way. He knew that last year's course had started with something like forty-five people and ended with only thirty or so. This year's was going to be much bigger though, at least sixty, because Maharishi was in a hurry to train teachers and get them out there. Rosalyn said that made sense. The way the world was going, there wasn't much time left to save it.

After the trays had been cleared away Larry and Rosalyn returned to their seats to try to meditate, or get some sleep. Since I wasn't sleepy, I took out the book I'd brought along, stuffing it into my plastic briefcase at the last minute, and opened to the place I'd marked, just a few pages in.

". . .framed panuncular cumbottes like a rudd yellan
gruebleen orangeman in his violet indigonation, to the
whole length of the strength of his bowman's bill..."

A few months earlier I'd read Ulysses and liked it, once I'd gotten into it, but *Finnegan's Wake* was proving a lot harder to get into. After a few minutes I closed the book at the same page and placed it in the netbag on the back of the seat in front of me.

By that time almost everyone else in tourist class had turned out their reading light and was either meditating or asleep. Although we'd picked up a few more passengers in Frankfurt, there was still only a handful of people in the plane, and it looked like most of them were meditators. You could tell by the way they sat with their eyes closed, not collapsing downwards into sleep or sprawling out with heads thrown back and mouths wide open, but sitting upright with their heads tilting forward, jerking back up every now and then as they realized they were having other thoughts and then, "We just put the mind back on the mantra…"

Eventually I put up the armrests of my seat, tucked my legs up beneath me, and tried to put my mind on the mantra too, despite the constant throbbing of the engines, their gross vibrations…

Instead of meditating, I found myself thinking of Rosalyn, and what it was about her that reminded me of Jill, despite the Brooklyn accent. Something in her face, the lips and nose, and above all her body, its compact fullness.

Jill was the girl I fell in love with during my freshman year in college, although the expression was weak. For me, "falling in love" was coming to the stupendous realization that there was someone in the world more important than yourself, which, if that was all I'd learned in college, would have been enough.

Jill was everything I was not and all those things were better. Instead of having to live and breathe in the stifling wasteland of LA, she'd been born and raised in the pristine air of San Francisco, "the City," as she called it—actually across the Golden Gate in San Rafael where her parents rented a little house perched on a steep hill overlooking the lights of Sausalito and the Bay. Jill's parents drank wine with dinner and had voted for Kennedy, whereas my mother drank Coke and had voted for Nixon and was convinced the whole 1960 election had been a Catholic-communist conspiracy. After getting to know Jill, every time I went home to LA for long holidays or summer vacation I shrank back into someone I was ashamed to be or to have been. On the rare summer weekends I took the PSA commuter jet up to visit Jill and her parents I grew into someone I could hardly believe was me.

Up at UCSB Jill and I would study in the new library made of pink cinderblocks, sitting across from each other with our shoes off and our feet touching, our toes running up each other's legs until we couldn't stand it any longer and we would go outside and lie on the grass beneath the jacaranda and the judas trees, the whole length of our bodies touching, breathing each other's breath, saying nothing.

At night we would stand on the cliffs overlooking the beach, engulfed in the sound of the waves below and the smell of eucalyptus and star jasmine and just a hint of the pitch oil that was constantly seeping out of the fault up at Gaviota and being carried by the currents down the coast. We would stand there for hours wrapped tight into each others' arms, our lips pressed together, pausing only to breathe.

On campus, if the weather was good on Saturday afternoons we would take the path down to the lagoon and on to the beach and wander up to the deserted dunes and spread our towels in a quiet hollow and make out until I came on her smooth stomach and we would race to the surf to wash it off.

During my sophomore year my brother Tom loaned me his '51 Ford while he spent the year in the Marines, down in camp Pendleton. We used the car to drive into Santa Barbara for lunch on Sunday afternoons because the dining halls were closed. The place we liked best was the San Roque Steak House because they would let us buy wine with the meal. After lunch we would drive back to Goleta and instead of going back out to the university I would turn off towards the foothills and find an orange grove and drive until the dirt road came to a dead end. Drunk on the wine and the scent of orange blossoms we would thrash around on the front seat, caressing each other until we both came and came again, and then Jill would take the pack of Newports out of her purse and we would both light up, sitting back and blowing out the mentholated smoke in two long streams that mingled as they rose, the way our bodies urged our blood to merge.

During those two years spent in a state of constant, exquisite, aching desire, revelling in this miracle of reciprocal love, it was another miracle we never actually made love, and that by the end of our sophomore year she and I were still virgins, so to speak. But this was the early 'sixties and the taboo of sex before marriage was still very strong. Stronger still was the fear of getting pregnant. The pill was not yet easily available and abortions in Tijuana were risky and expensive.

Yet another miracle was the fact that despite all the time Jill and I spent doing anything but studying, my grades were good enough at the end of my second year to qualify me for the University of California's Education Abroad Program in Bordeaux, the first year the program existed.

The weekend before I left for France I flew up to San Rafael for a last visit. After lunch on Sunday, Jill and I went out on the porch overlooking the

Bay, waiting until it was time for her to drive me back to the airport in her parents' old Plymouth. She was sitting in a worn wicker chair and I was standing beside her, with her head against my thigh. We had promised to write each other every day, even if we didn't send a daily letter. We did not make each other promise to be faithful. The idea was beside the point, unthinkable.

I left for France the twenty-seventh of August and returned to California one year later, to the day. During the first few months Jill and I actually did write each other every day, and throughout the whole year she was constantly present in my mind. Not so much her physical image. We knew each other too well by then to visualize each other clearly. The wallet photograph I brought along of her showed how she appeared to others but not to me. Yes, that was her perfect mouth, her smile, those were her blue eyes, but to me she was so much more than the sum of her physical traits. Much more effective at conjuring up her presence was a tiny vial of her perfume she had given me as a going away present. I had only to pull off the little plastic cap and raise it to my nose to go into an ecstasy of longing that would last for hours and produce a twelve-page letter full of poetry and promises. It was my first experience with psychotropics.

This is not to say I didn't throw myself fully into the experience of living and studying in a foreign place for a year, and in 1962 France was still a very foreign place indeed. Even though I had only taken four semesters of French at UCSB, and almost flunked the first two, within three months I was speaking French fluently and spending more time with my new French friends than with my classmates from California.

One of the friends I was spending time with was not French in fact, but Spanish, at least by origin, her two parents having fled to Bordeaux during the last days of the Spanish Civil War. Aurore and I met while sitting next to each other in the amphitheater of the *faculté de lettres* during the *cours magistral* on nineteenth century poetry. Afterwards we would go for a coffee at a local café to talk about Baudelaire whose name she said I didn't pronounce correctly. "*Pas Bau-de-laire*", she'd say again and again, "*mais Bau-de-laire*," showing me how and where to place the tip of my tongue against the ridge of my teeth, while I focused on the tip of her tongue and the ridge of her teeth. Aurore had very white teeth and full red lips and the reddish-brown hair that fell to her waist was what Baudelaire was talking about when he wrote,

O TOISON, moutonnant jusque sur l'encolure!
 O boucles ! O parfum chargé; de nonchaloir!
 Extase!...

My friend Mike called her "la belle Aurore," and the nickname was appropriate. Aurore had a full, sumptuous body and her dark skin seemed lit from within by the glow of the sun rising over Spain. That's why her parents had given her that name, she explained, in hopes that she would someday see the dawn of freedom and justice in their native country. After getting her *licence* she was going to become a journalist and write articles that would help bring down Franco.

We talked about this and other things over dinners at the "*restau- u,*" sometimes followed by long walks along the quais of the Garonne where cargo ships were tied up next to rows upon rows of barrels of wine. I told her about California and she told me about "l'Andalousie," where her family was from. We decided the two places were pretty similar, and equally fascistic, she added. Aurore was a card-carrying communist and invited me to go with her to party meetings but I never did. She accepted my invitation, however, a couple of times, to come up to the room I rented in an apartment off the Place Gambetta. I had to sneak her in after the landlady had closed herself up in her kitchen to watch TV. Madame Grassin had a rule about not having visitors after dark, especially female visitors, so we had to tread carefully up those stairs and once inside my room muffle our giggles and moans and keep our voices to a whisper.

More than once I wondered what my mother would have thought if she'd known I was in bed with a communist. But Aurore was also a realist, which is why each of these bouts of passion ended with our bodies entangled in sweat-soaked sheets and pieces of clothing and this beautiful dark-skinned young woman pushing me gently but firmly away. What would she do nine months from now, she whispered, "*avec un petit Américain?*"

Later I decided this was all for the best, the way it was meant to be. This way I would save the first time for Jill.

The following September, on Saturday night of Labor Day weekend, Jill and I were back on that cliff above the campus beach at UCSB. It was a balmy, breezy night and the breeze brought with it that same rich mix of smells replete with memories of our first two years together. We had stood in each other's arms, but were now sitting on a bench. Every now and then the headlights of a car coming up the hill and onto campus lit Jill's face. It was more beautiful than I remembered, maybe because of those little lines around her eyes that I'd never noticed before. She was telling me about Bill Smith, her old high school boyfriend who had started dating her again while I was away. We had come to a pause in the conversation. I knew she wanted to tell me something and I knew it was something I didn't want to hear. Her right hand, wearing a jade ring I'd found in a store on the Rue de Rivoli and sent her for her birthday, was sandwiched in her lap between the two of mine.

"So did you, um, . . ."

"Yes," she said, looking down at our hands. "And it was horrible. I hated every minute."

Another car came up the hill. A tear fell on my hand.

"And you?" Jill said.

I sighed, withdrew my hands and looked away. "It was with a girl from Spain," I said. "Her name was Aurore."

Maybe in India I would regain all that I'd lost since I lost Jill, or since the night I stood in the middle of the street in front of our dark house in La Cañada, watching the taillights of my mother's car grow dimmer, then bright, then dimmer still, then bright again, then disappear.

CHAPTER 9

Back home in Bombay

✳ ✳ ✳

I t was water below us. The Indian Ocean. The ripples looked like wrinkles in brown skin. I couldn't tell if the lighter splotches were bursts of foam or something floating on the surface. There was a thick haze and you couldn't see the horizon, just a fading in and out of dark, dull green, smoky gray and the gray-blue of the sky. Finally, way in front and over the wing, I spotted three triangular sails, which I lost sight of then glimpsed again as we swept over them, coming in lower. Then I saw offshore rocks, smaller boats and a wide yellow beach, then green coconut palms, and concrete villa-type houses along the beach and then streets and clusters of brown and gray shops and dirty, crowded huts.

We landed in the haze and you could already smell it, feel it grit between your teeth, taste it. It was not smog or industrial smoke, but endless dust, the breath of the land, the smell of the Orient.

Originally we were supposed to continue right on from Bombay to New Delhi, but our connecting flight first got delayed and then cancelled—or maybe there was no connecting flight in the first place—and then there was a long debate about taking a train. Finally it was decided we would all be put up in hotels and take the next scheduled flight to New Delhi the following morning. The debate was carried on mostly between Debbie and the Air India Representative in Bombay, with input from the Maharishi who finally nixed the idea of taking the train because he was worried about Mia Farrow's health and safety. I knew this because most of the time we were sitting around in the terminal waiting for something to happen I was sitting next to Debbie—when she wasn't off negotiating—and her friend Nadine.

I had gotten to know them both during the stopover in Cairo while our plane was being refuelled and the Maharishi was giving another press conference. I had gotten off the plane to stretch my legs and was standing in a little boutique looking at postcards of pyramids when the two of them walked up. Debbie asked me how I was doing. I told her that the transit lounge of the Cairo International Airport was the last place I'd expected to be that night. She smiled and raised an eyebrow and said, "Yes, Maharishi does tend to surprise people."

Both she and Nadine had gotten on the plane in L.A. During the Cairo stopover the Maharishi had asked them to keep an eye on Mia Farrow, who had decided on the spur of the moment to get off the plane too but not to participate in the press conference. Debbie and Nadine had managed to follow Mia as far as the ladies room in the first class lounge, but there she'd given them the slip and now they were worried about where she was and wondered if I'd seen her. I said I wasn't sure I'd recognize her if I had.

"Oh, you'd recognize her all right," Nadine said. "Just a sprig of a thing, but she's got those big round eyes and that big smile."

"When she wants to use it," Debbie added, raising an eyebrow.

Apparently Mia Farrow had not wanted to use her smile much during the long flight from L.A., nor had she been very cooperative with the Maharishi's wishes that she sit with him during the press conferences at every stopover. It was clear that Debbie and Nadine did not think much their guru's last minute decision to bring Mia along. "After all, she's only been meditating a month," Nadine added.

Before I could formulate a response an airport official ran up to tell Debbie she was urgently needed in the first class lounge. The three of them rushed off, leaving me to contemplate the postcards, one of which was of a sphinx that had been meditating 4,500 years.

※　※　※

In Bombay a crowd of Maharishi's followers had shown up at the airport to welcome their guru back to his native land. After he and his Hollywood trophy had emerged from the aircraft and descended the moveable stairs the devotees draped him and Mia in garlands of marigolds and bestowed a few on the rest of us as well. There was a short exchange of speeches, in English and Hindi, and we were all herded off to the terminal a hundred yards away.

The sun shone milky white and warm, and with the low white stucco buildings, half covered in brilliant bougainvillea, a few crows hopping around on the tarmac, a few little planes parked here and there, I felt myself transported in a wave of jetlag dizziness back to the Burbank Airport where I'd arrived home after my junior year in France. Now as then, I felt torn by conflicting emotions. Then—five years earlier—I'd been happy to be home after a year away, but at the same time I knew that place could never be home again. Now the emotional ambivalence was due to the strange feeling of being home at last—triggered by familiar sights and sounds—yet knowing I was farther away from home than I had ever been.

Inside the terminal we all found a place to spread out or sprawl out on benches or chairs with our feet propped up on piles of luggage, waiting for the final leg of the journey. As it kept getting delayed, more and more members of our party dropped off into sleep where they sat, no pretense of meditating this time—people slumped and sagged, threw back their heads and snored through wide-open mouths, oblivious to the shouts of hawkers walking by, the muffled roar and honk of traffic on the street outside, and the occasional noise of an airplane taking off or landing. There were not more than twenty or twenty-five of us, so I couldn't figure out why they were having such a hard time getting us up to Delhi. But maybe that was the reason. They didn't want to fly a whole plane just for us.

The sense of déjà-vu I'd had while walking to the terminal continued as I sat chatting with Debbie and Nadine. It turned out Debbie's husband Jerry was not only the head of SIMS, he was also the son of Al Jarvis, who had been a popular L.A. disc jockey in the 'fifties, and whose "Make Believe Ballroom" my brothers and I used to listen to for hours when we were kids. Al Jarvis also had connections with the Beverly Hills branch of the Christian Science church, and had known my parents. But most amazing of all, when I told Debbie I'd gone to UCSB she asked me if I knew Jack Schor, who she said was the head of SIMS-UCLA, and was now "transcending all the time."

Did I know Jack Schor?

During the first semester of our freshman year Jack Schor and I had rooms across the hall from each other in the same dormitory, and right away he became the kind of friend you can only make during your first year away at college. Without Jack Schor I would never have read *Jean Christophe* or listened to Glenn Gould. It was Jack Schor who offered me my first joint during our senior year. One morning I'd walked in on him and his girl-friend Judy rolling around on the floor of their Isla Vista apartment and Jack had said, "Oh my god Josiah! You gotta try this!" Jack called me Josiah and I called him Jacques, and during the first two years when we lived on campus we would sit for hours on the ivy-covered slope above the lagoon in front of De la Guerra Commons, often with Jill between us, swooning over sunsets that were even more spectacular whenever they sent up another missile from the Air Force base at Lompoc thirty miles up the coast. I was as close to Jack as I was to Jill but without the sex and we never broke up. In fact we were still exchanging letters, although as I thought about it I realized the last letter I'd gotten from Jack, which I still hadn't answered, must have been six months ago. In that letter he'd said that he was starting grad school but he'd said nothing about Maharishi or meditation.

Jack was one of the few people I'd told that the real reason I was going to Paris was to write. After a few months I'd sent him my first batch of stories and like a true friend he'd written back to tell me how bad he thought they were except for one. Jack had a high-pitched, maniacal laugh. Just watching him laugh made me laugh too, and sometimes the two of us would laugh for hours over things no one else found funny. If there was one person who would have understood my urge to laugh out loud during my initiation it was Jack, and now I had trouble picturing him as the head of the student meditation movement at UCLA.

On the flight from Paris one of the things I'd talked about with Larry and Rosalyn was the Maharishi's conservative dress code for young people. Larry said that he got away with his own shoulder-length hair because he'd told the Maharishi he needed long hair for his job, like the Beatles, but as a general rule any hair over the ears was strongly discouraged. The rule was not set in stone, Larry said, and a lot of people our age were hoping that as more and more of us joined Maharishi's movement he would loosen up a little, but for the time being anyone who wanted to work for SIMS, even as a volunteer, was supposed to eschew the hippie lifestyle and adopt the cleancut look of the 'fifties, which for guys meant short hair and ties.

For me, wearing a tie was a copout to the establishment, a conces-sion to the old guard who had gotten us into the mess the world was in now, including those who talked about "the business of scholarship," and

I couldn't help having doubts about an organization that made its young interns dress up like Mormon missionaries.

Jack Schor had thick, black, bushy hair that grew out and up instead of down. The last time I'd seen him in Berkeley, just before I left for Paris, he'd let his hair grow out about ten inches all around. With a bushy moustache and a pointy black goatee beneath his long hooked nose, he'd looked like a Jewish devotee of Angela Davis, which he probably was.

Maybe the Maharishi was right, his movement was like a whirlwind, sweeping the world, changing people, changing everything. It had certainly caught me up and swept me away, and Jack Schor too, apparently. But now, trying to imagine him back in LA in a suit and tie and a Marine crewcut, I wasn't sure I liked the way the wind was blowing.

After Debbie left for another round of negotiations at the Air India counter, I sank down on the bench with my feet up on the suitcase to try and take a nap. But no matter how comfortable I managed to get, sleep was still impossible. I was too keyed up, too excited about where I was.

Finally I got up and started walking around the terminal. I would have liked to go outside but I didn't want to abandon my suitcase, especially with the typewriter zipped up inside it, and I was afraid I might miss an announcement telling us to scramble for a waiting aircraft.

In a far corner of the lounge, I came across Mia and her sister Prudence sitting by themselves at a little table. Spread out in front of Mia were sheets of stationery, some with writing on them. It looked like she'd been crying but as I came up she wiped her eyes and smiled.

"It's so hard for me to write," she said. "I get so emotional."

As soon as she spoke I realized it was not the big eyes or the wide smile. It was the voice. Tinny and a little coarse. Savvy. Sexy. It was a voice right out of Hollywood in the nineteen-thirties. A very American voice. It had seduced America's number one voice, after all. The Voice.

"Yeah, I can imagine," I said, thinking immediately that the last thing I could imagine was writing Frank Sinatra a letter saying you never wanted to see him again, or you wanted to come straight home, or you wanted him to come and join you in India. Somehow I couldn't imagine Frank Sinatra in an ashram. Mia invited me to join them at the table, so I pulled out a chair and sat down. Prudence asked me where I'd joined the flight and I said Paris.

"You don't look French," Mia said.

I told them my little story—the reason I was in Paris, the lecture a month ago, the effect of meditation on the asthma, the midnight call from London, my last minute departure, how strange it felt now to find myself in India. Prudence listened intently and, like Rosalyn and Larry, seemed duly impressed. Mia yawned and stretched and said, "Yeah. It was kinda like that for me too."

Both seemed interested when I told them I was from Los Angeles, and had spent my first nine years in Cheviot Hills, a stone's throw away from where they'd been brought up. When I told them I found a lot in common between Bombay and Burbank they both laughed.

"Gee whiz!" Mia said. "I never would have made that connection."

I didn't tell her one more reason I felt close to home all of a sudden was that I was sitting close to her. Even though we hadn't been raised on the same side of the tracks, we came from the same town and spoke the same language with the same accent. What's more, I couldn't help thinking how similar we both were, physically. Especially in that setting, where blonds were a distinct minority. Mia could have been my sister.

But not her sister. The whole time I sat there almost the only thing Prudence said was "Wow!" And that in a voice you could hardly hear. From Larry I had learned that it was Prudence who had gotten Mia interested in meditation. She herself had already been meditating for a couple of years, and was obviously much more suited for it than Mia. In contrast to Mia's laid back, open, friendly manner, Prudence seemed to have a spring wound up inside her. Over the next two months that spring would get wound tighter and tighter until it finally broke. But now she just sat there listening, nodding, and every now and then saying "Wow!" in that thoughtful, quiet voice.

After a while I went back to the bench where my suitcase was waiting and Nadine had finally slouched into slumber and I sat back down and tried to do the same but once again to no avail.

Around noon local time, the time I would normally be waking up back in Paris, Debbie returned with a slip of paper containing a list of hotels where everyone was to spend the night. Raising her voice above the din inside the terminal, she told all of us within earshot to take our luggage outside where we would be put into taxis that would take us to our respective destinations.

My roommate for the night turned out to be Gert, a German SIMSer we'd picked up in Frankfurt. Gert was big and portly and had a close-trimmed, dark red beard. Even after a long flight with little or no sleep, Gert maintained an earnest air of placid self-assurance that I found annoying, probably because it reminded me of a lot of Christian Scientists I'd known. I also disliked the way he would join his hands and scrape and bow whenever he found himself within twenty yards of the Maharishi, who was about half his size.

The hotel Gert and I were driven to was on the outskirts of town, near the beach, presumably the beach I had glimpsed through the window when the plane banked left before landing. Although the hotel had opened only eight days ago, you had the feeling it was already being reclaimed by the jungle. Hanging on the door of the brand new elevator was a delicately handwritten sign that read, "Temporarily in Disrepair." Some of the marble steps on the way up to the second floor were cracked and chipped. The door to the room Gert and I shared only shut when you gave it a shove, and huge cracks ran up the walls and across the ceiling.

Later that evening, as I sat at a table typing up notes on the Olivetti, more than one cockroach skittered out from underneath it, and through the open window, not six feet away from where I sat, a lizard crawled in from the night and settled on the sill to watch, the light from the lamp behind me reflected back in its unblinking stare. It was only about four inches long, but with a fluorescent green body sprinkled on the top with bright red spots, it was unlike any lizard I had ever seen.

The notes I was typing up were things I had been jotting down since leaving Paris. Ever since my first year in college I'd been keeping a journal and more and more that journal was becoming a random collection of thoughts, observations, descriptions of things I'd seen or bits of conversation I'd heard during the day. I would usually jot these things down, as they happened, on a little notebook I carried around in my back pocket, or sometimes just on scraps of paper I found handy—the margins or blank pages of a book I was reading, the corner of a paper tablecloth, half a paper napkin I would carefully fold and stuff into my pocket or a corner of my briefcase. Later, usually at night before going to bed, I would take all these notes out from wherever I'd stashed them and copy them down, typing them up on loose sheets, along with the date, then adding those sheets to others in a binder.

The idea was each day to try to make sense out of these random thoughts and observations, hopefully putting some semblance of order into the chaos of the day's events. Sometimes it worked, sometimes it didn't. Sometimes the notes added a little chaos of their own, especially those inspired by a half bottle of wine over lunch, insights that at the time had seemed so significant but later caused me to wonder what in the world I'd been thinking. Those I usually discarded, unless they were truly strange. Me speaking in tongues. Maybe that's what Joyce was up to in *Finnegan's Wake*.

That evening it took me more than two hours to copy down the notes I'd accumulated during that long day—a day that had started out in Paris after all—adding from memory bits of the conversations I'd had with Debbie and Nadine, Larry and Rosalyn, Mia and her sister, as well as other things I'd seen and heard, such as the row of bulletholes in the windows of the airport van that took us from the plane to the terminal in Cairo, and that Larry explained as a souvenir of the Six Day War, leaning closer to add in a whisper, "Don't tell them I'm Jewish."

While typing away, listening to the night sounds coming through the window: cars and motor bikes going by outside, vendors' bells ringing, children laughing, parents calling them home, I was again struck by how familiar it all looked and sounded and felt. Except for the lizard eyeing me from the sill.

Earlier that afternoon, as soon as we'd checked into the the room, I'd lain down on one of the twin beds and immediately fallen asleep, waking up four hours later wondering where I was. After that, Gert and I had eaten an early dinner in the hotel restaurant—by far the hottest curry I'd ever eaten—then we'd gone for a sunset walk along the wide, flat beach. As we walked along I couldn't help thinking of the beach at Santa Monica, where my parents would take me and my three older brothers on Saturday after-noons. Maybe it was something in the quality of the air, or the feel of the sand beneath my feet. Only here there were no musclemen lifting weights, no groups of people playing volleyball, no nearly naked couples making out on towels spread out on the sand. Instead, there was a couple standing at the bottom of a set of crumbling concrete stairs leading down from the jungle that lined the shore. She was wearing a sari, he a shirt and tie but no coat. Maybe they had just gotten off work and had come to spend ten minutes together before they'd both be missed at home. By then fog was blowing in from the sea, and every time a cloud engulfed them they would come together and kiss. Standing arm in arm as Gert and I walked past them twenty yards away, they looked like a clouded vision from an expurgated version of the Kama Sutra.

Shortly afterwards I'd had to abandon Gert on the beach and race back to the hotel, suddenly taken with a case of dysentery that had me running to the toilet pretty much nonstop during the whole three months that followed, and then on and off for the next twenty years, causing me to reflect more than once that if I'd gotten nothing else from my trip to India, at least I'd come away with that.

CHAPTER 10

Dilly-dallying in Delhi

I n Delhi the next morning once again we walked the distance from the aircraft to the terminal, again surrounded by an enthusiastic, picture-taking welcoming committee, while a swarm of porters took care of our luggage, transporting it by hand or on hand-pulled carts or on top of their turbaned heads.

Things were better organized than in Bombay, probably because Maharishi had been expected to arrive two days earlier and people had time to get organized, and grow impatient. As I was soon to learn, Maharishi was always, always late—sometimes only an hour or so, as he had been for the introductory lecture at the Paris Hilton—sometimes by a couple of days. No one seemed to mind too much, at least none of his followers. I think some of them even took it as a test—part of the price one had to pay for attaining enlightenment.

As soon as our luggage had been amassed in the middle of the terminal waiting room we each sorted out what belonged to us and dragged it out to the street in front of the airport where taxis were waiting to take us to the place where all the waiting had been taking place, the YMCA Tourist Hostel, about a half-hour drive from the airport.

Because of its reasonable prices and central location, the YMCA had been chosen as the gathering place for everyone who was going to attend the three-month teacher-training course. Apparently I was not alone in thinking that after a short stay at the Y we would all move on to Maharishi's ashram, 250 kilometers to the north. Instead, it turned out that Maharishi had organized a "World Peace Conference" that would take place over the next few days and consisted of a number of public lectures and conferences and other activities in which we were all expected to participate. By and large everyone seemed to take this further little delay in stride, accepting it with a mix of resignation and indulgence. Maybe it was another test.

And so, during the next five days the New Delhi YMCA became the joint world headquarters of the SRM and SIMS, with planning sessions and organizational meetings and group meditations going on in crowded rooms all hours of the day and night, and endless lines of shoeless pilgrims holding flowers, people who arrived in droves in hopes of a private audience with the now world-famous guru. Outside there was a steady stream of cars and limos in front of the hotel, bringing dignitaries and high government officials and others who wanted to pay their respects to the Maharishi and maybe at the same time get a glimpse of or maybe even an autograph from one of his more famous converts. So far though the only celebrity among us was Mia, and she was never really among us, staying not at the Y but across town at the new luxurious Oberoi, along with her sister and anyone else who could afford it, or stand it. The Oberoi was like the Paris Hilton, only worse. A place where you could order hamburgers and dry martinis and sit around the pool watching western girls in bikinis. I went there once, but three months later, at the end of the course, and only to use the pool, because by then the weather in New Delhi was beyond hot.

By the time our contingent arrived from Bombay there was no more room at the Y, so Larry and I were put up in a small house a short walk away, where we shared a bare room on the second story with concrete walls and a concrete floor with a drain in the middle and two narrow beds and a door that opened out onto a small terrace overlooking a little yard on the ground floor enclosed on three sides by high hedges. The house was owned by by a middle-aged couple who were also followers of Maharishi, although the wife seemed more devoted than the husband, since she was always away at meetings, and he was always at home, at least whenever I was there. At fifty-five or so, with curly gray hair and a modest paunch, he had a quiet, friendly manner that reminded me of Jill's father. One afternoon Larry and I were sitting with him on the terrace looking at three children in the yard below playing what looked like an Indian version of hopscotch. A servant they called Mohan or Mohandas had just served chai and we were sipping it and munching samosas and watching the children, when the man raised a finger in the air and said "That is Transcendental Meditation!"

"Right on, man!" said Larry.

But most of the time we were in Delhi Larry and I spent at the YMCA, where we also took all our meals. While sitting around in the YMCA dining room, or waiting for another meeting to get off to another late start, I started getting to know and to make friends with some of my fellow teachers-of-Transcendental-Meditation-to-be. It turned out to be a pretty heterogeneous bunch, everyone having widely different backgrounds, doing different things, and hailing from different places in the world. The areas of the world most heavily represented were countries in Northern Europe, plus the United States and Canada, where the Maharishi had made the deepest inroads in the past ten years, and received the warmest welcome.

During the next five days I found myself fraternizing and eating a lot of my meals with a contingent of Scandinavians, who because of my blond hair and Norwegian mother seemed to adopt me as one of their own and called me Rikard. Among them was Berndt Schneider, approximately my age and size, with longish brown hair and a short scraggly beard, and Gunilla, an attractive young woman with long dark hair, salient cheekbones and blue eyes. Both Berndt and Gunilla were members of SIMS Stockholm, of which Berndt was president.

There were also three Americans, Tony, Tom, and Terry. Tony was a blackjack dealer from Las Vegas who spoke English with a strong New Jersey accent, since that's where he'd been raised. Terry was a forest ranger from California and spoke English like a cowboy. Tom was an actor from Hollywood who spoke English with whatever accent was required by the movie he was acting in, none of which any of us had ever seen.

So along with Larry, Rosalyn, Prudence, Mia, myself, and a few others, U.S. Americans were a majority among the younger people in the group, the next nationality probably being British, with a group of five or six including Geoffrey from London, Colin from somewhere north of there, and a pretty, winsome, blond girl named Viggie. There was an Irish poet named Kieran Kilroy who in addition to being a meditator was a devout Catholic and who, when he heard I was living in France, suggested that after the course was over we meet in Saintes-Marie-de-la-mer, to be on hand for the annual visitation of the Virgin.

Finally, there were two Australians, Jeremy and Ian, both of whom walked with a limp and the help of a cane, Ian because of polio at an early age, Jeremy because of a clubfoot. "The gimpy Aussies," as Ian referred to the two of them.

All of these people and more I met in New Delhi during those first five days, and over the next three months became quite close to many of them—to some quite close indeed. Somone I did not become close to was Tom the Actor, probably because he started hitting on Rosalyn as soon as we arrived, and worse, Rosalyn started responding.

In all, there were about sixty of us, including people staying at the Oberoi and other places around town, and like the small group of younger people I was getting to know, the group as a whole was quite diverse, with people from all walks of life and with a wide range of incomes—from the very wealthy who traveled with Maharishi wherever he went and whenever they could, down to those who, like Rosalyn and Terry and Tony, had to request a leave of absence from their jobs and spend all their savings to come. According to Debbie, I was the only one there on scholarship.

As a rule the group tended to split down the middle according to age, with SIMSers on one side and SRMers on the other. Perhaps this was only natural, it was after all the decade of the Generation Gap. But this tendency was also favored by the way Maharishi's movement was organized, with the SRM as the original, parent group, and SIMS coming along many years later, in an effort to attract younger people. During the next few days in Delhi these two separate branches were represented by the two leaders of each organization, Jerry Jarvis, Debbie's husband, who flew in from Scandanavia to attend the World Peace Conference, and Charlie Jackson, whom I had first seen pacing around the hotel room of the Continental, and who was one of those who traveled with Maharishi whenever they could. According to Larry, Charlie was one of the original SRMers, and whenever he was with Maharishi he followed him around like a faithful dog. While Charlie and Jerry were always polite with one another and seemed to get along well enough, I sometimes thought I could detect a muted sense of rivalry between them. At the end of the course this rivalry would break out into open conflict between the two branches of Maharishi's movement, bringing about some far-reaching and regrettable changes. But for the time being during those days in Delhi the two generations got on amicably enough, despite a tendency among certain members of the SRM to look down their noses at the SIMSers as newcomers and upstarts, for whom Transcendental Meditation might just be a fad or passing fancy, and who were therefore less deserving of Maharishi's time and attention. Many of the people in the SRM, after all, and probably most of them on the course, had been following Maharishi and practicing Transcendental Meditation faithfully for ten years or more.

One person on the course who did not fit neatly into her allotted category was a woman named Reumah, from Tel Aviv. Reumah was in her mid-forties and she got along as well with Larry and me and the other younger members of the group as she did with her contemporaries, if not better. One afternoon when neither of us had any meeting where our presence was required Reumah asked me if I wanted to join her for a little sightseeing in Old Delhi.

Happy to escape the madness at the Y, the two of us hailed a bicycle rickshaw out in front and asked the driver to take us to the Jama Masjid Mosque. On the way there, Reumah explained she was anxious to compare this mosque with the one in Jerusalem which she had visited many times and was one of her favorite places. Quoting from her guidebook, she said the Jama Masjid was built in the mid-seventeenth century and was the largest mosque in Asia, able to accommodate as many as 25,000 worshippers at one time.

The driver dropped us off at the bottom of a vast set of stone steps. At the top of the steps we came out onto a huge, flat plaza, paved with red sandstone, and in the middle of the plaza, about fifty yards from where we stood, one of the most beautiful buildings I'd ever seen. At first glance, and from a distance, it looked like a fragile, hand-carved, incredibly detailed bibelot, but a bibelot that took up the space of a football field. At each end two slender minarets rose 120 feet in the air, like gigantic knitting needles, each topped with a graceful turret. Above the mosque, between the minarets, were three onion domes. The largest dome in the center capped the vaulted central gateway, sixty feet high and forty feet wide, open like the mouth of God ready to receive the faithful gathered in the courtyard—all 25,000 of them—in one gulp.

Looking at the mosque from the top of the stairs, I was struck by the vast scale of the place, and the overall sense of peace and harmony and equilibrium. Maybe this was due to the symmetrical repetition of columns and arches and delicate geometrical patterns of white marble against red sandstone, whispering something over and over in a language I could not understand. By comparison, Notre Dame suddenly seemed cluttered and diminished in my memory, crowded in on all sides by all those statues of gods and saints and angels.

That sense of peace and harmony was shattered half an hour later when Reumah and I descended into the narrow, winding steets that surrounded the mosque on three sides, in order to "take a stroll through picturesque Chandni Chowk," which according to Reumah's guidebook, was a must after the mosque.

Chandni Chowk is not a place you stroll through. Up on the plateau where the mosque stood everything had been lightness and order and beauty. Down in the swarming, squirming chaos of the alleys and by-ways of Chandni Chowk all was confusion and noise. Searching for a taxi or rickshaw that could take us back to the Y, Reumah and I threaded our slow way through those narrow streets and alleys, all packed shoulder-to-shoulder with people, most of whom were shouting, many of them at Reumah and me. Getting jostled by people pushing past us, pushing our own way past skinned animals hanging upside down and covered with flies, being yelled at by merchants who wanted to sell us packs of batteries, cigarettes, hashish, statuettes, tugged on by hordes of barefoot, dirty, begging children, assailed by a mix of odors that was one moment tantalizing, the next disgusting—if not both at the same time—I no longer had the impression of being in familiar territory. It was as if I had stepped back into another century, or another world—bewildering, exciting, disorienting (or simply Orienting), and a little scary.

For Reumah it was not as overwhelming, she told me later. Israel could be like that in places too. By then we had finally found an available pedicab, and the driver was picking up speed on streets that were gradually getting wider and better paved and less crowded. As we were approaching Connaught Place, Reumah asked me what I thought of the inside of the mosque. I said I'd found it impressive, but not as impressive as the streets around and below it, although oppressive might have been a better word. Reumah said that she herself had been a little disappointed. She said she had been expecting something uplifting, sacred and holy, like the feeling she had in the mosque in Jerusalem. But instead she had felt nothing.

"Perhaps that is not the fault of the mosque," she added with a short laugh, "but with me."

She told me these past few days she'd been feeling confused, even depressed—a rare confession for a meditator, especially an SRMer. Reumah had been meditating for more than seven years, and for her, attending the course was the realization of a long-cherished dream, but she confided in me that so far the course was not living up to her expectations. The main problem, she admitted, was the people.

"I thought they were going to be easy to talk to," she said. "Since they were all meditating they would all be special." She looked at me and laughed again. "Like me!" She shrugged and sighed and looked away. "But, no. They are just more of the same, it seems. Petty and superficial and…" She shook her head, "concerned with such silly things!"

I knew what she meant. That morning while having breakfast I'd heard a woman behind me say to someone sitting next to her, "Ever since I arrived my meditations have been terrible, but my BM's have been just marvellous!"

I told this to Reumah, explaining what a BM was, and she laughed, saying she knew exactly who I was talking about. The woman was Mrs. Harrington, the mother of Colin, from Northern England, and the woman Colin's mother had been talking to was Mrs. Ostrovsky, one of two women on the course from Brazil, both of whom Reumah said she liked well enough, but did find, yes, a little strange.

Then there was the tall, blond, obnoxious American woman named Nancy who was staying at the Oberoi and who, according to Larry, had been with Maharishi a very long time and was very rich, married to some right wing L.A. lawyer. Whenever Maharishi came into a room she would elbow her way past everybody else until she was standing right in front of him, towering over him, at which point she would clap her hands together, her wrists and fingers glittering with jewels, and shout out "JAI GURU DEV, MAHARISHI!"

And of course there was Charles, also staying at the Oberoi, whose strange behavior I had already witnessed at the Continental in Paris. This time as soon as he saw me at the Y he had walked right up and said, "I told you so."

"Told me what?" I asked.

"That you're a lucky man."

I had to admit he was right though, I *was* lucky, and Reumah said she thought that was true too, but maybe for other reasons. I thought for a moment before I asked her what she meant. By then we had wheeled around and away from the noise and traffic on Connaught Place and were rolling down narrower, quieter streets, getting close to the Y. We were silent for a while, swaying gently back and forth, listening to the rhythmic click of the wheels, then Reumah turned to me and said, "I see that you are very close to your mother."

"You do?"

"Oh yes, and she is close to you. I can feel that."

Instead of replying that my mother was one of the reasons I'd left the States, I said it had been a long time since I'd last written her and that she would be surprised indeed to know I was in India, about to attend a three-month course on Transcendental Meditation.

"Appalled, would be more like it," I added.

Reumah mulled that over for a while and then suggested that I write my mother as soon as possible, telling her where I was and why I was there and that I was seeking God in my own way.

By then we had arrived back at the hotel and the pedicab driver had dismounted from his seat, waiting for us to climb down from ours. Just as well, I thought. If I'd had time to reply to Reumah I would have told her I'd had enough of God and what people had to say on the subject, especially my mother. The Muslims had it right, but why not take it one step further? Even better than not depicting the divine, whatever that was, why even talk about it? The less said the better.

CHAPTER 11

A stab at world peace

※ ※ ※

Nevertheless, the following morning I followed Reumah's advice and wrote my mother a letter. It turns out I had lots of time to write it because the meeting I was supposed to have with Maharishi at nine didn't take place until noon. It was actually a private audience. The night before, after Reumah and I got back from Old Delhi, there had been a planning session with Maharishi, Jerry Jarvis, and all the SIMSers. One of the main events of the World Peace Conference was going to be an appearance the following afternoon by Maharishi at the University of Delhi, where he was hoping to ignite the kind of interest among students that was sweeping Europe and North America, and establish a firm foothold for an Indian branch of SIMS. At the planning session, Maharishi explained that he wanted each of us to prepare a two to three minute presentation about how fast Transcendental Meditation was spreading in our home countries and all the good things happening as a result. The next morning he would meet with each of us one by one, to listen to what we had prepared, then we would deliver our presentations that afternoon at the University, as a part of Maharishi's talk.

That night after dinner I went back to compose my speech at the house where Larry and I were staying. It turned out to be a lot harder than I thought. Since I hadn't been back in the States for a couple of years, I assumed Maharishi wanted me to say something about Paris, but what could I say? The speech at the Hilton had been a near disaster, and since I'd only been meditating for a month I hardly knew anything about the movement in France, or anybody in it, or even if there was one. Finally I put together a little talk that started by briefly summing up Maharishi's introductory lecture, leaving out the gorier details, then describing the more enthusiastic reception at the Continental, and ended with some remarks about how the seeds Maharishi had planted in France would no doubt sprout and grow until one day even the naturally skeptical French would recognize the benefits to be gained from meditation and take to it in droves.

To a certain extent I actually believed this. I thought meditation was great—look what it had done for me! What I especially liked about Transcendental Meditation was that there was no BS about God attached to it. You didn't have to believe in anything to practice it. As my new friend Berndt was fond of pointing out, meditation was like brushing your teeth. You just did it twice a day and went on with the rest of your life. There was no religious crap thrown in, no belief system you had to adhere to. And while I was sure not everyone would have the same immediate, dramatic results that I had had, I did believe that everyone who took up meditation seriously, and who kept it up for a while, would eventually experience some sort of positive effects in their daily life. And if enough people did it, who knows? In the long run maybe it would help bring about peace in the world. Why not?

The trick was how to say this without sounding like I was preaching and trying to make converts, especially in India, of all places. The last thing I wanted to do was stand up in front of a bunch of Indian university students, who had their own long traditions I knew next to nothing about, and sound like I was reading a commercial. But as it turned out that's exactly what Maharishi wanted us to do, which was one of the reasons my meeting with him the next day was such a disaster.

The next morning I got to the Y in time for breakfast, then joined the rest of my fellow SIMSers in the room where they were sitting around waiting for their appointments with Maharishi. The room was a kind of library, with tables and chairs in the middle and benches along the walls, as well as a few shelves with the usual assortment of books that travelers leave behind. Half of one wall was taken up with windows that looked out onto a dry, scruffy garden. The room Maharishi was in also looked out onto the garden, although you couldn't see him through the windows because the curtains of the room he was in were partially drawn. Every now and then someone would come out and say someone's name and that person would go in.

By the time my name was called I'd had plenty of time not only to write a three-page letter home, but also to go over the speech I'd prepared the night before, making changes and adding finishing touches until I was actually fairly pleased with it. When I finally got up and walked into the room next door I was sure Maharishi would be pleased with it too.

He was sitting in the middle of a long, low bench covered with vinyl cushions. Over the cushion in the middle someone had placed the deerskin which Maharishi always sat on and which I'd first noticed on the blue sofa in the Continental in Paris. Larry told me that for one of Maharishi's recent appearances in New York it was he who had been in charge of the deerskin, picking it up from the seat of Maharishi's car and rushing it inside the lecture hall to place it on the chair down in front before Maharishi got there, then after the lecture, folding it carefully and rushing it back to the car out in front. Larry said he didn't know exactly what it was about the deerskin, but he did know Maharishi couldn't sit down without it.

I paused at the door for a quick salute and a "Jai Guru Dev," then strolled into the room and sat down next to Maharishi on the bench. Just like at the Continental, when I'd sat next to him to translate, my head was a few inches higher than his. I hunkered a little lower and unfolded the sheet of paper my little speech was written on. When I turned to look at him I didn't have to feel his vibrations to know something was wrong. He squirmed on his deerskin, jabbed a finger at the floor in front of him, and said "Indeed!" Realizing he'd been expecting me to sit on the floor, I quickly got up and sat down tailor fashion at his feet, hoping my little gaffe would be forgotten as soon as he'd heard my speech.

I started reading it carefully and slowly, pausing now and then for effect. When I mentioned Descartes I looked up to make sure he'd gotten the reference. Maharishi was looking at me intently, his brows furrowed.

"You know," I said. "A French philosopher? 'I think therefore I am'?"

Maharishi's expression did not change. I went back to my little text. By the time I reached the end and looked up again Maharishi had the same expression on his face. It was as if he was wondering if he'd heard correctly. For a while neither of us said anything. Then he cocked his head to one side and said, "You are not French?"

It was not until much later that I learned the reason Maharishi had invited me along to India had nothing to do with my vibrations or my aura or my high level of spiritual evolvement, but simply because he'd thought I was French and wanted a Frenchman along for his World Peace Conference. I learned this from Berndt, with whom I remained in contact long after the course was over. As the head of SIMS-Stockholm, Berndt attended a lot of the staff meetings in New Delhi, and was privy to a lot of course gossip. He told me that not only did Maharishi think I was French—even though on the night of the checking session at the Continental I'd told him I was American, born in California—but Berndt also related a rumor that had circulated shortly afterwards, to the effect that I had intentionally concealed my real nationality so as to be invited along. Of course this initial misunderstanding got me off on the wrong foot with my guru even before the course began, and gave rise to a lot more misunderstandings along the way. But I remained unaware of all of this, and for the most part blissfully so, until Berndt told me about it up in Stockholm a year later. When he did, it explained a lot of other things as well.

After Maharishi had digested the bad news that I was just another American (and a freeloader to boot), he had me read my speech again, this time stopping me after every sentence, sometimes after every word, to make suggestions for revision. It was my first experience with his desire to control everything that took place around him, down to the tiniest detail. No wonder his meetings got so far behind! But in the case of my little speech it was not the details Maharishi changed, or suggested I change, but the whole thing, top to bottom, content and style.

The first sentence of my original version read, "I am an American living in Paris." For reasons now obvious, Maharishi had me change this to "I am living in Paris," or, "better yet," he said, with a wobble of his head, "'I am from Paris.'" From there on, every expression or word that could have conveyed the slightest negative connotation he had me either delete or change to something more positive-sounding. The "naturally skeptical" French, became merely "inquisitive." "Aggressive political questions" became "expressions of intense curiosity." In my version I had described the lecture at the Hilton as an "animated confrontation"—already an understatement—but Maharishi changed this to "an introduction to the wisdom of the ages." I began to wonder if we were talking about the same event, and then to revise my own opinion of Maharishi's apparent equanimity the night of the lecture, after people had started shouting names at him and stormed out of the hall. *Maybe he hadn't seen what I had.*

For someone who had been brought up by people who preferred illusion to reality, this was not a comforting thought. At any rate, by the time Maharishi and I had finished going over my speech, it was even shorter than its original two minutes and sounded just like a commercial. I didn't see how I could read it in public and keep a straight face.

Luckily, I didn't have to.

We were sitting in a semicircle on the stage. There were about thirty of us, the entire SIMS contingent on the course, with a few exceptions, most notably Mia, who according to rumor had flat out refused. Her sister was there though, sitting in the middle, peering out at the auditorium through her big round glasses, looking as uncomfortable as the rest of us. All of the guys had been told to wear the standard SIMS uniform, coats and ties. The girls, poor things, were wearing saris. On an Indian woman who has worn one all her life, a sari adds grace to her already graceful movements. Not that Western women don't have grace of their own, but instead of enhancing it, five yards of fabric just get in the way. Most Western women wearing a sari look like they are constantly afraid it's about to come undone. When they walk it looks as if their ankles are attached by a short length of rope. When they sit down they seem at a loss for what to do with all that fabric, but at the same time afraid something will show.

That's how all the female SIMSers looked that afternoon. Afraid. And for good reason. That's how we all felt. It was a large auditorium and even before we filed onstage the hall was packed, almost entirely with men. Wearing turbans and dense beards, most male college students in India look a lot older than their counterparts in the West. And while the atmosphere did not seem openly hostile, at least not yet, it certainly seemed that most of the people in the audience had not come there for "an introduction to the wisdom of the ages."

Maharishi was sitting in the middle of the stage, a few feet behind the proscenium—the center of the half circle of disciples behind him. Also in attendance, but sitting stage left, was Charlie, Maharishi's official deerskin porter that day, and next to Charlie Jerry Jarvis, who had come along to be on hand at the end of the meeting, so that he could sign up new recruits and help set up the new SIMS center. Also sitting on the sidelines with Charlie and Jerry were a couple of deans or other officials from the University.

In front of Maharishi was a microphone on a short stand, and next to him, on his left, a tall one for each of us to come up one by one and speak into. The idea was for him to start the meeting by introducing each one of us by name—"Here is Berndt from Stockholm. . . And now Lawrence from New York. . ." After all of us had given our little speeches Maharishi would launch into his standard introductory lecture, to be followed by questions from the audience.

But of course it didn't turn out like that.

A few of us did make it up to the mike to stand beside Maharishi and give our speeches. Prudence did, and so did a dazzling blonde called Ingrid from Denmark, Gert from Germany, Berndt, usually so relaxed and composed but who on this occasion looked extremely uncomfortable. Each speaker started out by giving their name, saying where they were from, then conveying greetings from all their fellow members of the Students International Meditation Society back in . . . Soon it was obvious to everyone in the audience that all the speeches were canned. It was also clear that they were designed to convince everyone who had not yet started Transcendental Meditation to do so just as soon as possible.

The audience wasn't buying it. At first there was some polite applause after each little speech, but as each speaker kept repeating the same thing, the applause became mixed with hoots and boos, and then there was no applause at all. Finally, after only six or seven of us had gotten up to talk, and to the enormous relief of the rest, Maharishi cut short the side show and started in on his own talk. He began by chiding the Indian students for their lack of hospitality. This time he made no attempt to ignore the hostility, as he had done in Paris. But then how could he? The audience at the Paris Hilton was peaceful and subdued compared to this group, which was rapidly turning into an angry mob.

It was Maharishi's mention of "Mother India" that finally set them off. Before he could finish his sentence, one of the students down in front jumped up onto his chair, raised his fist in the air, and shouted, "How dare you lecture us about Mother India!" Then, still pointing at Maharishi, he turned to the rest of the crowd and gave an impromptu speech about "these self-proclaimed wise men" who abandon their country to become wealthy abroad by selling their traditions in the West. As soon as he'd finished another student sitting a few rows back jumped up on his chair, shook his fist at Maharishi and shouted something about "all you old men with long beards." He went on with an impassioned speech of his own, that drew cheers and wild applause, about "so-called religious leaders" in India who tried to divert poor people's attention from their misery by keeping them immersed in superstition.

It began to look like we SIMSers from the West were not the only ones who had come with prepared talks—giving credence to something Charlie would say later. Maybe attendance at Maharishi's talk had been assigned in Poli Sci 101, with extra credit if you gave a speech. Or maybe in India, as in Paris, it was not possible to just get up and start talking about "a great new movement that was sweeping the world," without taking into consideration the different political contexts that allowed that movement to spread in certain parts of the world, but not in others. Especially if you got up to talk to a bunch of university students. I wondered what would have happened if Maharishi had tried to stage a similar event at the Sorbonne. Which then made me wonder who had dreamed up this event in the first place. What a dumb idea!

By now everybody in the large lecture hall was on their feet and anything Maharishi tried to say was immediately drowned out by shouts of "Give your millions to the poor!" "There are too many holy men in India!" "Stay home and help feed the hungry!" People in the audience who were not standing on their chairs were waving them in the air. It looked like they were going to start throwing them at the stage, or take it by storm.

Time to call in the cavalry, and it galloped up in the form of Charlie Jackson. Finally unable to restrain himself any longer, Charlie ran to the front of the stage, where he started strutting back and forth between Maharishi and the raging crowd. It almost looked like he was inviting students to come up onstage and duke it out—John Wayne ready to take on the injuns—or that he was about to jump down there among them.

Rather than calming the audience, of course, Charlie's antics only stirred them up further. While Maharishi shouted "Charlie! Charlie!" at the top of his high, squeaky voice, trying to get him to go back to his seat, the officials from the University also jumped up and herded us all backstage, where we escaped out a back door and into the taxis that had brought us there and were still waiting, thank God, to take us back to the YMCA.

So much for World Peace.

Back at the Y the general reaction, especially among the SRMers who only heard about what happened, was one of shock and sorrow. Shock that Maharishi had been treated like that, and by his own compatriots in his own country, and sorrow that he had planned this great party, organized this wonderful opportunity for East to meet West, and it had all been spoiled. Charlie said not to worry. Charlie had arrived back at the Y an hour later, and by some miracle, still in one piece. After the debacle at the University he had ridden in the limousine that had taken Maharishi on to the next event, a reception at the home of "a high official in the Gandhi government." Charlie said that on the way there Maharishi had not seemed the least bit perturbed, and passed off the whole thing as his karma. According to Charlie, it had been a put up job from beginning to end, orchestrated by a handful of communists. He claimed that some of them had even brought knives with which they had been plotting to assassinate Maharishi at the end of the meeting. Which showed how ignorant they were. Everyone knew that Maharishi's mission had only just begun and nothing would happen to him until it had been accomplished.

But at least they had seen him, Charlie said. Everyone in the audience had had a glimpse of Maharishi's face and that would have to do for now. Those students at the University weren't ready yet. They still had too many bad elements among them. But when they were ready, "once the bad apples had been tossed out of the barrel," he said, sounding like Spiro Agnew, they'd remember.

His karma? How could an event involving hundreds of angry people have been one man's karma? There must have been something I was missing.

There might have been some other people on the course who thought the same way I did, but if so they kept these thoughts to themselves, or at least did not share them with me. And not having anyone to share my own doubts with, I pushed them aside, telling myself they must have been groundless, or that I was having them because I hadn't been meditating long enough, and there were lots of things I still didn't understand. Up in Rishikesh maybe I'd see the light.

❋ ❋ ❋

The conference that took place the following day was the final event in the Conference for World Peace, and for many reasons it was the best, as far as I was concerned, restoring my faith, such as it was. The event took place outside in a large field or fairgrounds, and a huge crowd showed up. Being somewhat indisposed that day, running a slight fever and running with more than usual frequency to the nearest toilet, I spent most of the time looking down at the proceedings from above, standing on a rooftop terrace of a house that also belonged to Indian followers of Maharishi, and which they had opened up for the day, so that members of our group could come and go, helping ourselves to refreshments that had been set out on tables on the second floor. It was a warm and sunny afternoon, and even though it was a weekday—Tuesday, January 30, to be exact—the house and the field it overlooked and many other houses in the neighborhood were draped with garlands and streamers, and there were paper flags flying everywhere. Contrary to what some of my fellow meditators believed, these decorations were not put up in honor of Maharishi but left over from India's independence day, celebrated on January 26. Still they seemed appropriate for this concluding ceremony, which was in some ways like a huge revival meeting.

There were a dozen or so of us up on the roof, for the most part SRMers, since most of the SIMSers were down mingling with the crowd. In the distance, about a hundred yards away, was a long stage with people sitting beneath huge parasols. Some wore suits, some wore yellow robes. Maharishi, all in white, sat in the middle. One by one, the people on the stage got up to speak into a mike. Some of the speeches were quite long and sometimes people in the audience would cheer or chant in response. From where I stood it was impossible to hear the speeches, but the wind brought snatches of them across the field and I could tell they were not in English but in Hindi. That also seemed right to me, and added to the atmosphere of the spectacle, which was both dreamlike and authentic. And everywhere there were all these happy, smiling people—sitting on the dusty ground, or standing, or milling about—what seemed like thousands and thousands of people!

I couldn't help thinking about scenes I'd read about in the Bible when I was a child—the feast at Cana, the loaves and fishes, the gathering on the banks of the Sea of Galilee—these multitudes that just happened to show up, swarms of curious people craning their necks to get a look, children sitting on their parents' shoulders, some people perched in the few leafless trees, others lining the paths and roadways, maybe waiting for a chance to touch the hem of his robe.

Why not? Aside from the miracles—which had probably been focused on and exaggerated over the centuries, if not simply made up, so as to attract new converts—Christ's message too had been pretty straightforward and simple and down to earth. Love your neighbor as yourself (because he *is* yourself). Judge not, unless you too want to be judged. (And god knows what fools judges are.) The kingdom of heaven is within you. (If you want to find it, go find a quiet place, close the eyes,… twenty to thirty minutes, twice a day.)

Maybe this was like back then. More than ever before the world needed something new and something fast, and preferably something simple, cutting through all the centuries of bullshit that had piled up around the world's organized religions. Maybe something like that was going on now, and we were part of it, whatever it was, and I was there.

It was a heady thought, and I knew some of the other people I was getting to know had that thought too, otherwise they wouldn't have been there. And although we didn't talk about it much, if ever, among us there was a little glimmer of hope at some level, simmering away, a flickering faith, that this just might be it, the something that the world so badly needed.

It was January, 1968. I was twenty-five. Anything was possible.

CHAPTER 12

The ride to Rishikesh

※ ※ ※

Early the following morning everyone was supposed to rendezvous at the Y for the trip up to Rishikesh. We were scheduled to leave at nine, but the show didn't get on the road until well past noon. Rishikesh was almost 250 kilometers northeast of New Delhi, over small, local roads that sometimes got very small and very local indeed and were often in bad need of repair. The plan was to go up in a caravan—consisting of about a dozen taxis and an aging bus—but the word caravan brings to mind an orderly line of vehicles, one after another, whereas this was more of a stampede—or a race—each taxi driver jockeying for first place every time the road widened a little or we came to a town, where instead of slowing down, it seemed that the general rule was to lean on the horn and step on the gas.

There was a law in India about driving on the left—no doubt left over from the British raj—but that day everyone drove all over the place, swerving wildly, and just in the nick of time, to avoid running into gaudily painted trucks, or buses, or people carrying things on their heads, or cows. Cows were by far the scariest, because they didn't get out of the way, and what would have happened if we ran into one?

In the taxi I rode in Larry sat up front and I sat in back with Reumah. For some reason that Reumah said had to do with unions in India, all of the men driving our taxis that day were Sikhs, all with tightly bound turbans and tight-knit beards. From what I gathered, Sikhs were sort of the Calvinist Protestants of India—reliable, good to have on your side in a fight, or driving your taxi through crowded streets—but dour, with strict rules about underwear and never cutting their beards. Ours seemed more dour than the others, but maybe that was because Larry kept asking him to stop all the time so he could jump out and take pictures.

"Check that out!" Larry would suddenly shout, pointing to a bullock cart being driven by a man holding a small boy on his lap. "Out of sight! Driver, stop the car!" Before the driver had stopped the car Larry would be out the door and running up to the bullock cart, his camera concealed behind his back. Larry's standard technique for photographing human subjects was to go right up to them, stop two feet away, whip out the camera and start taking pictures, the motor drive whirring away while the human subject, who might never have seen a camera before, stood or sat there with his or her mouth open. Larry explained to me once that it had something to do with capturing "the real person," but in the pictures he showed me a lot of the real persons had very surprised looks on their faces.

It's true that the farther north we went the more photogenic the faces became, as well as the scenery. As we got closer to the Himalayas the countryside and towns became more and more startling and colorful and other-worldly.

One of my favorite classes in graduate school had been on French medieval literature and as we made our way northward I felt like I was travelling deeper and deeper into the middle ages, a feeling I'd had with Reumah in Old Delhi as well. Of course this fit in with all the romanticized preconceptions of India I had put together over the last three years while reading books by Yogananda, Aurobindo, and Vivekenanda—all required reading for the counter culture seminar of the mid-'sixties. But still, while leaning out the window of the taxi, breathing the dust of the land and the smoke from burning cow dung, catching glimpses of people doing things the same way they had been doing them for thousands of years, with what looked like the same tools, I couldn't help get the feeling that I was being transported back to a place where symbols were closer to what they symbolized, appearances had not yet lost touch with reality, and I just might get in touch with my spiritual roots.

There were even bands of troubadours—although as our driver pointed out, it was not courtly love that they were interested in. We would come across them on the outskirts of towns—clusters of strangely dressed men, all of them wildly made up, many of them wearing dresses and saris. They would preen and pose in front of Larry's camera while he snapped their closeups and the driver drummed impatiently and disapprovingly on the inside rim of his steering wheel. Finally, one time when Larry was taking longer than usual to capture the real people beneath the makeup, the driver turned to Reumah and me in the back seat and suggested that all these delays might make us late for our rendez-vous up in Rishikesh, a suggestion which Reumah passed on to Larry when he got back into the car.

"Yeah, okay," he said, stashing his camera beside him on the front seat, "I'm running low on film anyway."

Everybody else in the group must have done a lot of sightseeing on the way up as well though, because by the time we got close to the outskirts of Hardwar, only thirty kilometres away from our destination, our taxi seemed to be one of the first in line, with only three or four in front of us, that we could see. By then it was beginning to get dark and as we got closer to the city the spectacle outside the windows of the taxi, which our driver ordered us to keep closed, began to take on aspects of a dream. Our driver explained that Hardwar was a holy city which every twelve years attracted millions of pilgrims for the religious festival called Kumba Mehla. This was a Kumba Mehla year and already the population in and around Hardwar had begun to swell, even though the beginning of the festival proper was three months away.

Lining the road and opening on to it were three-sided wooden stalls that got closer and closer together, and smaller and smaller, as the road narrowed and the traffic thickened. Wrapped in shawls and huddled around coal fires inside the stalls were small groups of people standing and squatting amid displays of powders and spices, saris and sarongs, religious articles and trinkets and mulicolored statues of Hindu gods, vegetables and fruit and flowers. But there were no fly-covered carcasses. From here on, until the high peaks of the Himalayas, the sale or purchase of meat was strictly forbidden.

Every now and then, as we made our way into the center of the city, a half-open door or canvas canopy revealed a temple inside, sometimes brightly lit with Coleman lanterns or fluorescent lights, more often dimly aglow with flickering candles. Inside you could see people bowing or saluting a gaudy statue on a dais at the back. In front of the shops and temples beggars lined the road, some of them deformed lepers unable to move, others chanting, shouting, tapping on the windows of the taxi, trying to get a handout or a look inside. Through the closed windows and wafting up through the floorboards came smells of woodsmoke and fried vegetables and incense and dust and open sewage. By now the driver had slowed to a crawl and was literally leaning on the horn, adding to the din of bells ringing, people shouting, monks chanting, radio music blaring. The taxi came to a stop at an intersection choked with trucks and tongas and pedicabs and carts and people and goats and cows. Outside my window, lit by a rare street light, stood a skinny man with a long beard, completely naked. The man was painted gray or blue from head to toe and between his spread legs hung two feet of rope. One end of the rope was looped around his genitals and the other end was tied around two or three bricks, dangling a few inches above the ground. The man seemed to be pointing at the taxi, pointing right at me, and he was shouting something over and over. The taxi lurched forward and veered left. I turned to see Reumah, also looking out my window, eyes wide and mouth wide open. She shifted her glance to me and clapped a hand over her mouth to stifle a guffaw.

"I guess he's seeking God in his own way," I said, shouting to make myself heard.

Luckily Larry hadn't seen the naked sadhu or he would have ordered the driver to stop and jumped out to flash pictures. As it was he kept clapping his hands and jumping up and down on his seat and yelling, "Far out!" or "Oh my God! Did you see that!"

Gradually the traffic began to thin out and we began to pick up speed as we headed out the other end of the city. Peering through the windows we could soon see trees, more and more of them, the first trees we'd seen in any number since leaving Delhi, and through the trees the occasional glow of a fire, now and then a light from a hut or a temple. I rolled down my window, letting in fresh, cold air the driver said would soon get colder still. Beyond the trees off to the right, he said, gesturing with his right hand, was "Mother Ganga." He explained that Maharishi's ashram was not actually in Rishikesh, but on a cliff above it on the other side of the river. He had only been to Rishikesh a few times before, he said, and never to the ashram, but he knew where it was, along with a number of other ashrams belonging to other gurus who like Maharishi, attracted many foreign visitors. The driver went on to explain that Rishikesh in Sanskrit meant the "City of Seers," and was, like Hardwar and Benares, a very holy town and very ancient. Most of the people who lived there he said were sadhus and sannyasis, men who, usually around the age of retirement, renounce all worldly pursuits, to spend the rest of their lives pursuing spiritual ones under the guidance of the guru of their choice, of which, according to the driver there were hundreds in the area. "Maybe thousands," he added, with a wag of his head.

Rishikesh turned out to be quite similar to Hardwar but smaller and less spectacular and overwhelming, with more temples in evidence and less ramshackle shacks along the road. We drove through it in ten minutes, despite the crowds still in the streets and the ubiquitous beggars and cows and priests. This time no one tapped on our windows and there were no naked blue men to give obscure warnings about sex.

About five minutes outside of town, our taxi pulled off the road at a turnout, beneath a dim streetlight, where three other taxis were already waiting. There was also a large, army style truck. Half a dozen porters were transferring luggage from racks on top of the taxis to the waiting truck. Some people had opened their suitcases on the ground and were taking out sweaters and coats and other small items. Among the people who had emerged from the taxis I recognized Berndt and Gunilla, and also Viggie. Ian, one of the Australians, was leaning on his cane.

Our driver eased to a stop and killed the motor and we all climbed out. A wind coming off the nearby mountains was bringing with it air that was colder than anything I'd felt since leaving Paris. Through the gathering darkness you could see lights along the bank rising up on the other side of the river. You could also hear the roar of the river below. When I'd heard that Maharishi's ashram was on the banks of the Ganges, I'd pictured scenes of chubby priests descending wide stairs into stagnant, tepid water, but once again my expectations took a jolt from reality. In fact Rishikesh is where the Ganges flows out of the Himalayas, and here it was still very much a mountain river, cold and fast and deep.

While we were waiting for our driver to finish untying ropes and loosening straps around the roof rack, Berndt came over, looking amused. He often looked amused, his face, like now, wearing a wry grin. As head of SIMS Sweden for the past couple of years, Berndt had organized several speaking tours for Maharishi in Scandinavia and he had learned to take in stride the vicissitudes and delays and sudden changes in plans that travelling with Maharishi always seemed to entail. "Larry, Rikard, Reumah," he said as he walked up, "Good trip?"

"Good trip," I said. "And you?"

"Oh yes. And now," he gestured towards the bank on the other side of the river, "we take a little walk."

"In the dark?" Larry said.

"How far?" said Reumah.

Berndt laughed and said he didn't know for sure. No one seemed to know for sure. "A mile or two, I think."

Berndt explained that normally we were to have crossed the Ganges on a ferry about half a mile down the river, but the ferry stopped running at sundown, so now our only alternative was to cross on a footbridge here and hike the rest of the way to the ashram. Berndt said we were to take with us some warm clothing and anything else we would need to clean up before dinner. The truck was going to take our luggage by an access road that crossed another bridge several miles upriver and led around to the back of the ashram through the forest, but it would take the truck another two or three hours to get there.

After our driver had untied the luggage, I helped him pull my own suitcase down from the rack, then laid it on the ground, zipped the top flap open and extracted the Olivetti, which I didn't want to be thrown around in the back of a truck. I also pulled out a heavy woolen sweater and put it on. Then I zipped the suitcase closed again, handed it over to a porter, and went to the edge of the parking area for a look at the bridge. Viggie was standing there too, her shoulders wrapped in a heavy shawl.

"Brrr," she said as I walked up.

Viggie was someone I had started becoming friendly with during long waits at the Y, and with whom I was hoping to become friendlier still. Gentle, soft-spoken, but funny and quick-witted, with long, light brown hair and pale blue eyes, Viggie had a physical softness which, together with a kind of aristocratic aloofness, made for a combination I found increasingly attractive, especially now that Rosalyn had been pirated away by Tom. Viggie nodded at the bridge just below and said, "What do you think?"

You got to the bridge by a set of steep stairs descending to a ledge about twenty feet below us. The ledge was lit by a hanging lamp that was blowing in the wind. The footbridge extended from the ledge off into darkness over the river, emerging on the other side where it ended at what looked like a tiny village, glimmering in the darkness a hundred yards away, with lights trailing off to the right, along the path we were to take. The bridge was just wide enough to accommodate two people walking abreast. On each side was a guide wire you could grab onto as you made your way across, and beneath that a safety net in case anyone slipped, although the safety net looked pretty flimsy.

Even more impressive than the bridge was what lay below, and which you could not ignore because of the constant roar and dampness rising up. Peering through the darkness about a hundred yards upstream, you could see white water of rapids, the source of most of the noise, but you could also hear the much more dangerous sound of gushing and swirling directly below us, where the river ran fast and deep.

"Piece of cake," I said. I had told Viggie about Charlie back at the Continental in Paris. Now she looked back at me and smiled, her eyes reflecting the colored lights across the river.

By then most of the other taxis had arrived, and finally the bus came lumbering up the hill. It groaned to a halt in the turnoff, and the door clanked open. As its passengers began to disembark, they started jumping up and down and clapping their arms around them to keep warm.

Maharishi's taxi still had not arrived, along with a few other taxis transporting about a dozen people, including Mia, who someone said had wanted to stop in Hardwar to do some shopping. A debate arose whether to wait for them, or start out on our own. There was no telling how much longer Maharishi would be and there was some concern about the older members in our group, who were tired after the six-hour drive, and anxious to reach the ashram. Finally someone volunteered to stay behind and wait for Maharishi, and the rest of us set out for the last leg of the journey.

Most of the people who had ridden up on the bus were SRMers, several of whom had had the wisdom that comes with age to bring along a flashlight, which they now fished out of their luggage, along with warmer clothes. One of these people was Colin Harrington, who as luck would have it had also been to Maharishi's ashram the year before, and claimed to know where it was. Using both hands to hold his flashlight, which he called a torch, he pointed it down at the ground directly in front of his feet and started down the steep, uneven steps, with his mother clinging to one of his elbows. The rest of us followed.

We regrouped on the little platform at the bottom of the stairs. There were thirty-five or forty of us, and almost everyone was carrying an overnight case, or a bulging purse, or a travel bag. I seemed to be the only one carrying a typewriter.

At the entrance to the bridge, blocking direct access, was a low barrier, with a banged up metal sign attached to it that said, "STOP," and then below that, in smaller, block letters, "VEHICULAR TRAFFIC, ELEPHANTS AND CAMELS, ETC." This was followed by two lines in Hindi. To Viggie, standing beside me, I wondered aloud what they meant.

"Yes, and what do you suppose they mean by 'etcetera'?" she added.

"Other large animals?" I suggested.

"But what if they can't read?"

Finally Colin and his mother started out across the bridge and the rest of us fell in line behind them, two-by-two or single file. I went single file, holding onto the guide rope with one hand, the Olivetti in the other.

Thinking back on this later, it made sense that that bridge was taking us from light into darkness and back out into light again, as well as from West to East, because for many of us that journey was a crossing over to the other side, from which there was no turning back.

Caught up in the excitement of our imminent arrival at the ashram, tired after our long drive, probably none of us realized what a fateful moment that was, but there were signs. For one thing, after we'd gotten a little over halfway across the bridge, the wind suddenly dropped off. As it came down out of the mountains, it must have swept along the western bank, which put the opposite bank in the lee and created an eery lull. There were still some ripples and puffs, but the hard, steady blow had ceased completely by the time we re-emerged into the light on the opposite bank. The sound of the river was also much diminished. You could still hear it clearly enough, but as if someone had turned down the volume, again quite suddenly, and now in addition to the sound of the water below, you could hear someone singing or chanting in a thin, high voice, and the tinkling of little bells.

The chanting was coming from a bony old man, sitting cross-legged on the ground, not far from where we came off of the bridge. He barely glanced up as we went by, apparently finding it perfectly normal that a stream of forty Westerners carrying hand baggage should exit the bridge at that very moment and file past him, looking down at him with curiosity. Maybe he thought his chanting had conjured us up. Maybe it had.

The sound of tinkling bells, and of some other louder, bigger ones, was coming from little temples clustered at the end of the bridge, and from caves carved into the side of the mountain that we passed by as we started out on the path leading off towards the right. In each little temple or cave was a brightly painted statue of a Hindu god, lit with candles or an electric bulb, or a couple of dim lanterns. Some of the caves were occupied by people ringing bells and softly chanting. Others were empty except for the gods, who seemed to beckon us inside as we went by.

After a quarter of a mile or so, the pathway widened to a rough dirt road, and we stopped to wait for stragglers. Here the only light was supplied by flashlights of those few people who had brought them along, and from the stars, which seemed to shine with a special brilliance and gave off a pale light of their own, filtering down through the trees. Somewhere along the way I had lost track of Viggie and was now standing next to Rosalyn, who for a welcome change was not standing next to Tom. Rosalyn was carrying a hand towel in which she'd wrapped a toothbrush. Next to her on the other side was Larry, who was holding a leather shaving kit and had two cameras dangling from his neck. By then our group had picked up a guide, a man who lived in another ashram not far from Maharishi's and who had offered to take us there, as Colin seemed to have lost his way. The reason we were waiting for everyone to catch up was that the guide said it was important from here on to stick close together because there were wild animals in the forest, tigers and panthers that went out prowling at night, not to mention poisonous snakes that might be crossing the path. This warning was passed on down the line, giving rise to audible gasps and little shrieks and exclamations as it worked its way down.

"Tigers!" said Rosalyn, her eyes wide.

"And lions!" said Larry.

"And snakes!" said I.

As the group started out again up the road the three of us linked arms and huddled closer, not wanting to be among those taking up the rear, but trying all the same to be cautious about where we put our feet, so as not to step on a stick that would turn out to be a snake. Tigers and panthers were one thing. I figured they would pick off the fatter ones first. But snakes were something else entirely.

Our guide had told us that if we listened carefully we might hear a tiger roaring in the forest, as they sometimes did at night, but all we heard as we walked along were barking dogs and once some rustling in the leaves which someone ahead of us said with a nervous laugh was "probably just a monkey."

After we had all trekked along in the dark for a quarter of an hour, the guide turned to take leave of us at a fork in the road that led to his own ashram. A couple of dogs quit barking and came out to greet him, and look suspiciously at us as we filed by on the fork to the right, the sound of the river gradually growing louder through the trees. Soon, as the man had said, the road came to a clearing, veered left, and climbed a hill towards a little settlement. This was Shankaracharya Nagar, a collection of wooden cabins and huts and a few larger structures just outside Maharishi's ashram.

In the starlight, with lights from candles and cooking fires visible through the windows of the wooden houses, Shankaracharya Nagar looked a little like a Gold Rush boom town that had been thrown up overnight. And that's what it was in a way, the gold in this case being the prospect of enlightenment that would draw westerners in droves over the next few years, to sit at the feet of Maharishi or other local gurus. Not to mention the real gold that would be given back in kind.

In addition to the collection of huts which housed the twenty or thirty people, mostly men and boys, who made up the permanent year-round staff of Maharishi's ashram, the little town included a post office, a laundry, and a little store, where we could purchase the amenities that would ease the hardship of our monastic lives, such as lemon drops and Cadbury chocolate and Peace cigarettes. There was a rumor that you could also buy Scotch in the store, but only at certain hours and by pre-arranged agreement.

CHAPTER 13

First night at camp

※ ※ ※

Entrance to the ashram was beyond the village through a wide gate at the top of the road, through which we streamed that night like tired sheep arriving at the fold. The ashram occupied about a dozen acres and was surrounded on all sides, except along the cliff where it overlooked the Ganges, by a high wire fence. The road we were on led straight through the ashram and out the other side, about 200 yards farther on, through another gate directly opposite the one we had come through. It was through this higher gate that the truck was supposed to arrive with our luggage. People were beginning to look at their watches and wonder when, and to worry. It was now past nine and if it took the truck three hours it would not arrive until midnight. If it arrived at all. Maybe the next bridge up the river was no more sturdy than the one we'd just crossed over and the truck had gone over the side and our luggage was now on its way to Calcutta. Although the Olivetti had grown a lot heavier in the last half hour, I was glad I'd brought it along.

To our left as we walked up the road was a series of low, concrete, white-washed buildings which contained the rooms where we would all be housed. The buildings resembled old fashioned "motor hotels" you can still see along old roads in California. Each building or block of rooms was shaped like an upside down U, built around a little courtyard. Running around the courtyard was a veranda about two feet off the ground with the roof extending over it, supported by slender columns. Every ten feet along the veranda was a door and a window for each room, three rooms in the wings extending out towards the road, six more along the inside wall, which made for twelve rooms per block. That night some of the doors leading into some of the rooms were open and the windows were lit and boys were scurrying in and out of them along the veranda, carrying what looked like bedding or pieces of furniture, while shouting and giggling among themselves.

Above us, hanging from branches of trees and stretching across the road, were strings of little paper flags and pennants, presumably hung there to welcome us to the ashram. Paths lined with whitewashed stones and marked by an occasional low lantern lit with a candle ran off to the right through the trees. In the distance, through brush and low-lying branches, you could see the lights of what a fast-spreading rumor identified as the ashram kitchen and dining room. Instead of heading immediately off in that direction, we were all herded into the courtyard of one of the blocks up at the high end of the road, not far from the other gate. Everyone laid down their burdens and sat down on the floor or on the edge of the veranda, exhausted, hungry, and cold.

Standing in the middle of the courtyard, lit by a gas lantern and holding a clipboard on which he was checking off names, was a man who introduced himself as Mr. Suresh. He was someone we would all get to know quite well in the days to come. As general manager of the ashram, Suresh was the man you went to whenever the toilet got clogged, or the pipes above your bed leaked, or monkeys were reaching through your broken window to steal your bananas, interrupting your long meditations. That night, speaking with a heavy accent and using flourishes that sometimes made him hard to understand, he began by welcoming us to Maharishi's Academy of Meditation, where he hoped we would find everything up to the snuff, even though in some of the rooms the finishing touch might not yet have been applied completely, because we were arriving somewhat earlier than expected.

The statement was an artful example of Indian bureaucratese, of which Suresh turned out to be a master, combining an apology with an excuse that at the same time managed to imply that the problem giving rise to the apology in the first place was our fault to begin with. In any case, it caused many of us to look at each other in surprise, since it was our impression we had arrived six hours late. And judging by the noise of sawing and hammering coming from the next block of rooms up the road, the finishing touches sounded more like heavy construction. Suresh went on to say that the lorry loaded with our luggage was well on its way and would be arriving soon, an announcement that brought cheers. He said that room assignments would be made as soon as Maharishi arrived along with the remainder of our group, which he also said was "imminent, if not beforehand." In the meantime, he suggested we all troop down to the ashram kitchen to be served out a good hot meal, a suggestion which brought more cheers and a round of applause.

On the way down to the dining area, everyone's spirits lifted by the prospect of food, I had the feeling we had all arrived for the first night of camp. With the chill air, the smell of smoke, the proximity of high mountains and the excitement of knowing wild beasts were prowling around outside the fences, it all reminded me of the summer vacations my family used to take in one of the National Parks in the Sierras. As it happened, I was walking next to Terry, the forest ranger. When I asked him if this place didn't remind him of Kings' Canyon or Yosemite, he laughed and said, "Yup. It sure does."

The dining area consisted of a kitchen—basically a large, three-sided wooden shed with a storeroom attached—and nearby a long, narrow dining room. In front of the kitchen on the edge of the cliff a row of tables was surrounded by flimsy wooden lattice-work that shivered and rattled in the wind coming up from the river. Here we were at the extreme southeastern tip of the ashram, diagonally opposite the gate we had come through and almost directly over the Ganges. While the older, hungrier members of the group started lining up in front of the kitchen, a bunch of us younger ones went to the edge of the cliff for a look at the view. Here the sound of the river was again a roar and the cold wind blew as it had when we'd set out across the bridge. Huddled together and standing as close to the edge as we dared, we could not see the river because it was pitch dark, but it sounded like it was straight below us. What we could see were the lights of Rishikesh in the distance, with a few others twinkling nearby, and straight above us an array of stars that looked like fireworks frozen in midair.

I was standing next to Viggie, who had wrapped her shawl tightly over her head and now said something I couldn't hear above the roar of the river. I put my head down and she put her mouth to my ear and shouted, "I said it's quite fantastic, isn't it!"

I nodded and shouted back, "Yeah, wow!"

There were about ten or twelve of us on the cliff that night, all SIMSers, waiting for the line in front of the kitchen to go down. In contrast to most of the SRMers, who were tired and cold and some even cranky after the day's long ordeal, not to mention the whole long week of delays down in Delhi, the mood among the younger crowd that night was almost giddy—again, we felt like a bunch of kids on their first night away from home.

Someone took out a pack of cigarettes and passed it around. Among meditators, smoking, like drinking alcohol, was one of those habits that was frowned upon but not flat out forbidden. Maharishi's theory was that the desire to indulge in such habits would go away naturally as the nervous system continued to refine itself through meditation. I was surprised to see how many still did smoke though, especially among the SIMSers, whose pleasure in lighting up was probably enhanced by the thought that this was a habit they would soon be leaving behind as they got close to cosmic consciousness. When I first got to Paris I had smoked Disques Bleus for a while. It was part of the rebellion against Christian Science in general and my mother in particular. I also liked the way my left hand looked holding a smoking cigarette over an ashtray, while my right hand held a pencil over a page. After a few months I'd given it up because of the asthma, but I still smoked occasionally and this was one of those occasions, the sense of cama-raderie among us heightened by this little ritual that also brought me closer still to Viggie, both of our hands touching and our faces inches apart as she lit her cigarette off of mine.

After we'd finished the cigarettes and flipped the butts out over the cliff, we all went back to the kitchen where the line had now diminished. In front of the kitchen was a table stacked with trays and silverware and bowls, from which you helped yourself then went inside to get served. Inside, along one wall, was a bank of charcoal fires on which that night were huge bubbling pots of vegetables and rice and dhall. There was also a table with salad and chutneys and a large bowl of yogurt or "curds," and a platter of warm chapa-tis. The idea was to have your bowls filled at the charcoal fires then help yourself to condiments, grab a handful of chapatis and rush back outside before you fainted from smoke inhalation.

As soon as you left the kitchen, you made a dash for the dining room, twenty yards away. The dining room looked a little like an old-fashioned diner, except it was the length of two train cars instead of one. It looked as if they had found a table long enough to accommodate forty people, plunked it down on a slab of concrete, then built the dining room up around it, with waist-high windows all around the sides. That night, with lanterns hanging on the walls between the windows, and candles down the length of the table, it looked quite cozy. It also turned out to be surprisingly roomy. By the time those of us who came in late had found a seat and were scooping up dhall with our chapatis, it looked like everyone who had crossed the bridge that night was sitting around the table, sharing our first ashram meal.

While we were eating Suresh came down with the happy news that our luggage had arrived and could be picked up at the upper gate. He also said that since it was so late there would be no group meeting that night with Maharishi but that the course would officially begin the following morning with a lecture at 10:00 in the auditorium. With the help of a couple of assistants, he then started reading off names and passing out pieces of paper with our room assignments. On mine was written Block 1, Room 2.

Block 1 was all the way down at the other end of the ashram from Block 6, where the truck had dropped off the luggage, so half an hour later, while lugging my suitcase down the road, I passed in front of all the other blocks of rooms. By that time there were lights on in many of them, mostly from candles or flashlights. People were walking around on the verandas, poking their heads into each other's rooms, laughing and talking in various languages. Other people who had already settled in and had taken blankets off their beds to wrap around their shoulders were coming back from the kitchen holding mugs of steaming cocoa in both hands. As they went by they called out, "Good night! Gute Nacht! Jai Guru Dev!" I even heard someone call out "Bonsoir!"

Block 1 was about ten yards from the gate we had all come streaming through a few hours earlier. I turned into the courtyard and climbed the three steps onto the veranda. Each door had a little card tacked to it with a number on it. Room 2 was one room in from the last wing that extended out towards the road. The door was unlocked. I pushed it open and stepped inside. While I was feeling my way around, someone came in behind me with a flashlight. It was Geoffrey from London. Down in Delhi I had learned that Geoffrey was a solicitor, and that in England that was nothing to be ashamed of. He was about thirty-five, with a pointy brown beard and a shock of matching brown hair that he kept brushing back from his forehead. Geoffrey had been meditating for over five years and pronounced Maharishi "Mahawshi." Despite a tendency to make pompous pronouncements worthy of the most conservative SRMers, Geoffrey seemed to prefer the company of the younger set and, like Reumah from Tel Aviv and Tony from Las Vegas, he seemed more of a SIMSer at heart. He now informed me that he was my next door neighbor on my right. Silhouetted in the doorway, he also said that the electricity seemed to be off in our block as well. He shined his light around my room until he found a little stack of candles on the corner of a table next to the bed. Next to the candles someone had thoughtfully placed a box of matches. Geoffrey kept his light trained on the candles while I lit one, dribbled some wax on the edge of the table, and held the candle there until it stood on its own. Geoffrey said we'd be sharing the same washroom out in the back, along with the chap who lived in Room 1 and who had not shown up yet. "I take it we're all chaps," I said, and he said yes, as far as he knew. In the dark it was easy to hide my disappointment. I'd been hoping the accommodations were co-ed and my next door neighbor would be Viggie.

I lifted the suitcase onto the bed and followed Geoffrey out the rear door to a kind of covered patio with a concrete floor that dropped off to an open yard three feet below. Geoffrey's flashlight picked up a wire fence about ten feet away and beyond that trees and brush. In the space between the fence and our washroom was a fifty-gallon drum perched on a column of cinder blocks, with the remains of a fire underneath. Geoffrey said he presumed that was our water-heater, and added, "I hope you weren't planning on a warm shower." He said he'd tested both taps in the sink and they were ice cold.

With his light he pointed out the other conveniences: a long low concrete sink along one wall, an enclosed shower stall to the right, and to the left a water closet with a toilet but no seat, something Geoffrey said he intended to take up with Mr. Suresh first thing in the morning. He went on to say that although each of our rooms was equipped with a flimsy electric radiator, for use when there was electricity, he doubted they gave off much heat and if they did he thought it would be a miracle if no one set fire to their room or got electrocuted in the next three months.

"But then it's miracles we're here for, isn't it?" he added with a sudden change of tone and a wide grin that in the dim light struck me as slightly manic. With his smallish build, the brown hair converging down to a pointed beard, Geoffrey looked a little like an elf, a meticulous, slightly manic elf.

While we were talking someone came into the room next to mine and started banging and thumping around inside. A faint light shone beneath the back door and a few seconds later it burst open.

"Hallo?"

Geoffrey shined his light on the face of Gunar, the Norwegian artist. During the last few days in New Delhi Gunar had made himself scarce with a Norwegian woman who was a few years older and was named Eva. Gunar said he had just helped Eva move into her room up in Block 5. While he was there the electricity had actually come on, he said, then gone off a few minutes later, probably when everyone plugged in their electric heaters. Gunar said his own room was exactly like the rooms he'd seen up in Block 5, furniture and everything, so all the rooms must be identical, except those up in Block 6, which he said were the luxury suites, and where construction was still going on. Gunar said that all the rooms in Block 6 had electricity that actually worked and rugs on the floor and bathrooms attached with real bathtubs and even air conditioning for when the weather got hot, or so he'd heard. He said Mia Farrow and her sister were already settled in up there, and so was that tall American woman with all the fancy clothes and jewelry whose name he couldn't recall.

"Nancy," I said.

"Nancy, ja!"

There was a knock on my front door and Larry came through it, holding a kerosene lantern. Behind him was Tony. "You guys got hot water?" Larry asked.

"Apparently not," I said.

"At least not till tomorrow," Geoffrey added.

Larry said the room next to his was empty so he moved into it, since the view was better and the mattress a little thicker.

Gunar repeated what he'd heard about the rooms up in Block 6, and Tony suggested we all go up there to see if there were any vacancies, "Cause dis place ain't no Caesar's Palace, lemme tell ya."

The remark brought a laugh from Larry and me, a quizzical look from Gunar, and a few steps back from Geoffrey, who, after a slight pause, said, "Well I don't know about the rest of you, but I intend to stay where I'm allotted." He then used his flashlight to look at his watch and announced it was well past his bedtime, a remark which essentially broke up the party.

After everyone had left I closed the doors of my room, lit a few more candles, and started to unpack. The room was not large, about ten by fifteen feet, with barely enough room for the bare furnishings. In addition to the table and the bed, which was basically a wooden plank with four legs and a thin mattress on top, there was also a chair to go with the table, a set of shelves built into the wall, and a rigid armchair with a wooden frame and white plastic caning. The armchair did not look like it had been made with meditators in mind, but the bed was generously supplied with pillows and thick, woolen army-style blankets that would serve as padding.

I put the Olivetti on the table but did not take it out of its case. It was too late and I was too tired to type up my notes for the day, and it would have made too much noise anyway. The next morning I would look for a place where I could type without bothering anyone.

After I had transferred the contents of my suitcase to the shelves and pushed it under the bed, I undressed, put on the long underwear I had luckily stuffed into the suitcase in Paris as an afterthought, put a turtleneck on over that, blew out the candles and got into bed. I always enjoyed drifting off to sleep in new surroundings, but that night there was no drifting.

CHAPTER 14

Setting out along the pathless path

※ ※ ※

The next morning I awoke to a bloodcurdling scream. After getting my bearings, I got out of bed and pushed aside the thin curtain to peer out the window. No human sacrifice was going on in the courtyard in front of my block of rooms, nor in the area across the road that I could see. In fact all was peaceful and quiet and full of morning sunlight. I yawned and rubbed my eyes, figuring what I'd heard must have been the last vestige of a dream dredged up from eight hours of deep, uninterrupted sleep, the first full night of sleep I'd had since leaving Paris.

It was cold in the room, and even colder in the open air washroom where Gunar was leaning over the sink, brushing his teeth. He smiled through foam and tried repeatedly to say something I finally realized was "Jai Guru Dev." I repeated the greeting and made for the WC. In the back yard three boys were standing around a smoky fire they'd managed to start beneath the fifty-gallon drum. One was breaking lumps of charcoal with a rock and handing them to the other two who were feeding them into the flames while trying not to burn their fingers. When they saw me they all gave me big smiles and joined their thin hands and called out "Namaste Sahib!"

When I emerged from the WC I asked Gunar if he'd heard a scream a few minutes ago. He stopped banging his toothbrush against the rim of the sink and looked at me quizzically and said "Ice cream?"

"Nevermind," I said, convinced the scream had been a dream. I stepped into the concrete shower, turned on both taps and stuck my hand into a weak, tepid flow that soon turned cold. Gunar said there was nothing like a cold shower to get you started in the morning. His own had been quite warm, he said, but it hadn't lasted very long. Geoffrey had already taken his and gone off to breakfast. Gunar suggested we walk down together. It was not even 8:00 and the kitchen served breakfast until 9:00. He said he had already been down there looking for Eva but she was still asleep.

On the way down to the dining area we were joined by Terry and Tony, each of whom had a good start on a full beard and both of whom had only brought along electric razors. I said they were welcome to my Gillette, which I only used once a week anyway, but both of them were debating letting their beards grow for the course, especially Tony whose beard was black and heavy and who didn't relish shaving with cold water.

It was a beautiful morning, still quite cold, but bright and clear. Gunar said he'd heard it had snowed during the night in the mountains just above us and as we walked along I noticed frost in the leaves along the path. All around us up in the trees crows were jumping around from branch to branch and cawing loudly, accompanying us on our walk down to the kitchen. Terry said that outside his washroom that morning he'd seen a family of monkeys skittering across the tops of the trees, and he'd also heard the cry of a peacock.

"Does a peacock make a noise that sounds like a child getting its throat cut?" I asked.

"I guess you heard him too," he said.

It was a wonder no one else had.

Tony said he had the feeling meditation was going to be interesting in this place, "What wit da monkeys an da peacocks an da crows." I asked him if there were a lot of meditators in Las Vegas and he said actually quite a few, and for good reason. "It helps ya keep yer sanity in dat place."

Unlike Terry and Gunar and myself, and for that matter almost all the younger people on the course, Tony had a family back home—two small kids and a wife. His wife had let him come on the course, he said, because she knew he would come back a better husband and a better father. "Or so she hopes," he added with a grin. Still, he had to admit he sometimes wondered what he was doing there, and he was having qualms about the long separation from the ones he loved. But for now he said, rubbing his hands together as we walked, he was looking forward to a "big plate of bacon and eggs!"

Down in the dining area twenty or thirty people were scattered around having breakfast, some inside, some out, sitting at the tables along the edge of the cliff. Everyone sitting outside was wearing overcoats, and some had added blankets from their beds. A few were sitting outside in armchairs they had moved to spots where the morning sun was streaming down through breaks in the leaves. Viggie was one of them, her pale face tilted upwards, eyes closed in meditation, or simply absorbing the warmth.

Before going on to the kitchen the four of us went to the edge of the cliff for a daylight view. The town of Rishikesh was about a half mile away, on the other side of a smaller river called the Chandrabagha which fed into the Ganges and that morning looked like a strip of aluminum foil laid along the lower edge of the white houses and temples in the distance. Below us, the Ganges curved around towards the right to flow on towards the town. Beyond the town and the surrounding forest you could make out the beginning of India's northern plain, stretching as far as the eye could see, and at that hour through a veil of mist that was rising and evaporating in the morning sun.

Just below us, on the other side of the Ganges, was a kind of rocky peninsula, no doubt under water when the river was high, and fifty yards beyond that the beginning of a thin forest of low brush that shone light green in the morning sunlight. In among the brush, farther up, were scraggly trees, through which you could see the crude huts of sannyasis who lived there close to the river. From some of the huts thin columns of smoke were rising. Standing on the edge of the river directly below us, knee deep on the opposite shore, an orange-robed sannyasi was stooping down to scoop up water, rising back up and raising his hands towards the sky, stooping down again. . . There was no wind that morning and the river too seemed calmer than it had the night before, so that we could talk to each other in a normal tone of voice, or even in a whisper. None of us said a word though, caught up in the spirit of that still and holy morning.

While there were no bacon and eggs for breakfast, there were thick slices of homemade bread toasted over an open fire and covered with butter and cheese, or honey or jam or peanut butter. There was also oatmeal or cold cereals in little individual boxes and containers of juice and milk, and chai or hot chocolate or instant coffee, and yogurt and all the nuts and dried fruit you could eat, along with apples and bananas and oranges and sometimes mangoes. Although some people complained about the vegetarian meals at the ashram being too bland or too monotonous or not nutritious enough, to me they were always satisfying and tasty. Maybe if I'd been paying for those meals I might have complained too and wanted more for my money, but for me they were a gift, after all, and I had the feeling the gift was coming not only from Maharishi or the SRM or SIMS or whoever was footing my bill, but also from the earth—these simple meals that required no creature living on it to be killed, to keep this creature living on it too.

After breakfast I went back to my room to meditate for an hour before the morning lecture. Although I hadn't had a recurrence of asthma since the day I started meditating in Paris, I was a little worried the dampness and the cold would bring on an attack. Rather than trying the armchair, I piled up blankets and pillows on the bed against the wall and wrapped myself up and sat down among them, tucking my feet up under me to keep them warm.

Right away, I went to a space where I would be spending a lot of time the next three months. While repeating the mantra, I soon felt the muscles around my eyes relax, as my breathing got slower and slower. After a while I began to feel again that old familiar sense of fulness and well-being that used to come over me while driving the MG, less immediate and sharp perhaps, but also less evanescent. It started with a sense of swelling or expansion of my folded hands, and gradually led to a kind of lightness of my whole body, as if I were being lifted gently upwards, towards some sort of presence hovering above me. And then I became aware of what seemed like a shaft of cool air on my forehead, between and just above my eyes. The sensation was so real and distinct that I wanted to raise my hand and hold it in front of my face to see if it was a draft in the room, maybe coming through gaps in the window. But as soon as I began to move, as soon as the muscles of my arm began to act on that impulse to raise my hand, the sensation vanished. And as soon as I settled back down into that state where I had been just before, a state of suspended animation, where my breathing was so faint it was as if I were not breathing at all, it would start up again, that cooling shaft of air, as if it were being blown through a tube and hitting me right between and above the eyes.

After meditating for what I thought was ten minutes I opened my eyes and looked at my watch and saw that it had been over an hour and if I didn't hurry I would be late for the first lecture.

Early in the course, in the courtyard of Block 1.
(Photographer unknown, but probably Larry Kurland.)

The lecture hall was in the middle of the ashram, with paths leading to it from every direction. Inside, it was a large, high-ceilinged, airy building, with a dirt floor covered with mats, and enough space for about a hundred people, sitting on the same kind of armchairs everyone had in their rooms. When I arrived, a little over half of those chairs were already occupied by people wrapped in blankets, most of them sitting down in front. Judging by the way their heads were bobbing up and down, many of those people had been there for a while. I went down the central aisle and took a seat on the left, next to Terry, who opened his eyes and smiled as I spread my own blanket on the chair then sat down and wrapped myself inside it like a sausage. Down in front of the hall was a low stage completely covered with white sheets. In the middle of the stage was a low wooden bench. Set up on an easel behind the bench was a large painting of Guru Dev sitting lotus fashion on a gilded throne, over which was a large umbrella. The painting was draped with garlands of marigolds, which despite the cold nights were growing in bunches all over the ashram. In front of the wooden bench was a small table, also covered with a white sheet, which held a vase of flowers and a microphone. All along a low shelf around the back of the stage were potted plants and more vases of flowers and incense holders with sticks of incense in them and thin threads of smoke rising up, filling the air in the hall with the scent of sandalwood and jasmine. The air also smelled of smoke produced by charcoal burners that had been made out of large tin cans and placed at intervals along the walls down each side of the auditorium, to take the chill off the morning air.

Up in the ceiling, running down the length of the hall, were iron pipes that served as rafters. All of them were decorated with strings of different colored paper pennants, like those hanging from the trees up by the road. Close to the ceiling were rows of windows, all of them closed. On the other side of some of the windows pigeons had gathered and were hopping around, peering through the glass.

As I was getting warm, settling into the armchair, a few other latecomers arrived and took seats. It was almost 10:30 when Maharishi himself arrived, accompanied by Nancy, Mia, and Prudence. As they came forward and started down the aisle we all stood and turned and joined our hands in front of us in greeting. Maharishi was smiling broadly, as usual. Mia was smiling too, although the smile looked a little self-conscious or embarrassed.

Prudence as usual looked a little dazed, and Nancy as usual looked like she was in complete control.

Behind them were three bramacharis, or celibate monks. Two of them were carrying stacks of notebooks that they passed out to everyone as they made their way down the aisle. The third bramachari was carrying Maharishi's deerskin. He was shorter than the other two, shorter even than Maharishi, and his head was shaved. Later I was to learn that he was a lawyer who had given up a prosperous practice in Delhi to devote his life to Maharishi.

Down in front the three women took seats that had been reserved for them in the first row, while Maharishi stepped up onto the stage, preceded by the bald bramachari who rushed forward to drape the deerskin over the bench. Maharishi sat down, arranged his robe around his crossed legs, pulled his tan shawl tighter over his round shoulders, and helped himself to a flower from the vase in front of him. With his other hand he reached forward and tapped the mike. "This is working, yes?"

It was not working, no. The bald bramachari hurried over to a console in the corner, where he started flipping switches and twisting knobs. A series of yelps and shrieks came out of the speakers down in front, causing people to cover their ears and Maharishi to wince and laugh. Finally the bramachari found the proper adjustments. People unstopped their ears. Maharishi leaned towards the mike and in his high voice squeaked out, "Jai Guru Dev!"

"Jai Guru Dev," came the answer in almost perfect unison, then we all sat back down. Maharishi waited until everybody had gotten comfortable and the room had grown silent, then waited thirty seconds longer, and said, "Now, we all meditate. Ten, fifteen minutes."

After the group meditation, Maharishi began by asking if anyone had had problems settling into their rooms. To my surprise, nobody raised their hand. Gone were the complaints and grumblings I'd overheard during breakfast about freezing water, broken windows, leaking pipes and lousy food. Maybe this was one of the miracles Geoffrey had alluded to the night before. Finally one woman down in front raised her hand. The woman was a stout Australian SRMer named Edna. On the middle finger of Edna's raised hand was a ring the size of a walnut made entirely of diamonds. Timidly, although Edna was not a timid woman, she asked about the noise of construction still going on up in Block 6, along with shouting of the workmen.

Edna's room was in Block 5, and she said the noise was interfering with her meditation. Nods and noises from other people in the auditorium indicated she was not the only one.

Maharishi hooked his left thumb through the string of beads around his neck and waggled his head back and forth. He said that some last minute renovations were still necessary, but he would talk to Suresh and have him tell the carpenters to perform the noisiest operations while we were meeting for lectures, and to keep the shouting to a minimum. In the meantime, there were underground cells or caves just outside the auditorium—Maharishi pointed to his left—where people could go and meditate in perfect silence during the day. Normally, the caves were for meditation when the weather got hot, but if you had one of the boys install a coal heater and took blankets to wrap yourself in, there was no more peaceful place to meditate.

Maharishi went on to say that the primary objective of this three month course was to give us all experience in deep meditation. He explained that in the beginning there would be three lectures per day, the first at 10:00 a.m., the second in the afternoon, before tea, and the third at 7:00, after dinner. Whenever we were not attending lectures or eating meals, we were supposed to spend the time meditating, going over our lecture notes, or studying Maharishi's commentary of the Bhagavad Gita, which was available in the ashram print shop down in the village.

As the course continued the number of lectures each day would diminish until there would only be one, in the afternoon or evening. This was because every day we were to spend more and more time meditating, even skipping lectures if we so desired. Around midway through the course Maharishi said that many of us would be meditating around the clock, only taking time out for meals, which could be delivered to our rooms, or to sleep, although most of us would find that the need for sleep would also greatly diminish as our nervous systems relaxed with the effect of long meditation. After the midpoint of the course, in about six weeks, the number of lectures each day would increase back to two and then three, and we would gradually lessen the time we spent in meditation, as we began to prepare ourselves for return to our home countries.

After outlining the overall structure of the course, Maharishi said he was now going to give the first lecture, which he wanted us to write down word-for-word in the notebooks we had just been given. Many people sitting down in front had brought small cassette recorders and one of them now asked if she couldn't just tape the lecture and listen to it afterwards. Maharishi considered this for a moment, his head tilted to one side, then said that for this first lecture it was important for each of us to write it down word-for-word, so that it left as deep an impression as possible in our memory. Dutifully each of us opened the pink and blue notebooks that had been passed out by the bramacharis. When all of us had a pen or pencil poised over the first page, Maharishi began to speak. Following his instructions to the letter, I even recorded the occasional grammatical lapses.

"Purpose of this course, is to gain the wisdom for life which will present the most effective march towards fulfillment... Path to accomplish this purpose seems to be a path in time, but it is a pathless path, easy, not difficult, because the way of approach is so delightfully simple and natural that we will not encounter any difficulty..."

CHAPTER 15

Mia goes AWOL

※ ※ ※

Within a few days almost everyone had settled into a routine that despite certain hardships and discomforts was for the most part quite pleasant. Basically, that routine consisted of waking up, followed by early morning meditation (for the early risers) followed by breakfast, then meditation, then morning lecture, then lunch, then meditation and/or nap, followed by afternoon lecture, then tea, then meditation, dinner, evening lecture, meditation, sleep. To add variety to this daily schedule, one could sign out of the ashram with the guard at the lower gate, next to block 1, and stroll down to the makeshift village to check or send mail at the improvised post office, drop off or pick up clothing at the improvised laundry, or buy amenities at the improvised general store—amenities which in addition to Peace cigarettes and Cadbury chocolate bars included items such as additional candles, matches, incense, and postcards of Hindu gods or goddesses with which to decorate our Spartan walls.

Since people were supposed to spend as much of their free time as possible in meditation, reading was discouraged, unless the reading matter was Maharishi's Commentary on the Bhagavad Gita. The Commentary was a thick hardback, bound in white and gold imitation leather, that Maharishi advised us to read, "to elewate the mind," whenever we found it difficult to meditate. Despite my limited budget, I bought myself a copy, anticipating long periods of boredom in the weeks to come. Whenever I sat down to read Maharishi's Commentary, however, instead of finding it elevating, I found it boring, even a little depressing, maybe because at least unconsciously I kept comparing it to another commentary of a sacred text I had grown all too familiar with during my childhood. As much as I had come to loathe Mary Baker Eddy, I would have had to admit that her prose, in comparison to Maharishi's, was both more poetic and more substantial.

Like his dictated discourse during the opening lecture, Maharishi's written works lacked the charm and spontaneity of his off-the-cuff remarks during interviews and informal talks, and they did not stand up well to scrutiny. The more I studied his annotations to the Bhagavad Gita the less they seemed to make sense, and if I wanted mystification after all I could always close myself up in my room and haul out *Finnegan's Wake*. Still, no doubt like many of my classmates on the course, I kept faithfully plugging away at the Commentary, figuring I must be missing something, and that something would dawn on me sooner or later, maybe with the dawn of cosmic consciousness.

Because that's what the lectures three times a day were all about, their constant, recurring theme, the point of reference Maharishi always came back to, the reason we were all there. Enlightenment in this lifetime. Here. Now. Just close your eyes and you were there.

Well, almost.

Well, most of us.

Well, maybe some of us. Presumably.

Was that why I was there?

Yes, absolutely, without a doubt. After being brought up in that pseudo-religion, growing up in a country that paid lip service to God and family but believed only in More—More money, More fun, More toys, More guns—and in the meantime was busily killing off more and more families in Vietnam, I knew there had to be another way. While reading Huxley and Watts and Laing and even Proust and Joyce, it seemed to me that I'd caught glimpses of that way, glimpses that had been confirmed whenever I'd peeked over the rim with the help of a little grass or acid. And during my short but unforgettable epiphanies, while driving my MG, or staring at the back of Notre Dame, or sometimes lately while repeating the mantra, hadn't I experienced that Other Way directly? From what I understood, when I attained cosmic consciousness I would live those moments all the time, they would be a part of me, even while I was asleep.

So yes. Bring it on. Lemme at it. What did I have to do? Take the wafer? Swallow the pill? Keep repeating the mantra? I'm your man.

Or was I?

The other reason I was there was that Maharishi, thinking I was French, had raised his finger and invited me along.

As it turned out, this was something I had in common with Mia Farrow, although I didn't know it at the time. Thinking she would sit with him on all the press conferences between LA and New Delhi, and end up attracting millions more to his movement, and in time become as devoted to him as her sister, Maharishi had invited Mia along too, free of charge and very much at the last minute.

So far though, she hadn't been living up to expectations. At the beginning of the afternoon lecture on Saturday, the third day of the course, while everyone was settling into their armchairs and getting ready for the group meditation that always preceded the lectures, Maharishi noticed that Mia was missing. When he asked where she was, someone down in front said she had gone to town.

"To town?"

"Yes, to Rishikesh."

"Alone?" Maharishi shifted position on his deerskin. The person offering the information was an American woman named Ginny who had accompanied Nancy from California and who also lived up in Block 6 with Nancy and Prudence and Mia. She said that after lunch she had talked to Mia who said she needed to go for a walk to be alone. "She said she was going to town to take a look around," Ginny said, "and asked me if I needed anything."

Maharishi looked confused. It was the same look he had given me at the YMCA in New Delhi when I told him I was an American. For a long moment, he sat there with his head cocked sideways, digesting this news. Then he turned to his left and beckoned to the bald bramachary sitting on the floor next to the amplifier. The bramachary leaped up onto the stage and leaned down. Maharishi said a few words to him in a low voice. The bramachary nodded and said something in return. From where I sat it sounded like "atcha," a handy Hindi expression which, when accompanied by joined hands and a brief head wobble, meant "you got it," or "gotcha."

The bramachary threw his shawl around his shoulders, raced back up the aisle and out of the auditorium.

Focusing again on the people in front of him, as if suddenly remembering who we were and why we were there, Maharishi said by way of explanation, "She does not realize. It can be wery dangerous. Everywhere in India there are people who…" He paused, looking for the right word, "They are like savages."

Even though he had spoken in a low voice, away from the mike, all of us in the hall heard what he said, because by then we were all watching him intently. It was as if we were all stunned, not by Mia's absence nor by what Maharishi said, but because he was so visibly upset, so obviously worried. Another woman down in front raised her hand. It was Edna, the Australian with the colossal diamond ring. Today she was wearing a colossal watch to match. On the end of that waving arm there must have been a thousand diamonds. Maharishi nodded at her absently. She stood up and said, "Maharishi, we're here to meditate, and I think that's what we should do! Not walk around."

As soon as she sat down another elderly woman sitting just behind her stood up in turn. It was Mrs. Harrington, the woman with the good B.M.s and the bad meditations. Instead of talking directly to Maharishi, she half turned to address her remarks to all of us sitting in the hall. "Personally, I feel we have come all this way to come to India to be with Maharishi and we can walk in our own countries. I don't think it's necessary to walk anywhere. We should spend the time in meditation. That's what I think personally." She sat down to general noises of assent and scattered applause.

Sitting in the same row as me but a few seats to my left was Reumah. I leaned back and caught her eye and we exchanged a little smile. I was glad that Prudence wasn't there that afternoon. Normally she sat down in the front row along with all the other notables, but already she'd started skipping lectures to spend more time in her room to meditate. I wondered what she would have thought of all her fellow meditators ganging up on her sister.

The next person to stand up was Herr Schraff, sitting a few rows back. Herr Schraff was fifty-something and both his hands were shriveled, as if they'd been badly burned. While still in Delhi the rumor circulated among us SIMSers that at the end of the war Herr Schraff had been on a Nazi U-boat when it was hit by an American torpedo. Immediately, he had grasped the large wheel that opened the valves that let in water so the submarine could submerge. Even though the wheel had been scorching hot, he'd managed to turn it, enabling the U-boat to plunge to safety just in time, and for him to survive the war and twenty-three years later come to Rishikesh. I don't know why that story went around or if there was a grain of truth to it, but when you looked at the little man wearing his wrinkled hat with the sun visor he'd probably bought especially for the trip and which he rarely if ever took off, the story stuck. Now he stood up in his turn and said, rather bravely in fact, that he had walked down to the river that morning to meditate, "Und it vass vonderful!"

After the laughter had died down Maharishi pulled the microphone towards him and said, "With all dat great noise of the Ganges it is impossible to meditate." If we wanted to meditate outside, he said, better to go up to the roofs above our terraces and meditate while sitting in the sun.

Herr Schraff sat back down. People shifted in their seats. "And now," Maharishi said, after a short pause, "we just close the eyes…"

It was not a good group meditation. For one thing there was Maharishi's reaction to the news that Mia was MIA. To see someone normally so imperturbable suddenly not taking it easy, looking in fact very worried, was a little jarring, even for me, and cast a dark little cloud of foreboding over the whole assembly.

For another, instead of one or two pigeons that afternoon who had found their way into the auditorium, there were five or six of them. The pigeons roosted up on the iron-pipe rafters draped in paper flags and garlands, where they would coo and fly around and disturb everyone's meditation, and sometimes even shit on the meditators below. Today two ashram staffers had been given the task of trying to shoo them back outside. They were running around barefoot with long bamboo poles, trying to knock the pigeons off the rafters as soon as they alighted, but all that did was make the birds fly around faster, and get tangled up in the garlands and flags. And while the pigeons inside beat their wings and flew around in a frenzy looking for a way out, the pigeons outside flocked to the windows in ever growing numbers, ducking their heads and cooing loudly, as if cheering on their brother birds, or more likely looking for a way to come inside and join the fun.

Finally, as if that were not enough to keep the mind off the mantra, there was Arjuna. Arjuna was a little black floppy-eared puppy Mia had found and adopted soon after she arrived at the ashram, naming him after the mythological Hindu warrior Maharishi was fond of and had already talked about a few times during the lectures. Normally, during lectures or meals, Arjuna sat contentedly in Mia's lap, but in her absence he would run around yapping and chewing on the legs of chairs, or people, begging to be picked up. Which was what he was doing now. As he was Mia's pup and therefore enjoyed diplomatic immunity, no one dared suggest he be taken outside and shot. As a result, throughout the group meditation, every now and then an SRMer down in the first rows would let out a yelp or a muffled curse and give the dog a kick, causing Arjuna to yelp before moving on to another armchair.

Finally I gave up trying to meditate and opened my eyes. Sitting in the row directly in front of me were the three Swedish SIMSers, Soren, Berndt, and Gunilla. They were meditating like pros, apparently oblivious to the mayhem going on five rows down, or the cooing and flapping up in the rafters.

Gunilla was sitting just in front of me, her shoulders wrapped in a blanket, the end of her long dark braid suspended just a few inches above my bended knee. Tall, slender, and well-built, within a few days down in Delhi Gunilla had become the focus of attention of almost every male on the course. While I enjoyed talking with her during my conversations with Berndt and the other Scandinavians, Gunilla's beauty was not the kind that I was sensitive to. Maybe she was a little too tall, too exotic, too beautiful, or maybe I just figured she was out of my class and therefore inaccessible. At any rate, in those days all of my fantasies were more likely to feature Rosalyn, or more recently Viggie. But as I sat there unable to meditate I focused instead on the nape of Gunilla's neck not two feet away, and at the dark, wispy little hairs that had escaped the braid.

Above us a pigeon gave a coo of alarm and fluttered from one pipe to another, losing a feather on the way. I watched as the feather floated slowly down and down. It looked like it was going to light directly on the top of Gunilla's head, but instead it just missed, finally coming to rest on the floor in front of my chair.

CHAPTER 16

Dewotion

※ ※ ※

"Jai Guru Dev!"

"Jai Guru Dev!"

"It is easy, yes?"

"Oh yes, Maharishi," came the response, as people stirred and stretched and opened their eyes.

The topic of the lecture that afternoon was devotion, or rather the lack thereof, the topic inspired no doubt by Mia's desertion. Maharishi waited until we had all opened our notebooks and were waiting with our pens at the ready, or for those with cassette recorders lined up at the foot of the stage to come down and switch them on, then he pulled the mike closer still, leaned back against the wooden backrest of his bench, and said, "Dewotion,…"

The fingers of his right hand were twirled around the string of small red beads that hung around his neck, while he held his left hand slightly aloft, pressing the forefinger against the thumb, to emphasize the point he was about to make. His gaze was abstract, a little dreamy, the right eye gazing at the relative world, the left eye taking in the absolute. Clearly, Maharishi had recovered full composure. Maybe he wasn't even thinking of Mia at all.

"Devotion is responsible for final alchemical change, the transformation of ordinary waking state to most celestial state. Dat is, God Consciousness…"

In an earlier lecture, the one where he'd talked for the first time about Krishna and Arjuna, Maharishi had introduced the concept of God

Consciousness, describing it as one step higher than Cosmic Consciousness, and saying it was the most highly developed state a human being could attain. He had described Cosmic Consciousness as fully experiencing both the relative and the absolute simultaneously, whereas in God Consciousness those two states merge and you become "one with the gods," as Arjuna had done through devotion to Krishna.

Maharishi waited until everybody writing had finished writing, then he went on.

"Just by living God Consciousness, Being and Celestial, for a time, the mechanics separating the two become au-to-ma-ti-cal-ly clear."

While waiting for the clatter of pens to cease and for everyone to look back up at him, Maharishi tapped the fingertips of his right hand into the knuckles of his left, which he held in a loose fist. Ploppety-ploppety-plop.

"This clarity is Supreme Knowledge."

There was another pause, and then he said, "This is clear, yes? There are no questions?"

It was a way he had of asking for questions. Obligingly, a hand went up down in front. The hand belonged to Walter Kuhn, a graying, sixtyish, hatchet-faced German who lived in Santa Barbara and whom, after our initial exchange of introductory banalities down in New Delhi, I preferred to avoid. Towards SIMSers Walter tended to be officious, condescending and often downright bossy, whereas to the inner core of SRMers—people like Nancy Nixon and Charles Jackson—he was self-effacing and obsequious. To Maharishi, when he was not being ingratiatingly "helpful," he was simply abject. He grovelled. Whenever Walter said anything—question, comment, or command—he preceded it with the word "Now." Sometimes, imitating a tic he had picked up from his guru, he would also press the index finger against the thumb of his extended hand, as he was doing now.

"Yes?" Maharishi said.

"Now," said Walter, forefinger on thumb, "if I understand correctly, Maharishi, to get from Cosmic Consciousness to God Consciousness, what you need is devotion."

"Dat is correct. Dat is the only way."

Another hand went up, this one flashing diamonds. "Maharishi," Edna said, "could you please explain again the difference between Cosmic Consciousness and God Consciousness?"

Maharishi wobbled his head and smiled. "In Cosmic Consciousness you see the world through rose-colored glasses. In God Consciousness you see the world through gold-colored glasses."

Unfortunately, no one asked the question which occurred to me only after I was back in my cell that night going over my notes. Devotion to what? To whom?

But that was because the answer was obvious, at least to everyone there but me. To Maharishi, of course. Or, if one preferred, to the tradition of masters, represented by the portrait of Guru Dev ever present in the background, set up on the easel behind Maharishi's bench, looking over his shoulder as it were.

Maybe the reason Maharishi kept harping on this topic—and it was to come up again and again in the next three months—was that it was a hard concept for us Westerners to get a grip on, and before sending us out into the world to teach Transcendental Meditation, he wanted to make sure we gripped it firmly.

One of the Indian bramacharys was a very tall, very dark-skinned, very long-haired young man named Devendra. He seemed to be a kind of personal valet to Maharishi, always on hand, if Maharishi showed signs of being thirsty, to rush forward with a brass bowl of freshly squeezed grapes, along with a little napkin for Maharishi to wipe his lips on after his drink. Or ready with a shawl to place over Maharishi's shoulders if he showed signs of getting cold, or with a large umbrella, when the lectures took place outside and Maharishi was sitting in the sun and the sun got too bright or too hot. For as long as an hour or even two, Devendra would stand there holding the umbrella, the sweat dripping down his placid, smiling face and seeping through his white cotton shirt, turning it brown beneath his beard, the stain growing larger and larger the longer he stood there motionless.

Even though it didn't seem as though Devendra could speak or even understand a word of English, whenever Maharishi or anyone else said something that made Maharishi laugh, Devendra too would laugh. Whenever he turned serious or frowned, Devendra's expression too would cloud over. It occurred to me that another of Devendra's duties, the main one perhaps, was simply to be there, providing a model of devotion to the rest of us.

Early on in the course, during one of the first lectures to be held outside, a number of blanket-clad older women in the audience complained timidly that they were cold, because the branches above them were depriving them of the mid-morning sun. Maharishi leaned towards Devendra, pointed towards the branches hanging over the women, and uttered what could not have been three words in Hindi. Devendra took a few strides towards a large tree behind the women and leapt up into it like Tarzan, but without the warcry, then proceeded to rip away the offending branches, some of which were as big around as my upper arm.

In fact Devendra looked a lot like Tarzan, but a Tarzan without his Jane, since as a bramachary he had taken a vow of celibacy. Technically speaking, we were all bramacharys, as Maharishi was fond of pointing out. He never went on to say, however, that this meant we should also be practicing celibacy. In fact the topic of celibacy was not one he ever said much about, explicitly. Unless that's what he meant by "socializing," which was something he said a lot about at the beginning, and tried to discourage all of us from indulging in.

The image of Devendra leaping up into the tree on that peaceful sunny morning made a deep and lasting impression on my mind and also caused me some discomfort. Deep down I had to admit that by comparison with Devendra I felt little or no devotion to Maharishi or Guru Dev and I wondered if I ever would, or could.

During lectures, whenever people started spouting gibberish which was obviously intended to show how devoted they were—something that happened regularly—I would gnash my teeth and vent dark thoughts on the left-hand pages of my notebook. Public displays of self-abnegation as soon as Maharishi entered the room—the way some people would bow and scrape, or others rush up to be first in line for a flower—made me want to gag. It was one thing for an Indian to prostrate himself at the feet of his guru, but for a Westerner to do that—an Anglo Saxon, an American, a Californian!—was to me against the grain, unnatural, revolting! And after three weeks in India the more I saw Westerners around me going through the motions of devotion the less I felt inclined to do the same.

Another reason for my discomfort at the image of Devendra ripping away the branches was that I suspected Maharishi must have known about my lack of devotion, and how could he not? If you had God Consciousness—and to talk about it with such authority he must have been at least at that level, if not higher—couldn't you see into the hearts of those around you? In which case, what would prevent him one of these days from beckoning Devendra over, pointing at me where I sat in the back of the class, and saying, "Take that boy there, the young American with blond hair and no devotion, and fling him over the cliff."

But as far as I could tell, everyone else on that course, even the most Western of us Westerners—Charlie Jackson and Nancy Nixon for example—had a pretty firm grip on the concept of devotion, ranging from the blind and abject variety of a Walter Kuhn, who would have thrown himself over the cliff if Maharishi told him to (but not without first holding up his hand, forefinger pressed against thumb, to ask, "Now, if I understand correctly Maharishi, ...") to the tempered if not tepid variety shared by most of the SIMSers and a couple of SRMers like Reumah and Tony. The devotion of the latter tended to take the form of an overriding affection for Maharishi that allowed them to indulge and accept, at least for the time being, some of his more outlandish statements and preconceptions—his unwavering support for the War, for example, or his blanket condemnation of drugs and anyone who took them—even though it was thanks to drugs that 95% of the SIMSers had ended up as his followers and made him famous. According to all the SIMSers I had become friends with, the often embarrassingly reactionary statements Maharishi came up with—his comment about "the happy hungry man," for example, that had caused a near riot at the Paris Hilton—were due in part to his ignorance of Western culture and history (before the year was over Maharishi would proclaim to the world at large that Transcendental Meditation had ushered in the Age of Enlightenment, not knowing—not having been told—that this age had taken place two centuries earlier) and also in part to the benighted and odious advice he had been receiving all along from the old inner circle of SRMers, most of whom, when you dared to talk to them about politics, seemed to consider Goldwater a dangerous liberal. Now that SIMS was by far the larger and more vital of the two branches of Maharishi's movement, and was outstripping SRM in new initiations every day, all that would soon change—Viggie, Berndt, Reumah, Larry and others were sure of it. It was just a matter of time. They had that faith.

So did I, I suppose, but for me the faith took the form of hope, hope that they were right and that I was, by some karmic wrinkle, in the right place at the right time.

One thing I knew for sure was that I was not bored. Looking at the daily schedule of activities at the ashram, one might assume that the first lesson one had to learn on the course was how to cope with boredom, but this was definitely not the case for me, nor as far as I could tell, for the great majority of my classmates.

One notable exception was my fellow-freeloader and not-so-devoted compatriot Mia Farrow, who admitted to a few of us, during one of the first cocoa sessions, that she was "bored out of her skull."

The cocoa sessions were a pleasant addition to the daily routine that started during the first nights of the course and soon became a nightly event. After evening lectures ended, usually around ten, virtually everyone would troop down to the smoky kitchen to fill thermoses or cups with tea or hot chocolate, which they would then take back to their rooms. But a few of us, mostly SIMSers, got into the habit of taking them to the dining room instead, along with platefuls of crackers and cheese, to sit around for a while chatting and smoking, sometimes even playing cards. Maybe it was these cocoa sessions that got Maharishi started on the topic of "socializing," having been tipped off by a disapproving SRMer. Socializing, Maharishi said, was a waste of psychic energy that we could otherwise channel into our meditation. But trying to keep a bunch of twenty-to-thirty-year-olds from getting together to talk once in a while was an uphill battle, to say the least, and Maharishi had the good sense not to belabor the issue or ban the cocoa sessions outright, probably sensing that doing so would have led to mutiny, and for the time being he had enough mutiny on his hands with Mia.

Mia's confession about being bored came the night after she'd returned from spending the afternoon wandering alone through the streets of Rishikesh. It was only after she got back to the ashram that she learned how upset Maharishi had been by her unannounced departure—which seemed both to annoy and amuse her.

After combing the streets and temples and alleys of Rishikesh, the search party organized by the bald bramachary had come back empty-handed. Maybe because Mia had disguised herself as a pilgrim, draped in a shawl from head to foot, and barefoot to boot.

"It's a pretty wild place, believe me," she told us, warming her hands around a cup of steaming chocolate, while in her lap Arjuna gnawed on a crust of bread.

That night there were eight or ten of us sitting around the table in the dining room, including Berndt, Larry, Rosalyn, Ian the gimpy Australian, and Sarah and Ben, both from Canada. All day it had been clear and warm but as soon as the sun went down the weather had turned stormy and now bursts of rain were spattering against the windows and the wind was howling down from the Himalayas, making it that much cozier in the narrow, candlelit room.

"Wild how?" Ian asked, leaning forward with his elbows on the table, his red face and moustache redder still in the glow from the candle in front of him.

"Well, there are all these sadhus for one thing," Mia said. "Sitting in the street with their begging bowls. As if anyone had anything to give them. I mean, everybody is walking around in rags. You'd think it would be depressing, but it's not. Everybody looks so happy."

Another gust of wind caused the windows of the long narrow room to rattle in their casings, and all the candles on the table to flicker. No one said anything for a while, then Sarah yawned and looked at her watch and sighed. She said she knew she should go back to her room to meditate, but she had this terrible urge to go out dancing.

"Well don't stay out too late," Mia said. "You know how Maharishi worries." She fed Arjuna another piece of cheese. The puppy gulped it down then licked her hand. Another gust of wind-driven rain rattled the windows.

CHAPTER 17

Down by the riverside

※ ※ ※

Afternoon lecture the next day was cancelled because Maharishi was giving a private conference to some bigwigs who had driven up from New Delhi. Rumor had it they were rich businessmen or government officials—three big black official-looking Ambassadors were parked outside the upper gate beyond Block 6. Taking advantage of the time off, a few of us from Block 1—Terry, Geoffrey, Larry, Tony, Soren and I—walked down to the Ganges. I had always been attracted to rivers and bodies of water, an attraction Geoffrey and Larry immediately attributed to the fact that I was Aquarius—one of the prime topics of conversation at the ashram being astrology—and now there was the added attraction of forbidden fruit. Not that trips down to the river had been forbidden per se, following Herr Schraff's confession, but like socializing, they were discouraged.

On the way down the path we stopped off at the Post Office to check our mail. The Post Office was a small house with a table inside and a mountain of mail piled up on top of it. Behind the mountain sat a small man reading a copy of *Time*. As we entered he put down the magazine, stood up, and gave us a joined-hands "Namaste!"

After we had repeated our names several times, and finally written them down on a "chit" the man gave us, he nodded "Atcha!" and retired to a back room. Moments later he returned with an aerogram for me, and a small packet of letters for Larry, tied up with a piece of string. "Dynamite!" Larry said, as the man handed him the packet, registering no surprise that the American word for thank you was a dangerous explosive. A few minutes before, while we were all signing out at the ashram gate, Geoffrey had picked up and trimmed the leaves off a small straight branch which he adopted as a walking stick and was now pointing dubiously at the pile of mail on the desk. "Erm, nothing for the rest of us?" he asked.

"No sahib," the man said with a slight bow. "So sorry."

Trailing behind the others as we continued down the sandy path, I opened my aerogram, which was from David. He began by saying he had deposited my check from IBM into my account at the Credit Lyonnais and did I want him to send me a money order? Did I ever! My outlay for Maharishi's Commentary had reduced my supply of cash to a small wad of rumpled rupees that looked like well-worn Monopoly money and had about as much real value. In the not-so-unlikely event of my being banished from the ashram I'd have to find myself a begging bowl and join the happy hungry millions.

In the second paragraph David related going to dinner and a movie the night before with Rose and Vivian, the two Jewish-Brazilian sisters David and I had met at the American Center and gone out together with a few times, both of whom now sent me their good vibrations and were anxious to hear all about India. David ended the letter by saying that he was still seeing his analyst twice a week and filling drawing pads with pictures of his demons.

I folded the letter and slipped it into my shirt pocket, a little taken aback by how far away all this seemed: Les Deux dragons, the dark little Chinese restaurant they'd gone to in the rue Monsieur-le-Prince—the cinema they went to afterwards on the Carrefour de l'Odéon, the images of Vivian and Rose and even of David. They were like photographs in an old album I'd forgotten about long ago and that I'd inadvertently opened when I unfolded David's letter.

I caught up with the others where the path opened out onto the gravel and sand and smooth stones that lined the shore. Here the river was strangely quiet, making even less noise than it did when you were up in the ashram standing on the edge of the cliff. Now all we could hear, in addition to the faint sound of chanting and tinkling bells coming from the ghats of Swargashram up the river and around the bend, was the sound of water gurgling along the river's edge, together with the steady, urgent whisper of the deep, fast-moving water in the middle. Even though its source was less than

100 miles away as the crow flies (and more than a mile higher up), here the Ganges was quite wide. While Geoffrey walked around poking his stick at pieces of driftwood or the dried-up bodies of dead scorpions, the rest of us walked to the water's edge and picked up some flat stones and tried skipping them across, none of them even getting halfway.

Scorpions were a problem at the ashram we had all been warned about. That morning while putting on my trousers one had fallen out of the left leg and skittered across the floor and escaped beneath the crack in the door before I could smash it with my shoe.

During one of our dinner table conversations down in Delhi everyone was trying to guess my rising sign. "I'd say Libra," said Viggie, but Jeremy from Australia said he'd be willing to bet it was Scorpio. In addition to doing horoscopes, Jeremy was an avid reader of the *I Ching*, which he would consult to find out answers to the most trivial questions. Everything is locked in symbol, he said, all you needed to unlock them was the right tool and there was no better tool than the *I Ching*.

While Geoffrey continued exploring with his stick, pushing it into crevasses and under rocks, the rest of us sat down a little ways from the river on a half-circle of small, smooth boulders that looked like they'd been put there for us to sit on. Larry took out the fresh pack of cigarettes he'd bought at the company store on the way down and passed it around. One of his letters was from a publisher in New York to whom before leaving Larry had floated the idea of a book the publisher now said he might be interested in. It was to be a book of photographs of the kinds of things that catch your eye while making love.

"You know," Larry said, "clouds going by outside a window, a lamp on the nightstand beside the bed, part of a shoulder against a pillow. That kind of thing."

"Yeah, I get it," said Tony. "A used rubber lyin' on the floor, next to an old sock, in a corner a wad of wet tissues… Very poetic."

Apparently none of us thought much of the idea except Larry but it brought up the subject of sex, about which all of us, apparently, had been thinking a lot.

"I wonder if they think about it as much as we do," Soren mused, meaning the female course participants.

"Are you kiddin'?" Tony said. "Of course dey do." He went on to say that if he didn't have a wife and two little kids back home in Vegas and was unattached like us guys he would be doing something else at night besides night meditation. Or at least he'd be out there trying. "All these beautiful girls," he said, "it's a bachelor's paradise!"

At that point Larry stunned everyone into silence by announcing that of all the women on the course the one he found the most sexy and would give anything to crawl into the sack with was Nancy.

"Nancy Nixon?" I asked, aghast, while everyone else kept trying to think of anyone else on the course named Nancy.

"Right on, man! She's so fucking hot! You can feel it when she walks into the room." Larry was sure that in bed Nancy would be "dynamite!" and he was willing to bet he was going to find out firsthand before the course was over. While the conversation turned to what sort of evidence Larry would be required to produce as proof, I slipped off my sandals and headed for the water's edge. The image of Larry and Nancy naked in bed together was not one I wanted to dwell on, but I couldn't help wondering how she would react every time Larry grabbed his camera to snap another picture for his book.

The water felt exactly like the melted ice it was, but still it called to me. In two or three weeks, when the weather got hot, I would come back down in the heat of the day and slide into it and let the current take me down to the next bend. In the Ganges they said you could find blind porpoises or enormous snakes, not to mention remains of cremated bodies. Or worse, they could find you. But I was sure that was farther down, where the river flowed by Benares and beyond. Here the water was clear and cold and unpolluted.

About fifty yards upriver from where I was standing something was sticking out of the water near where the river smoothed out after a stretch of rapids. Two big birds, attracted by whatever it was, were wheeling around it, one of them now and then landing nearby to peck at it until the other drove it away and landed in its turn. Using the larger rocks that lined the shore as stepping stones, I headed up the river for a closer look.

As I walked I also looked more closely at the rocks. Rather than massive lumps of worn granite one normally sees along mountain rivers, these were rounded, igneous boulders, all black or dark brown or copper-colored. Many of them resembled enormous cannonballs. They also looked very old, smoothed down by centuries of water and ice. It was almost as if, back when the Himalayas were active volcanoes, each one of these rocks had been sucked up from the molten middle of the earth by a gigantic ice cream scoop then plopped down here along the banks of the river to cool, and bear witness nowadays to that pre-human age, showing how close we were to it, and it to us.

As I made my way up the river on those round rocks, some of them half-submerged in the icy water but all of them warmed by the sun, a strange feeling started coming over me. With each step it felt as if something was coming up through the balls of my feet, passing from the molten, hardened flesh of the rocks into my own. I picked my way carefully at first, then, as I gained confidence in my footing, picked up speed. The faster I walked the more intense the feeling became.

Maybe it was the subject of the conversation I had just come away from, or the effects of three days of progressively deeper meditation, but that feeling was definitely sexual. Not focalized in my genitals, rather it was a general excitement radiating throughout my whole body, extending to my fingertips. Carried away by this feeling, I went faster and faster, trusting in my inner ear and my peripheral vision and my dumb luck to keep from falling, until I was doing a kind of dance, leaping from boulder to boulder, with—each time I touched down—this infusion of something pulsing up through me, producing a thrill that was both physical yet somehow transcended my physical body. It occurred to me that if I kept this up I was going to have a prehistoric orgasm, unlike any I had ever known.

But I could not keep it up. For one thing the feeling was too intense. For another, I was exhausted. And finally, I ran out of rocks. I landed on the last one and collapsed, out of breath and soaked in sweat.

As I sat there feeling my heartbeat slow back down, I saw a man across and up the river. He was kneeling in the water, washing clothes, or maybe washing himself, and softly chanting. Because of the glare of the sun off the water I couldn't see him clearly but I could clearly hear his high-pitched invocation to the goddess Saraswati as it mingled with the gurgling of the river rushing around my ancient boulder.

Directly in front of me, about ten feet away, was the thing sticking up out of the water that had attracted my attention. It turned out to be a ribcage and part of a skull of what looked like a mid-sized animal, all of it now picked nearly clean. Later when I described it to Terry he said it was probably the carcass of a deer, killed by a tiger while drinking upriver at the water's edge, then left there after the tiger had eaten its fill, to be carried downstream when the water rose with the next heavy rain.

One of the two birds had flown, but the other had decided to stick around, about ten yards farther up, perched on a stone too far for me to leap to. The bird stood with its back to me but with its head turned sideways, its long beak pointed towards the monk across the river, its left eye fixed on the ribcage and on me. It held its wings akimbo, keeping them at the ready, airing its underarms. During the whole time I sat there looking at it, and after I got up and walked away, the bird remained completely motionless, a scrawny phoenix poised for flight.

CHAPTER 18

Like dat, like dat

※ ※ ※

That night at the cocoa session Mia was conspicuously absent, her absence made all the more conspicuous by the presence of her puppy that we all kept passing around. There were a lot of us that night, at least a dozen, sitting as usual around the far end of the table. At the other end sat a few SRMers, proof that the cocoa sessions were catching on. Among them was Herr Schraff, talking quietly with two other women, also from Germany, one of whom was a practicing MD from Hamburg named Gertrude, the other a cheerful, plump little woman with very short hair called Annaliese. In Delhi Reumah had introduced me to Annaliese because she was a healer and Reumah thought that since I had grown up a Christian Scientist we might have something in common. When we shook hands Annaliese had taken both of mine in hers and looked them over for quite a long time and then looked up into my eyes and told me I had "healing hands."

The reason for Mia's absence that night was explained by Sarah, who was sitting at the very end of the table next to Berndt and Gunilla, and who had heard from Edna who had heard from Ginny that Mia had gone off on a safari with Nancy.

"On a safari?" someone said.

"With Nancy?" said someone else.

"My goodness!" said Gunilla. "You mean with guns? To hunt lions and tigers?"

"I guess so," Sarah shrugged. "What other kind of safari is there?"

From what she'd heard, the safari had been organized by Avi, a tall, suave, good-looking Indian friend of Nancy's who owned a travel agency and who had made himself useful when the group was down in Delhi, arranging rooms at the last minute in the Oberoi for Mia and Prudence, and other notables who showed up late. Apparently Avi had suggested the idea of a safari to Nancy who had proposed it to Maharishi who had given his reluctant consent when Nancy told him that otherwise Mia was liable to leave the ashram for good and return to Hollywood, or worse, go off on another barefoot tour on her own at the spur of the moment.

Berndt gave a short laugh and a sigh. "Ja ja," he said. "Well at least she won't be bored."

The reason boredom was not a problem with any of the rest of us, as far as I could tell, was that when you were sitting there in long meditation (and despite the time spent socializing, all of us were logging in more and more hours of meditation every day), you weren't just sitting there. Things were happening. What was happening exactly, according to Maharishi, was something called "unstressing."

The theory, which he had explained already a few times during lectures, and would have occasion to enlarge upon in lectures to come, was that as soon as you closed your eyes and started repeating the mantra, everything that happened from then on was part of a process of purification, making it possible little by little for the mind to perceive finer and finer levels of existence as clearly as it perceives the "grosser levels" that until then captivated it—held it captive.

The main events in this process are thoughts. During the Q&A sessions at the end of the lectures, it was clear that thoughts were still the most common complaint, just as they had been for the new initiates in Paris at the Continental—all these annoying, extraneous, random thoughts that got in the way and made people forget to keep repeating the mantra.

Maharishi's point was that during meditation no thought was extraneous and that on the contrary they served a useful and necessary purpose. The nervous system of the average adult in the modern world, he explained, was full of "areas of stress" or "knots of tension" or even "icebergs" that over the years had built up to cloud one's vision and cause it to focus only on the gross phenomena that can give it only momentary and superficial satisfaction.

These areas of stress (which I assumed in psychotherapeutic terms were neuroses or complexes), were caused by past events that had produced shocks to the system. Such shocks could be due to good or bad events, but they always leave a deep impression and a lasting effect. Quoting Maharishi directly from one of those early lectures, during long meditation "the stressed areas begin to unstress themselves as thoughts. These are thoughts which bring the mind out of transcendence,... Each thought neutralizes some stress in the nervous system, until eventually you have completely normal nervous system. Then you reflect Bliss Consciousness."

Putting it another way, and quoting from another lecture, "Thought is horizontal actiwity, mantra wertical. Thought is waluable because it cultures the mind to operate on lower and lower levels. So when stress is encountered, we stop the mantra, sit easy. Stress will disappear. Don't worry about it. When you become aware of not saying the mantra, start it again."

So much for the theory. As for the practice, once you accepted thoughts as a part of meditation it was usually quite pleasant to sit there and entertain them, or let them entertain you—these disparate, pop-up memories, fantasies, half-dreams, some of which were logically connected, with a beginning, middle and end, but at other times and more often, they seemed to have a life and logic of their own, bursting onto your mind-screen as flashes of light and color, now and then congealing into faces of people you knew or didn't know, while sometimes your inner ear might pick up voices saying things that if you tried to capture them and bring them back to the surface would make no sense whatsoever.

In fact what happened most of the time during long meditation was very much like, and perhaps identical to the kinds of things you see and hear when you're about to go to sleep and have started to let go of the world you were awake in and connected to, floating in that in-between state Proust spends the first six pages of his novel describing and the next 3,128 trying to recapture and make sense of.

But for us in long meditation the one rule of thumb—in addition to "putting the mind back on the mantra" whenever you remembered it—was just to let the thoughts come, not holding on to them, and above all, not trying to figure out where they were coming from or why you were having them.

During meditation we stopped worrying about making sense.

And it was, as I said, quite pleasant most of the time, for most of us. For some, these waking dreams would become waking nightmares. But this was later in the course.

For the time being we kept going to lectures and meals, and meditating in between, with a little socializing on the side. Soon the lectures became less and less like lectures as such, on a topic Maharishi had thought about and prepared for, and more like general assemblies over which he presided and which he usually began, after the group meditation, by asking how long people had meditated and what if anything they had experienced during that time and if they had any questions.

In other words, the lectures tended to become extended Q&A sessions, with the answers often taking the form of off-the-cuff digressions that could last as long as an hour and consisted of a more or less equal mix of practical advice and theoretical background, with frequent references to Hindu theology and Vedantic philosophy thrown in. Before the end of the first week we all knew for example that the illusion of the world as we know it was called "Maya," and the forces that maintained that illusion were the three Gunas: Sattwa (creation), Rajas (destruction), and Tamas (which supports the activity of the other two). We had also heard the story about Arjuna's exploits on the battlefield several times.

On the practical side, we learned that we should never sleep with our heads pointed north. And we should always meditate facing the sun during the day and at night facing north. The best hour of the day to meditate, wherever you happened to be in the world, was 4 a.m. To the dismay of a woman who liked to meditate with her cat on her lap, Maharishi told her to kick the cat out of the room, because cats usurp human vibrations for their own evolvement, and prevent people from transcending.

Maharishi began one lecture by saying, probably in answer to a question about hot water and the relative lack thereof at the ashram, that after meditation we should avoid taking baths or showers. This is because when people meditate the skin secretes a beneficial fluid called "ojas." After one has meditated for a certain length of time, this clear fluid can actually be seen on the surface of the skin as a kind of glow or sheen. When pressed further, Maharishi said this fluid was "the most precious substance the human system can produce," and accumulates in the body when one practices bramacharya.

In other words, as we SIMSers concluded that night down at the cocoa session, this had to be some sort of stored up, recycled sperm or coital fluid, a conclusion which gave rise that night to a number of wisecracks about the relative dullness of each other's skin, and to a series of ojas jokes that lasted the duration of the course, of which the best was Rosalyn's:

"Knock, knock."

"Who's there?"

"Ojas."

"Ojas who?"

"Ojas open the door, you know who it is and what I want."

※　※　※

Thus, early on, as the lectures became increasingly focused on people's experiences during deep meditation, it became clear that the course had no fixed curriculum as such, or rather that the curriculum was us. In fact what none of us knew at the time was that this was the first (and, as it turned out, only) teacher-training course where Maharishi had people meditate nonstop for longer and longer periods—one reason he would always start the lectures by asking how long we had meditated and what, if anything, we'd experienced. And so the whole course was in effect a three-month-long experiment in which we were the unwitting human subjects.

At the same time it was obvious that Maharishi was sincerely and rather touchingly concerned for our safety, comfort, and well-being. When some people complained about the buffalo curd not tasting like western-style yogurt, the next day and every day thereafter a plentiful supply of western-style yogurt was available in the kitchen. When some said they would like to go to town to buy comfortable clothing, more suitable for the climate, Maharishi had a bunch of tailors come to the ashram instead, with bolts of cloth that they would lay out in the morning on the roof of the lecture hall, or down in the village, so that people could choose the fabric they wanted for the kurta or dhoti that would then be made to order and delivered to their door. When Maharishi heard that someone had a cold or upset stomach, he would see that a doctor went to their room. He even engaged the services of a husband and wife masseur-sseuse to give people massages if they got stiff during long meditations. If Maharishi tried to discourage us from wandering away from the ashram, after all, it was because he didn't want anyone to get eaten alive by a tiger, or poisoned by a snake, or drowned in the river, or robbed, raped, and murdered by bands of savages. (All the more reason to discourage us if we happened to be rich and famous and the news of our being eaten, poisoned, drowned, or robbed, raped, and murdered was to make world headlines the following day.)

During the first few weeks of the course I continued to keep a daily journal, consisting for the most part of notes I would jot down during the day and then type up later on the Olivetti. So as not to bother my block-mates, I would take it down to the edge of the cliff and set myself up in an armchair with the Olivetti in my lap, to type away while sitting in the sun. With the Ganges curling around beneath me, colorful birds I'd never seen before lighting in the trees above me, and curious monkeys perched on nearby branches to get a closer look at whatever I was clattering away on in my lap, it could have been a less distracting place to sit and write, but hardly more beautiful or exotic.

But as the days wore on these trips to the cliffside with my Olivetti to update my journal became less and less frequent, until I finally gave them up altogether. I continued to write every day, in the form of lecture notes and records I kept in another notebook of what was going on in my medita-tion, and I used the Olivetti to type an occasional letter, but my journal as such ceased to exist on Monday, February 12, to lie dormant until I would take it up again two months later.

When I had started keeping a journal as an undergraduate, following the advice of my favorite English professor (the one who told me if wanted to write I should just write), it was in order to make writing an everyday habit. At first I saw it as a daily chore, but gradually it became a daily neces-sity, a way of keeping the events of the day from slipping through my fingers and if not stop, at least slow down the march of time. By the time I went to Paris my daily journal was fullfilling a need to leave my mark, to be able to say if only to myself that I had been here and seen this and done that, so that later I could say, if necessary, yes, that's where I was then and why I am here now. In Paris my journal became a kind of lifeline, proof and validation of my existence.

So why, as soon as I had settled into life at the ashram, did my lifeline cease to be important? How could I suddenly start living without it?

It had first to do with my concept of time, and how life at the ashram distorted it, or maybe made us see it as it was—an illusion, maya. (Error, as Dr. Carberry would have said.) In an environment where suddenly everything was done for you and all you had to do was eat, sleep, and meditate, time ceased being a factor you needed to factor in, or even think about. After the first few days, all the days began to merge into one another, since each day was pretty much a replica of the day before. And time—the driving force that until then had measured out my life in minutes, hours, and days—ceased to exist. The enemy disappeared.

Another reason the journal stopped being a priority was that the longer you meditated every day, the deeper you penetrated into a kind of fuzzy otherworld in which keeping track of the days and the paltry events that filled them seemed irrelevant, even a little silly.

Finally, and quite simply, the more time I spent meditating the less time I had for doing anything else, such as keeping a journal, and doing the kind of reflective, critical thinking a daily journal seems at times to favor, if not require.

It didn't occur to me until about ten years later that in abandoning my journal I was abandoning a part of myself that would have come in handy in the weeks to come. If I'd kept at it maybe things would have turned out differently.

❇ ❇ ❇

Halfway into the second week of the course, during a morning lecture, Maharishi proclaimed the official beginning of the phase of long meditation. From now on, he said, we should strive to meditate nonstop for longer and longer periods. To encourage us to stay in our rooms during that period lectures would gradually be phased out, beginning the next day with the morning lecture, then in ten days the afternoon lecture too, so that during the middle of the course only evening lectures would be given, and attendance at those was not required. Maharishi said that if there was a special event or evening lecture he wanted all of us to attend, word would be sent around to everyone.

During the day Maharishi suggested we meditate in our rooms, or up on the rooftops above our verandas, or if we needed to get away from noise and distraction, we could take a blanket and a pillow to "the caves," the little labyrinth of windowless cells under the concrete floor of the outside "amphitheater."

Maharishi made it clear that first morning that no one was expected to begin meditating twenty-four hours a day right off the bat. In fact, he advised against it. Rather, we should ease ourselves into it gradually, "like dat, like dat," a few more hours every day. Soon we would find ourselves reluctant to stop.

And so, little by little, day by day, like dat, like dat, I gradually eased into it. It was a little like sliding into a river and letting the current take you, hoping any monsters that might be down there would leave you alone.

CHAPTER 19

Fireworks over the Ganges

※ ※ ※

Right away I was surprised at how easy it was to sit and meditate for three, four, and soon even five or six hours at a stretch. From time to time, accompanying the random thoughts and childhood memories and dreamlike visions, I would feel little jolts and twitches in the muscles up and down my back. These were almost like small electric shocks, in fact maybe that's what they were, but they were not at all unpleasant. "Jumps and jolts" had already been brought up during the lectures, and Maharishi had explained them as a positive symptom of unstressing, something to do with "kundalini rising." For me, these little jolts sometimes took the form of a distinct tap on my shoulder, as if someone behind me wanted to get my attention. The first few times this happened I actually opened my eyes and turned around, expecting to see somebody there. After a while though I got used to this too and decided to just let kundalini rise.

Sometimes as I meditated—and this could happen right away, as soon as I sat down, or two or three hours into it—the mantra seemed to get so fine as to be almost imperceptible. Maharishi had a phrase for this state which I found quite appropriate. "Innocent awareness," he called it, when you were no longer repeating the mantra, but "innocently aware of it," as it seemed to continue repeating itself. At these times I could have sworn I was not saying the mantra but hearing it. Something else I heard, or listened to, whenever I paid attention to it, was a very faint but constant ringing just above my left ear, like the ceaseless ringing of a microscopic bell. If I chose to I could also see this ringing, in the form of a tiny, unbroken, shining silver thread. At those times it seemed to me that I was practically no longer breathing—Maharishi had said it was possible to stop breathing entirely during meditation and even for the heart to stop beating—and I would feel again that cool shaft of air on my forehead, just above and between my eyes, right where you see the third eye painted on tantric images and statues, or the dark daub of red dye on the forehead of practicing Hindus. Whenever that happened I told myself it was something I should bring up at the next Q&A, but it was several weeks before I finally did so.

To avoid having to go to the dining room for meals during the long meditation phase, we could have them delivered to our rooms, using order forms that were available in the kitchen. The forms were printed on little quarter page slips of pale purple paper, with boxes to put an X in after "breakfast," "lunch," "tea," or "dinner." Beneath each meal there was a short list of items to check off, and blank lines provided at the bottom for special requests such as extra chapatis, peanut butter, cheese, dried fruit, etc. Once you filled out the form you had only to tack it to the front of your door and someone would come by and pick it up and the meal would be delivered more or less when you'd requested it, around the time your stomach began to growl and your banal thoughts or dreamlike visions or celestial fantasies were beginning to feature Big Macs or thick, juicy steaks.

To me it was always a delight to open my door and find a tray waiting on the floor of the veranda in front of it, a tray that had been assembled down in the kitchen and delivered and placed there _for me_. Even though the meals were not what one would expect from room service at the Continental or the Oberoi, the fact that somebody had wrapped the chapati in coarse paper and placed it here—next to the dish covered with a bowl to keep warm underneath it the still steaming vegetable stew and beans and rice, and next to that the little silver dish of curd that I had ordered in the space provided—was always strangely moving, maybe because it was a link to the world of the living, a reminder and reassurance that I was _alive_, bringing me out of the evanescent otherworld I'd been floating around in for a timeless five or six or seven hours and back to the earth and my life as a creature on it, where there were other creatures looking out for me.

※   ※   ※

One night, shortly after the beginning of the long meditation phase and a short while after I'd put my empty dinner tray back outside and had sat back down in the pillows and blankets stacked up in that angular armchair and was beginning to drift back to wherever I'd been before I'd gotten up to eat, there came a gentle tapping on my door. It was my next door neighbor Gunar, telling me that tonight was a special lecture that Maharishi wanted everyone to attend.

When I got to the lecture hall it looked like everybody was already there. In fact I'd never seen it so full. It also looked like some sort of celebration was in store. Balloons were hanging from the rafters, along with fresh paper flags and pennants. The place was also smokier than usual because of extra incense and candles burning on the ledges along the walls and all around the dais down in front, which was also festooned with an abundance of fresh flowers. Guru Dev's portrait was draped in garlands of marigolds, and many other kinds of flowers, including roses, were standing in vases and strewn around the floor. Down in front I saw Avi and some other people I didn't know sitting with Nancy, so apparently the safari was over, but Mia was nowhere to be seen. Maybe she'd gone back to California, or been eaten by a tiger. But then why would we be celebrating?

There were also a lot of people milling around the back of the auditorium, mostly staffers and people from the nearby village, all of them with broad, expectant smiles.

I found an empty seat halfway down the aisle, next to Viggie. "Fancy meeting you here!" I felt like saying as I sat down, having spent the better part of the afternoon and evening dreaming or fantasizing or simply having pestering but not at all unpleasant thoughts about Viggie.

When I was settled she gave me a look that brought back one of those fantasies with startling clarity. I had been sitting in a chair like the one we were both sitting in now, but outside in the sun, and instead of sitting next to me Viggie was kneeling on the ground in front of me between my legs. Giving me the same look in the dream that she'd just given me for real, Viggie started running the long fine index finger of her right hand up the inside of my left thigh. When she reached the zipper she pulled it slowly down. Emerging out of the open fly, like a fern unfurling to full size, was not what we'd both been expecting, but a yellow flower, just like one of the "soucis" I had brought for my initiation at the Continental. When I looked up the person between my legs was no longer Viggie but Eileen, who said, "Calendulas, how lovely!"

For the lecture that night, Viggie had wrapped herself in a sari, another sign something was up. Normally Viggie never wore a sari but that night all the women were wearing them. From the folds of silk in her lap Viggie extracted a little plaster-of-Paris statuette of Hanuman, the monkey god. In answer to my quizzical look, she said it was a gift. "A gift for Mia, for her birthday," she whispered, and then giggled. She said that before I'd arrived Nancy's friend Ginny had come around with a basketful of little trinkets that she'd distributed to everyone in attendance, saying they should keep them hidden until Maharishi gave the word.

There was a murmur at the back of the hall. We all stood up and turned around and joined our hands as Maharishi came through the door with Mia. They both smiled broadly as they proceeded down the aisle. When they got to the front Mia sat down in the empty chair in the front row next to Prudence while Maharishi stepped up on the stage and sat down on the bench in front of the microphone. Selecting a rose from the table in front of him, he announced that tonight was a very special night. "But first, we just take it easy. We just close the eyes."

After the group meditation that evening, instead of asking for questions, Maharishi beckoned Mia forward and had her kneel in front of him, facing the audience. While she sat there beaming brightly, holding the red rose he had given her, Maharishi placed a paper crown on her head, or tried to. The crown was cut out of a flat piece of paper with two bits of string for tying the ends together, and Maharishi was having trouble holding the crown on Mia's head while tying the ends together in the back. Seeing the difficulty, the bald bramachary jumped up onto the stage and held the crown in place while Maharishi tied the two strings. Atcha! After the crown was firmly fixed on Mia's head the bramachary withdrew amid applause and laughter.

With Mia sitting cross-legged in front of Maharishi's bench, people then proceeded one by one to bring her gifts and place them in her out-stretched hands. With each offering Mia opened her wide eyes wider still and, while turning the little plaster statue or plastic bracelet or tin trinket around in her hands, exclaimed "Oh wow!" or "Well, just look at that!" It was a performance that played successfully to both audiences: those who believed that she was happy to be there, and those of us who knew she'd rather be anywhere else.

After everyone had bestowed their presents and they lay in a heap at Mia's side, Maharishi gestured towards the back of the auditorium to bring on the next act. There was some scrambling and shuffling, and some orders in Hindi that included what sounded like a few muttered oaths, and then two of the kitchen staffers came down the aisle carrying between them a wide board bearing a huge sheet cake, complete with candles and a message on the top in different colored frosting that said "Happy Birthday Mia!" The candles were bigger than the American birthday variety and they left behind a trail of smoke, but the cake itself was a masterpiece. How the people in the kitchen were able to make it with their primitive facilities was a mystery. No wonder they had all turned out that night to observe the effects of their handiwork.

The cake was laid at Mia's feet and everyone fell silent while she closed her eyes and made a wish then blew out the candles, all twenty-four of them, sending up a little cloud of black smoke that merged with all the smoke already hanging in the rafters.

After the cake had been cut into small pieces and distributed on little paper napkins, Maharishi checked to make sure the mike was on then pulled it towards him and said into it, "Now, let's have some spontaneous expressions of joy!"

After a long moment of squirmy discomfort the woman sitting in front of me jumped up and spontaneously expressed her joy at being there and her gratitude at her "dear, dear husband" for letting her come. The woman was a dowdy, sixtyish American whose name I didn't know and who until then had only spoken to express quiet but deep disapproval at the absence of hygiene in the kitchen and the lack of appropriate toilet paper in her bathroom and the cracks in her windows and the lumps in her mattress and whose dear husband must have been only too glad to get rid of her for three months.

Following this expression there were a few others, similar in tone, and then Geoffrey, sitting in the same row as me and a few seats over from Viggie, stood up and proved he was a lawyer by delivering a long and tedious soliloquy about "the Faerie Queene of the Aquarian Age," that actually made Mia blush and brought a round of applause—whether at what Geoffrey had said or that he'd finally stopped saying it was unclear.

Geoffrey's eloquence effectively put an end to the spontaneous outbursts and a long moment ensued during which nobody said anything. Finally

Maharishi announced into the microphone that it was now time for the fireworks.

Fireworks?

Viggie and I just looked at each other and laughed.

Re-wrapping our shoulders in blankets and shawls, we all stood up and trooped outside to regroup in a ragged semi-circle in front of the auditorium, with Mia and Maharishi in the middle and Nancy and Avi and the other guests standing around them. Twenty or thirty yards away, along the edge of the cliff, a bunch of staffers were shouting among themselves and thrashing among the trees and bushes, apparently taken off guard by our earlier-than-scheduled exit from the auditorium, or, more likely, as it turned out, unfamiliar with the finer points of pyrotechnics.

It was clear and breezy outside but not as cold as it had been the past few nights, or since the course had begun for that matter. Tonight the wind was directly out of the south, bringing with it warmer air and traces of the dust that I had smelled for the first time when I landed in Bombay. Kerosene lamps and torches had been lit and shone flickering light on everyone's expectant, happy faces and there was once again that feeling of sitting around the campfire that to me brought back family memories of Camp Curry in Yosemite.

Suddenly there was a loud pop and a flash on the edge of the cliff and a roman candle began to spout sparks ten feet into the air. Everyone shouted and laughed as we watched the fountain of glittering spray rise up and fall and scatter on the ground, causing those standing nearest to draw back. When another roman candle went off five feet away from the first, Viggie tugged at my sleeve and in a loud whisper suggested we go get Mia's pup and give it to her. Ever since Mia had gone away on safari, Arjuna had been penned up in a storeroom next to the kitchen to keep him away from people's ankles during lectures. "Good idea!" I said, diverted from the fireworks by the touch of Viggie's lips against my ear.

We trotted off down the path that led through the thin forest towards the kitchen, our way lit by a full moon. As soon as we were out of earshot, Viggie shouted out, "Poor Mia!" and before I could catch myself I shouted back, "Yeah, really!" By the time I thought of something else to say that might make Viggie realize I was capable of conversation we were standing a little breathless in front of the storeroom door with Arjuna yapping and whining on the other side, trying to gnaw and claw his way out. Unfortunately, the door was fastened shut with a heavy padlock. While Viggie crouched down in front of the door to try to soothe the puppy, I ran back to the auditorium to see if I could find someone with the key.

By then the fireworks had begun in earnest, with several loud booms in quick succession, followed by piercing shrieks and flashes of light and echoing booms up in the sky. As I got closer the noises coming from the spectators sounded less and less like cries of delight and more and more like shouts of alarm. When I got to the clearing around the amphitheater I realized why. While some of the rockets were going straight up, others were going off at crazy angles, a few of them actually grazing the tops of the trees above the ashram. And while a few of them burst into showers of sparks, as fireworks were supposed to, many of them just exploded in midair with a resounding boom that echoed off the nearby hills. When I reached the fringes of the group in front of the lecture hall there was another loud pop out by the cliff, followed by a whoosh as something raced over my head. "Oh my God!" said Mrs. Harrington, standing nearby.

A little farther on I spotted one of the boys who worked in the kitchen. He was watching the proceedings from behind a tree and laughing so hard it looked like he was about to fall down. I went up to where he was standing and, shouting to make myself heard, asked him if he knew where the key to the storeroom was. When I started barking like a dog the boy laughed harder still, before he finally got the message with the help of gestures and images I traced in the air. "Ah yes, sahib, key! Yes, yes." He motioned for me to wait there and ran off not towards the kitchen but towards the cliff.

Just as he ran off there were two simultaneous booms as two rockets, leaving a fiery trail, took off not up, not out over the ashram, but straight off horizontally towards the town of Rishikesh. Three seconds later one went off in a shower of sparks that rained down over the sanyassis' huts on the other side of the river, while the second continued on towards the town and exploded shortly afterwards with a blinding flash and a deafening boom. That was followed almost immediately by a much closer, louder explosion that sounded frankly like a bomb and sent staffers huddled around some bushes running off shouting in every direction. The thought occurred to me that maybe the fireworks had been bought from army surplus and included some outdated mortars and grenades. At any rate the whole thing was beginning to take on aspects of a military operation, if not the start of a slave rebellion. Out of the cloud of smoke caused by the last explosion the kitchen boy came running back towards me, holding the key in his outstretched hand. He was no longer laughing, and looked a little singed. I thanked him and snatched the key and ran off towards the kitchen.

When I got back to the storeroom Arjuna was yelping and yapping even more frantically, no doubt because of all the explosions. As soon as we got the lock off and the door open, Viggie scooped him into her arms and tried to calm him down while I closed the door, reinserted the lock over the hasp and pocketed the key, all the while trying to explain to Viggie what was going on. But when we arrived back at the lecture hall no explanation was necessary.

By now the group assembled in front no longer looked like a bunch of meditators having a party, but like a gaggle of refugees under attack. The size of the group had diminished appreciably, probably because a lot of people had escaped back to their rooms for safety, and those who remained were huddled together in little squads, not knowing whether to laugh or run for cover, perhaps reluctant to give up the field out of loyalty to Maharishi. Only Maharishi in fact looked like he was still enjoying the show and he seemed to be enjoying it immensely, the laughter bubbling out of him with each misfired rocket or defective roman candle. Towering a foot-and-a-half behind him, Nancy looked on aghast with one hand over her mouth. Beside her, Avi looked positively paralyzed—just the guy you'd want to have along on a safari—while the other guests he'd brought along peered out from behind the door of the auditorium where they'd retreated for cover. Standing next to Maharishi, Mia also looked amused, and genuinely so, for the first time that evening, while Prudence stood beside her taking it all in, maybe trying to reconcile what was going on before her eyes with everything that was going on inside her head during all the deep meditation she'd been doing lately.

Dodging in and around the wary onlookers, Viggie and I went up to Mia and Maharishi and deposited the shellshocked puppy in Mia's open arms. Mia shouted in surprise and showered Arjuna with kisses and thanked us profusely, while the dog, delighted at being reunited with his mistress, coated her cheeks with saliva. Meanwhile Maharishi looked on in approval and nodded happily and said "Wery good! Wery good!"

As Mia was cuddling her puppy there was another off-sounding explosion out by the cliff and someone close by yelled "Watch out!" Viggie and I turned around just in time to see a rocket hurtling three feet off the ground directly at us, as if it had been aimed. Luckily for us, the rocket took a dive for the ground where it veered left and skittered along twisting and hissing like a mad dragon before it finally hit Gunar in the foot and knocked him down.

This basically put an end to the fireworks. After a moment of shock, and while the rocket sputtered out harmlessly against the trunk of a large tree, everybody ran over to Gunar and crowded around him as he lay there writhing on the ground and holding his foot and shouting he was okay, he was okay. Over my shoulder I saw Maharishi conferring briefly with the bald bramachary who ran off, then Maharishi came forward too and stood over Gunar who continued to protest in a high voice that he was fine, really. Soon Gertrude, the German MD, arrived. She was carrying a little first-aid case and looked like she'd just been roused from sleep—in which case I figured she must have been dipping into her first aid kit, because how else could anyone have slept through what had just happened?

Gertrude kneeled next to Gunar and after a while proclaimed that nothing was broken and he would be back on his feet within a few days, to which those of us remaining gave out a cheer and Gunar chirped, "You see? I told you." Gertrude then put a bandage on Gunar's foot—the size of the bandage lending doubt to what she had just said—and then Gunar was helped to his feet and back to his room and the party was over.

By then Mia and Prudence had disappeared and Nancy and Avi and the guests had gone off somewhere and Maharishi had retired to his bungalow and all that remained of the night's festivities was a lingering scent of cordite and the still-burning torches that a couple of staffers were extinguishing one-by-one.

There was no cocoa session that night because the kitchen was closed for the celebration, but Viggie and I wandered back over there anyway, on the pretext of returning the key to the storeroom and also, I hoped, because Viggie wanted to stay in my company as much as I wanted to stay in hers. By now her physical closeness and the sweet, clean scent coming off her had filled me with a hopeful anticipation that was beginning to make me weak in the knees and trembly all over. The thought that she might feel the same way and that something might actually happen between us that night was beginning to take shape in my mind, but at the same time something in me kept pushing that thought back, keeping it at bay. What if Viggie didn't feel the way I did? And if she did, why start something that in all probability would turn out badly? Since breaking up with Jill all of the relationships I'd had with girls had turned out badly.

Still, there was this trembling in my knees.

When we got to the kitchen it was all dark and shut down and locked up and there was nobody around. I hung the key to the padlock on a nail next to the storeroom door, along with a note saying "thank you" and "namaste," and then Viggie and I, without a word, headed for the cliff.

With the full moon reflecting off the Ganges and the temperature quite mild now that the wind had stopped blowing, it reminded me inevitably of the cliff above the beach at UCSB. As we stood there looking at the moonlight on the water and the rocky bank below and at the lights of Rishikesh winking in the distance I wanted to tell Viggie about that other cliff in California, and the hours I'd spent on it with Jill. I wanted to tell her about Jill. I wanted to tell her about my mother driving away in the night. I wanted to tell Viggie about that flower popping out of my fly. I knew this was all connected and had a reason but I didn't know exactly how and I thought maybe if I just started talking, blurting it out, the connections and meaning would all fall into place.

Three or four times I reached out to put my arm around Viggie's waist and draw her towards me but each time I pulled it back and clasped my hands behind my back and counted to ten before trying again. Finally I cleared my throat until I found my voice and then all it said was, "Crazy night, huh?"

Viggie laughed and sighed and said, "You're right. It was a crazy night." Then she touched my arm and said goodnight and walked away, taking the path that led back to her room.

I fumbled in the dirt at my feet until I found a rock that fit and then I threw it out over the cliff as hard as I could. I listened for a long time, much longer than the rock would take to fall, but all I could hear was the rush of the river.

CHAPTER 20

Encountering an iceberg

※ ※ ※

A few days later I got a letter from my mother. Someone had slipped it under my door. I figured it must have been Larry, since he went to the post office every day, and it couldn't have been Gunar because he was still laid up with his bad foot. It turned out the injury was not as benign as Dr. Gertrude had said and was causing Gunar considerable pain and interfering with his meditation and his sleep. But he bore it stoically, hopping on one foot whenever he needed to use the bathroom, and glad to be getting through this bit of bad karma. As welcome compensation, his friend Eva from Block 5 was spending a lot of time with him, nursing him along. While I sat in my room meditating I could hear them chatting quietly and sometimes softly laughing. It was a strangely soothing sound, this occasional murmuring in my ancestors' native language, my mother's mother tongue.

I didn't see her letter until I got up to pee, after meditating nonstop since lunch. By then the light outside my window had begun to fade. Mom's letter was postmarked less than a week before and addressed to the Academy of Meditation, Shankaracharya Nagar, so I knew she'd gotten the letter I'd sent her from New Delhi, giving her my new address.

My mother's handwriting was beautiful. No matter what inane, misguided, annoying or infuriating things she said in her letters, they were always a pleasure to look at at least, if not to read. That day, as I slit open the envelope, I prepared myself for the worst, expecting to get hot under the collar as soon as I read the first few words. But instead the letter just made me sad. After it made me laugh out loud.

It turns out mom already knew I was in India when she got my letter. A few days before it arrived she was standing in line at the checkout counter of her local Ralph's, thumbing through the latest copy of Life, when she came across a full page color photograph of Maharishi getting off the plane in Bombay and next to Maharishi Mia Farrow and next to Mia me.

It was a picture only a mother would recognize. I wasn't exactly beside Mia but a little behind her, with a little less than half my face showing and only a corner of my right eye, but that was definitely the top of my head and my hair and my cowlick and my ear and my cheek and my neck and more than enough for my mother to turn to the woman standing next to her in line and point to the picture and cry out, "THAT'S MY SON!"

After telling me this story, mom went on to talk about a day, "many years ago," when she and my father were sitting on the beach in Santa Monica and happened to see Mia Farrow's parents there as well. "They were such a lovely couple. Daddy even went over and talked to them. John Farrow was so nice and polite. I remember he and Robert talked for quite a while. And Maureen O'Sullivan was just beautiful, just like in her movies."

As I continued reading, finding no word of reproach at having joined a dangerous cult and fled to a Godless country, only more about Mia Farrow's parents and other Hollywood celebrities she and my father had known, and even letting it drop that she happened to know that Mia's parents were "sympathetic to C.S.," it began to dawn on me that mom had written the letter under the illusion that the real reason Mia had come to India was not to be with Maharishi but to be with me.

In 1932, When my mother was eighteen, she broke her father's heart by leaving home in Escanaba and going out to Hollywood to be in the movies. The closest she got was working as a secretary for a director at Warner Brothers, who one day, while she was taking dictation, asked her if she wanted to stand in for Mary Pickford in a movie he was shooting. Stand in for Mary Pickford's hands, that is. By that time Miss Pickford was beginning to show her age and her hands could not be made up as easily as her face. It would just be a few close-ups, the director said, but it could be the beginning of a beautiful career.

In the end mom declined the offer. She said she thought it came with strings attached, and by then she was going out with my father, but I know she always looked back at that moment as a crucial turning point in her life, the moment she chose to become a wife and mother instead of the star she had been destined to become. Now as I re-folded the letter and slid it back into the envelope I realized it had been written in hopes that my trip to India was a little detour on my way back to Hollywood, where with the help and support of my new girlfriend I would fulfill the ambition she herself had been cheated from because she'd had to raise my brothers, my sister, and me.

I put the letter on the table and blew out the candle I had lit to read it by. Tomorrow I would haul the Olivetti down to the cliff and write my mother a letter telling her not to worry about a couple of Sinatra's goons showing up on her doorstep. But tonight I was going down to dinner and then to evening lecture and then on to the cocoa session to socialize. It was going to be nice to mingle with people who had no illusions.

Portrait of the author's right ear.

(Photograph by Raghubir Singh, from *Life Magazine*, Feb. 9, 1968, p. 59.)

※ ※ ※

The following day, after meditating all morning, I went down for a late lunch and then to the auditorium for the lecture. As I looked around before the session began it looked like almost everyone else had shown up too, except for Prudence, of course. Mia wasn't there either, but that wasn't because she'd shut herself up in her room to meditate. Over dinner the night before, someone said that the morning after her birthday she'd left the ashram to join up with her brother in Goa. I didn't know where Goa was, but to me it sounded a lot like "go away," which was probably just what Mia wanted to do after all the hoopla of her birthday.

I was surprised at my own reaction on hearing that she'd flown the coop though, and this time probably for good. Surprised to realize I would miss her. Ever since our little conversation at the Bombay Airport I had a kind of fraternal affection for her. I also felt that with her departure I'd lost a companion in crime. The crime of no devotion. From now on I was on my own.

When introducing the long meditation phase, Maharishi said that people should feel free to come and see him down in his cottage at any time day or night, in case they encountered any "difficulties or obstructions." At the time I wondered what he meant, but I found out that afternoon. We all did.

Even before the group meditation I sensed that something was wrong, but I couldn't have said what. Within seconds after Maharishi had given the signal to start and we'd all closed our eyes a loud groan escaped from someone sitting near me. The groan quickly became a scream, and then stopped. In that hall full of people sitting together, starting to drift inwards, it was a strange and strangely startling sound. You wanted to forget it happened and start over, which we all did, but after another minute or two of silence, as we were just beginning to get a group buzz on, the same person screamed again, this time louder, making all of us open our eyes and bolt upright in our chairs.

The scream had come from Jeremy from Australia, sitting two rows down and two chairs over from me. He was sitting pushed back in his chair with his eyes wide open, looking straight ahead at something no one else could see. He was holding his cane at arm's length in front of him, horizontally, as if using it to keep whatever it was away. And now, as if that threatening presence were starting to move forward, Jeremy whimpered and shrank back into his chair and closed his eyes and screamed again.

Over his scream and louder still came the voice of Maharishi, with an urgency I'd never heard before and which in a way was just as unsettling as Jeremy's scream. "Don't anyone touch him!" Maharishi said into the mike.

At that point Jeremy literally jumped halfway out of his seat—it looked as if his arms and legs and torso were attached to strings and the strings had been yanked upwards. Arching his back, Jeremy twisted sideways in a violent convulsion, at the same time grabbing at his throat with one hand and flailing his cane in the air with the other. Everyone sitting around him shrank back, some of them holding up their arms to ward off blows from the cane. But then the cane clattered to the floor and Jeremy put his other hand to his throat and sank back into his chair with a loud, rasping gurgle. Then he gasped and screamed again, his voice rising to a shriek as he said "No! No! Don't…" and then something else I couldn't understand, and then he started to whine and say something totally incomprehensible and finally he fell silent.

Maharishi was leaning far forward on his bench and looking at Jeremy intently. Speaking into the mike, he said calmly, "Where is the pain?" Jeremy twisted again in his chair and gave a kind of grunt as if he'd been punched and then he shouted, "When I close my eyes… I feel it crushing me! Then my head fills with blood, and… I can't say the mantra,… It's horrible!" Jeremy screamed again but the scream this time was stifled, as if he were being choked.

"Close the eyes and feel the horror," Maharishi said. "Where it is in the body?"

Jeremy's reply came in short loud bursts. "…My feet!… my legs… my thighs… It's crushing me!" he said. He shrieked again, and then fell silent and his body went limp.

After a space of time that could have been a few seconds or much longer Maharishi finally said, "It's all right. It's going to come out." Again he gave orders for no one to touch him but no one was about to. Everyone sitting around him was still drawn back in horror.

At least another full minute passed, maybe two, during which nobody said anything or moved. Finally Jeremy sat up in his chair and coughed. He took off his glasses and cleaned them with a handkerchief and put them back on and looked around.

"And now, we just take it easy,…"

Less than an hour later, over tea, Jeremy remembered nothing of this. He said he'd had trouble meditating that morning, all morning long. Each time he sat down and started repeating the mantra he could feel something start to come over him and knew it was unpleasant, so he'd finally stopped trying to meditate altogether and decided to come to the afternoon lecture to see what would happen there. But nothing did, or so he thought. All he remembered was the group meditation and the discussion afterwards, but nothing that had happened before.

"You don't remember anything crushing you, anything causing you pain?" I said.

Jeremy shook his head, "No."

"Far out!" Larry murmured. We all looked at each other.

During the discussion after the group meditation Maharishi had explained what had happened as a particularly severe case of unstressing, and it was only when people started asking pointed questions that Jeremy realized with some embarrassment that they were talking about him. He said he did feel a little sore in some parts of his body and had felt stiff when he got up to leave the lecture hall. Sitting next to him, Ian laughed and said he'd probably feel stiffer tomorrow. "The way you were jumping around in that chair, I expect you'll be feeling it for a week at least."

To me the whole thing was reminiscent of stories in the Bible about casting out demons. I recalled Maharishi saying "It's going to come out," and wondered what "it" referred to. Maybe he'd seen something the rest of us hadn't. A gargoyle popping out of Jeremy's mouth or one of his ears.

It's true that Jeremy did have something diabolical about him, at least in my view. Down in Delhi when he'd made the crack about my rising sign being scorpio he'd looked almost satanic, or so I'd thought at the time. I wondered if he felt different now, after this exorcism. Cleansed. I did notice he still needed his cane to walk.

In any event, the scene in the lecture hall, as troubling as it was, restored my faith in Maharishi, which had been severely shaken lately, especially after his request for "spontaneous expressions of joy" during Mia's birthday. That afternoon I had been impressed by how quickly Maharishi had taken control, and seemed to know exactly what was going on.

But for some of the others sitting around the table that afternoon, the incident had the opposite effect. During the discussion, Maharishi had said he was glad we had all been there to see it, because as teachers of meditation we might one day have to deal with similar problems in people we initiated who, as soon as they closed the eyes and started repeating the mantra, might encounter similar "icebergs." When and if that happened we were supposed to take it as it comes, he said, "to save the psychology by quiet reassurances." As he had done with Jeremy, we were to tell the person to stop repeating the mantra and put the mind on wherever the pain was in the body, until it came out and the knot of stress came undone.

But what if it didn't? What if, while we kept repeating quiet reassurances, the person went stark raving mad? And more important, what about the rest of us now? Maharishi had said that such severe cases of unstressing were very rare in people who just started to meditate, or when one meditates for "only twenty-thirty minutes." But during longer meditations he said it was not uncommon to come across large areas of stress at deeper levels. In which case, what was in store for the rest of us in the weeks to come? It was Tom the Actor, sitting across the table from me and on Jeremy's other side, who gave voice to these troublesome thoughts. "Sure," Tom said, "Maharishi says he's down there in his bungalow for all of us whenever we need him, but what if something happens so that we don't even know where we are, let alone where he is?"

The only person with a response to this remark was Geoffrey, to my left. Clearing his throat to get everyone's attention, not lifting his eyes from his cup of tea, but speaking loud enough for everyone to hear, he said, "As soon as you begin to doubt him, everything starts to come apart. But it's all in you. If you start to question it, to think, 'Ah, he's just an old man who doesn't know what he's doing,' then that's exactly what he will become. And all of this will come to naught."

No one said anything for a while, then Tony shoved back his chair and said, "Amen!" and then, as an afterthought, "Jai Guru Dev!"

Everyone burst out laughing, but the laughter had a hollow ring.

CHAPTER 21

A troupe of troubadours

※ ※ ※

Two nights later I got to the lecture hall early and took a seat just a few rows back from the front row, which, I happened to notice as I sat down, was partially roped off. Vaguely I wondered what was going on this time but I didn't really care. All I cared about was getting back to wherever I'd been before I stopped meditating to go down for dinner and now wanted to get back to on a full stomach.

Soon Terry came in and sat down next to me and the empty spaces in the hall began to fill and I closed my eyes again to get a head start on the group meditation. Right away, the mantra was like beads on a string that kept going by until I grabbed onto one and it pulled me down and down, maybe not to the place where I'd been before dinner, but someplace just as interesting. As I bumped around down there I was aware of other people coming in and sitting down around me and then there was some brouhaha and laughter at the back of the hall and Terry, keeping his voice low, said, "Holy shit! Get a load of this!" Since Terry was a man of few words and all those words carried weight I figured it was worth coming back up to take a look for myself and when I did what I saw at first glance looked like half a dozen gypsies traipsing down the aisle, or maybe a troupe of transvestite troubadours like the ones we had seen on the way up in the taxi when Larry had made the driver stop so he could get out and take pictures. But then I saw that the women were real women, and that they were blonde, and they were beautiful.

There were three of them and their long hair wafted backwards as they drifted forward down the aisle. All six of the newcomers had very fair skin, so they were definitely not locals, and under their overcoats and shawls they were dressed in colorful loose clothing—the women in long silk dresses and one of the men in what looked like blue and green striped pyjamas, and then it hit me that the reason the guy in the pyjamas looked familiar was because he was John Lennon and the guy beside him was George Harrison. The third guy I didn't recognize, but he was big and heavy-set and definitely not Ringo or Paul.

They reached the front of the hall and nodded and smiled at Maharishi who was already sitting on his bench up on the stage, and then while two bramacharys fell all over themselves removing the rope from the reserved seats, George and John turned to the rest of us and smiled and nodded and waved and there was a spontaneous expression of joy as everyone applauded. Then they all sat down and Maharishi, beaming like a magician who'd just pulled the most prodigious rabbit out of his hat, leaned forward into the microphone and said, "We just close de eyes…"

It seemed perfectly natural having two of the Beatles there with us that night, along with their entourage. But then, given the state most of us were in, it would have seemed perfectly natural if the Father, the Son, and the Holy Ghost had come down the aisle and taken seats in the front row—to meditate along with the rest of us during the group meditation, to turn in their chairs and crane their necks during the Q&A to see who was asking questions, and during the lecture, to ask a question or two of their own. None of them took notes, I noticed, because they had all come equipped with cassette recorders that they'd propped up on the floor in front of the stage while the bramacharys did their thing with the rope.

If anything was a little out of the ordinary that night it was that Maharishi's lecture seemed a little more focused, a little more like a lecture per se. He started out talking about karma and evolution. As usual, he put a lot of emphasis on doing what comes naturally, saying that natural action led to "natural flow of life towards fulfillment." When he said that reading newspapers was a bad idea because it could produce "life-damaging karma," he drew a laugh from all of us, including John and George and the others sitting with them in the first row.

Throughout the lecture all of them listened attentively and nodded politely and for the most part stayed awake—in itself something of an accomplishment, since they had left London the day before and stayed in New Delhi only for a short night's stopover before taking a taxi caravan up to the ashram, where they'd arrived that afternoon.

This we learned from George, who after the lecture came down to the kitchen with a bunch of us for cocoa. He said he wanted to take some back to the others, who had retired to their rooms after the long trip, but then he said the others would probably not need cocoa to get to sleep and would all be asleep by the time he got back to their rooms anyway so he decided to stay up for a while with us to smoke Peace cigarettes and socialize. He himself wasn't the least bit sleepy, he said, since he was so wired about being here.

"The others," in addition to John, were George's wife Pattie and Pattie's sister Jenny Boyd and John's wife Cynthia and their road manager Mal Evans. George said Paul and Ringo and their wives would be arriving too in a few days. The whole thing was a kind of gift the other three had decided to give him for his birthday, pretty much at the last minute. He wasn't sure how long Paul and Ringo were going to stay, especially Ringo, who had a new little baby at home and who "hates travelling anyway," but he and John intended to remain the whole length of the course, another two-and-a-half months, and George was hoping to stay on even longer, if it could be arranged, to visit some places he'd been wanting to see. He said he really wanted to go to Hardwar during the height of Kumba Mela in mid-April, and he had this fantasy of taking a raft down the Ganges to Benares.

Colin, standing next to him, asked him when his birthday was and George said the twenty-fifth.

"Of February?"

"Yeah."

"That'll give us time to warn the sanyassis," Terry said. We all laughed and told George about the birthday party Maharishi had organized for Mia Farrow, with the misfired fireworks, and George laughed too and said, "He's such a child, really."

There were about a dozen of us that night, all SIMSers except for Geoffrey, and instead of going into the dining room we ended up standing around in the dark in front of the smoky kitchen, with the ceaseless rush of the river below us and the light of the waning moon filtering down through the branches above. For the last few days the weather had continued to get warmer and the night was mild and clear and it was good to be alive and even better to be young.

After the death of my father two other events had changed my life and those two events had altered the lives of a lot of other people my age as well. The first was the assassination of JFK and the second was the release of Sergeant Pepper—a kick in the gut followed four years later by a shot in the arm. The first had brought us down, proving the world was a bad place controlled by evil people. The second lifted us up and told us something we badly needed to hear: that the real world was full of light and color and love and laughter and here in front of me, not five feet away, was the guy who'd written and sung "Within You and Without You."

George Harrison did not act like someone who had the slightest inkling he'd helped make the world a better place. If anything, he seemed humbled by it all. What it was like to be a Beatle, he said, was getting up on stage with your guitar and wiggling your hips (so we could see what he meant, he gave us a little demonstration), "and all these girls start screaming and climbing the fence!"

He explained that the wire fence dated from their appearance on the Ed Sullivan show—"a really nice guy, by the way"—because after that if they didn't have a fence in front of the stage the girls would climb up onto it and mob them. "It was just unbelievable!" he said, laughing. George joked about John's comment at a recent press conference that the Beatles were more popular than Jesus Christ and how their record sales had dropped as a result, especially in the south of the U.S. "But it's true, you know," he laughed. "We are!"

Rosalyn asked him if "The Fool on the Hill" was about Maharishi and he said no, Paul had written it before they'd even heard about Maharishi. But that's the way it was, he said, from the very beginning. It was an idea in the air that was about to happen and for some reason they were in the middle of it.

George told us how he'd gotten into the guru thing through Ravi—Ravi Shankar—who was teaching him the sitar and whose name George pronounced "Rawwvi." Apparently Ravi didn't think much of George's choice of guru, but according to George, Maharishi was a groove, and when their manager Brian Epstein had committed suicide he had been a real comfort to the four of them. George said that ever since he had started meditating he'd been wanting to come on this course in Rishikesh and now here he was and he couldn't believe it.

"Are you going to become initiators?" Geoffrey asked. "The four of you?"

George said he couldn't speak for the others, but as for himself, sure, why not? But there was so much going on it was hard to find time for anything new. Just taking the time off to come here had already created a lot of problems. "But you've got to do the things you need to do, you know?"

We all agreed, then took our cups back to the kitchen and said goodnight and went our separate ways.

※ ※ ※

The next day was my birthday. To celebrate I skipped early morning meditation and went down to the kitchen for an early morning breakfast. On the way there I passed a bramachary going the other way in a hurry, probably on his way to Maharishi's bungalow. As he went by he flashed me a bright smile and said "Namaste!" Sunlight was gliding in at a low angle through the trees, which like the deciduous trees in Southern California this time of year were already back in leaf. On the roof of the auditorium a bunch of crows were crowing about something and in the distance, from behind the blocks of housing, came the echoing cry of a peacock, as blood-curdling as it had been the first time I'd heard it on my first morning at the ashram, over two weeks earlier. I'd finally caught a glimpse of the peacocks a few days before. There were two of them, one male and one female, and they were strutting around beyond the fence outside our washroom when they turned to look at Gunar and me, looked down their noses as it were, as if to ask what we thought we were doing there.

The seventeenth was also Gunar's birthday, which even though he was born a year before me, meant that we had "many things in common," as he assured me—a little too often and too enthusiastically, as far as I was concerned, since I always found Gunar a little crazy. When I'd stuck my head in his room that morning to wish him happy birthday and see if he wanted anything from the kitchen he'd given me a goofy smile and pointed at his still bandaged foot and said his birthday gift was that the bandage was coming off today, or so he hoped.

Down in the kitchen I loaded a plate with singed toast and butter and buffalo cheese and marmalade, poured myself a mug of chai, and moved on to the outside dining area where so far there was only one other person and that person was John Lennon. He was sitting at the far end of the table, looking out over the cliff towards the town in the distance lit by the rising sun beyond a rising curtain of mist. As I sat down a few chairs away we exchanged good mornings and I asked how they'd slept. John said he hadn't slept much himself, but he thought the others were still asleep and would probably keep on sleeping until noon.

It looked like John had been there a while. In front of him on the table was an empty mug and a saucer full of cigarette butts and some loose sheets of paper and a notebook he'd been writing in with a black marker. He looked at the notebook now and read over what he'd written then gazed back out at the horizon and then back down at the notebook and continued writing, leaning into it. Obviously John Lennon was not someone who liked to make small talk and that was fine with me since I also liked to be alone with my early morning thoughts and I couldn't imagine making small talk with John Lennon anyway.

After breakfast I went back to my room where, according to my meditation notebook, I meditated from 8:15 to 1:00, and then from 1:30 to 5:45, noting only, "Monkeys a little distracting," followed by, "Nothing startling."

After the lecture that night there was a surprise birthday celebration for Gunar and me. Although it was not on the scale of Mia's—to everyone's relief there were no fireworks, and the two cakes were unassuming mounds of semolina, the kind of cake you'd be happy to have and not eat—my twenty-fifth birthday was one of the best. What better gift, after all, than being sung "Happy Birthday" to by John Lennon and George Harrison—nevermind the chorus of spaced out meditators—or sharing my humble cake afterwards down in the dining hall with George, his wife Pattie, and Jenny Boyd?

※　※　※

As George had predicted, Paul and Ringo arrived two days later, on the nineteenth, showing up at the evening lecture with Ringo's wife Maureen and Paul's girlfriend, Jane Asher.

Nothing changed by having the Beatles there at the ashram, and at the same time it changed everything. Nothing changed in the sense that all of us, or at least everybody I knew, kept on doing what we were supposed to do, gradually increasing the number of hours we meditated every day. So did the Beatles, except that since they'd arrived two and a half weeks late they didn't start right in at eight or nine hours a day. Instead, they spent extra hours in the morning and afternoon with Maharishi, down in his bungalow, to catch up on what they'd missed in the lectures. When I heard about these make-up sessions I couldn't help wondering what they consisted of since it wasn't as if they'd missed the basic principles of calculus or something.

For many of the older people, however, the Beatles' arrival was nothing short of a disaster. A common complaint heard among the SRMers those days, although I never heard it expressed openly at the lectures, was that since the Beatles arrived Maharishi was no longer there for them. The same complaint had been voiced about Mia, but now instead of one star to compete and contend with there were four of them, not counting all the people who had come along with them and who also got first class treatment, as well as the other celebrities who showed up at the ashram within the next ten days, including Donovan and Mike Love of the Beach Boys.

The way these disgruntled SRMers saw it, they had come to India not only to become teachers of Transcendental Meditation but also to accelerate their own spiritual growth while sitting at the feet of their master and soaking up his vibrations for three months. But now, not only was it impossible to sit at Maharishi's feet, sometimes they couldn't even stand at the back of the room, since it was crammed full of all these noisy young people, some of whom had only been meditating a matter of weeks. At lectures nowadays, the people who until then had managed to more or less monopolize the Q&A could hardly put a word in edgewise, and when they went down to see Maharishi in his cottage they were told they'd have to wait for hours or come back the following day. It was a discouraging turn of events. By coming to Rishikesh, these old-time SRMers thought they had moved into the fast lane to samadhi, and here they were, stuck in traffic.

They also objected to the carnival-like atmosphere that had descended on the ashram, with all the noise and confusion and opportunities for distraction this implied, including an attendant and troubling relaxation of the high moral standards that until then Maharishi had always so staunchly supported. Soon after Paul and Ringo arrived, word went around that a small number of SRMers, led by Nancy's friend Ginny, had been so scandalized by Maharishi letting Paul and Jane Asher share the same room, even though they were not married, that they decided to go down and confront Maharishi directly, asking him why he condoned this moral laxity. Apparently Nancy had been able to talk them out of it at the last minute, saying it wouldn't do any good.

To us younger people, even more shocking was that anyone could be shocked by such a thing. And this was perhaps the biggest change that came about as a result of having the Beatles at the ashram. It widened the gap between the Spiritual Regeneration Movement and the Students' International Meditation Society, or showed how wide that gap had always been, and for a while at least, as long as the Beatles were among us, it tipped the scales towards the SIMSers.

During the next six weeks a heady, youth-driven spirit of what-might-be held sway at the ashram, at least for those of us young enough, or idealistic or naive enough to be swayed by it. For me it was kind of a sneak preview of what was to happen in Paris a couple of months later, where I would also find myself a witness and occasional participant.

Soon after arriving George had set up a little organ on the roof of the lecture hall and that soon became a popular hangout, before or after lectures or in between long meditations, where some of us SIMSers would gather to socialize and listen to George play the organ or strum on his guitar and sing along with him and in between songs, talk about the future of the world.

There were all kinds of possibilities and all of them seemed within our reach. Within the next ten years, with the Beatles leading the way, as they right then seemed ready and willing to do, if just one, or maybe ten, or maybe even twenty per-cent of all the people in the world under thirty took to meditating twice a day… Just that. Nothing else. No religious mumbo-jumbo. We'd have to get rid of the initiation ceremony, or at least tone it down. Get rid of the fee, too. Make it free. Just give what you can afford and give it a try…

We thought about it, seriously, and talked about it intently, Berndt, Rosalyn, Larry, Jenny, George. Us youthful plotters up on the roof, with the sun going down across the river, the monkeys looking on, the crows cawing, the music playing. Before John wrote *Imagine* we imagined.

And yes, it was like an on-going rock concert/folk festival, only better. A preview of Woodstock but without as many people and lasting fifty-three days. Of course you had to keep meditating. But that was the deal. We all did that, the Beatles too, and that was fine. That only made it better when we came out to celebrate and sing along.

And it's true you had to deal with all those hordes of gawkers flocking to the ashram, all those curious, obnoxious people climbing or cutting the fence to get a close look at the Beatles or, if they were lucky, an interview. But the reporters came and took their close-up pictures and went away again and wrote their silly, irrelevant stories and the people back home in the rest of the world thought they knew what was going on but they didn't have a clue.

Neither did Maharishi, unfortunately. One evening we went down to his bungalow and tried to clue him in, this little delegation of what the world could be, consisting of George and Geoffrey and Larry and Terry and a couple other people and me. Maharishi agreed to see us right away. George Harrison was our spokesman, after all. We trooped into the little room where Maharishi received visitors and all sat down on the floor and told him as a first step he should relax the ban on drugs. Recently the rule about not taking any drugs before you could learn to meditate had been extended from three days to three weeks and there was talk of extending it even longer. While talking about it up on the roof of the auditorium we discovered that if that rule had been in effect when all of us sitting there had learned to meditate the only one to have learned would have been me, and that was because at the time I hadn't wanted to take anything else on top of the Tedral and Theophyline. Not to mention the wine. Yeah, how about wine? There was no rule about that. And that was because Maharishi said one's taste for alcohol would drop off naturally the more one experienced the infusion of the absolute. Why wouldn't the same rule apply to acid and grass? In the end we determined that the ban on drugs was a plot devised by old guard SRMers to discourage young people from learning to meditate and eventually cause SIMS to go bankrupt. Force out the competition. Which was why we marched down to Maharishi's cottage.

Sitting at his feet, we explained to him, George explained to him, that the three-week ban on drugs was just turning off a lot of people who would otherwise love to start meditating right away. Maharishi listened politely and tilted his head sideways and laughed, and when we said our Jai Guru Devs and got up to leave and regrouped outside before returning to our rooms to continue our long meditations we all agreed with George that it had been a good meeting and Maharishi had taken us seriously and listened carefully to what we had to tell him and we had taken the first step on the pathless path towards a world without war.

CHAPTER 22

Maharishiville

※ ※ ※

During the deep meditation phase of the course a lot of things happened that I was unaware of because I was shut up in my room paying attention only to what was happening inside my head, or wherever. And many of the things I know did happen because I was on hand and saw them or took part, are tinged with a dreamlike, sur-realistic aura, as if I were stoned at the time—which in a way I was, we all were. But then some of those events were pretty dreamlike to begin with.

One afternoon I was sitting on the edge of the cliff with my Olivetti in my lap trying to compose a letter to someone I'd gone out with at Stanford, but instead just gazing at the river and the gleaming temples of the town in the distance. I was perched in a little hollow, a drop-off ledge where I had dragged an armchair and where I didn't think I'd bother anyone and no one would bother me because the spot was slightly lower than the rest of the clifftop and shielded by a couple of trees and a big rock. But while I sat there wondering why I couldn't get beyond "Dear Sharon," someone jumped down, landing a few feet away, and stuck his arm out over the valley below us.

"Maharishiville!" he shouted. "Can you dig it?"

It was Mike Love. Even though it had been quite warm that day and the air rising up from the river had not yet started to cool things off, Mike was wearing a full-length, heavy woolen cape complete with a cowl that he had pulled up over his head. He looked like a monk who had just leaped out of a monastery in the Middle Ages. A very wealthy monastery. The color of the wool was a perfect match for Mike's reddish beard, and the cape was lined with white silk.

I had met and talked with Mike a few nights before, after his ride up from New Delhi. The reason he arrived at the ashram later than he'd planned, he said, was that his tailor wanted to make him a complete wardrobe suitable for the climate and it had taken her longer than she'd thought. Apparently she thought the ashram was a lot higher up in the Himalayas.

Mike was, well, a beach boy, and since we'd frequented some of the same beaches when we were kids and even knew some of the same people, it turned out we had quite a bit in common. Mike had a house in Redondo Beach a few blocks away from a place my two older brothers had shared for a couple of years and where I'd brought Jill for a depressing weekend of no sex. Mike even owned an MG TD that he promised to let me take for a spin when I "come back home to California." Generous, affable, openhearted, easy-going, and quick-tempered, Mike Love was in many ways a typical American, and I found it both touching and ironic that he had sought out my company that night, his first night at the ashram, because I was an American too, and better yet, an American from California.

Now, after Mike had removed the cowl and stood there looking down at me, I asked him what he was talking about.

"Maharishiville!" he repeated. He took off his cape and laid it over the back of my chair and sat down on the rock beside me. "It's gonna be so bitchin'!"

Mike explained that he and some other people he knew, people with a lot of money, were going to start a foundation that would one day, "and I mean soon, man—two, three years," finance the construction of the World Capital of Transcendental Meditation. In place of the huts and shacks of Rishikesh, they were going to build a regular little city, with skyscrapers and parks and freeways. There'd be an airport, a modern train station, helicopters flying all over the place. He pointed to a spot beneath us and across the river where a couple of sadhus in loincloths were washing their orange robes. "Right there we're going to build the stadium."

"The stadium?"

"Yeah, man! It's gonna be fan-fucking-tastic!" Mike explained that Maharishi would have to have someplace to welcome the millions of pilgrims who would flock there every year.

"But how about this place?" I said. "The ashram."

"This place?" He glanced over his shoulder at the lecture hall and gave a disparaging snort. "This place'll be a museum by then."

I too looked back at the lecture hall through the trees and had to admit it looked a little quaint all of a sudden. I asked Mike if he'd talked to Maharishi about all this and he said he had and Maharishi was all for it. He looked at my typewriter.

"Whatcha writin'?"

"Just some notes."

"Thoughts that come to you in meditation?"

"Yeah, sort of."

Mike admitted that all the thoughts he'd been having during meditation since he arrived were pretty gross. "I mean, about as gross as you can get, man. You wouldn't believe it."

The next day, sure enough, the helicopters arrived. Only one at first, but one was enough. It was mid-morning when I first began to hear it. I had found that in doing long meditation it usually took between two and three hours to really get into it, for something in my head to shift into high gear. I had just gotten to that point, probably along with fifty or sixty other people sitting within a radius of 300 yards, when I realized that the throbbing I'd been hearing was not coming from somewhere within, but from somewhere without, like from up in the sky, and it was a helicopter, and it was coming here.

When I came out onto the veranda Tony and Terry and a few other of my blockmates were already out there, trying to figure out what was going on. We looked at each other and shrugged, unable to make ourselves heard above the noise. By now the helicopter was so low that the wind it sent down was blowing new leaves off the trees, their branches bending and swaying wildly. After hovering for a while the chopper took a slow, low circle over the whole ashram, then headed off up the Ganges, where it hovered again, then started back down the narrow valley. It looked like it was trying to find a place to land somewhere along the river just below us.

Was it the Marines? Had the war in Vietnam suddenly spilled over, as everyone said it was going to? China was not that far away, after all.

By now other people roused from meditation were streaming past Block 1 on their way to the lower gate. Terry and Tony and the rest of us joined them, anxious to see what was going on down at the beach. Some people were laughing as they trudged along, others were visibly annoyed, but the majority seemed vaguely curious and resigned to whatever next was in store. The general consensus was that it was just another obnoxious news crew trying to get a scoop and sneak a look at the Beatles doing something newsworthy. Some of us thought it might be another celebrity arriving in style.

"Bob Dylan!"

"Yeah!"

Now that the Beatles were here there were rumors that Dylan might be next.

"Bob Dylan and Joan Baez!"

"Now you're talkin'!"

"Right on!"

My theory that it might be the Marines caused Herr Schraff walking in front of me with Annaliese to laugh out loud. "You think the US Army would be interested in our little ashram?"

"How about Jesus Christ?" someone said. Perhaps a friendly dig at Kieran Kilroy, who was a devout Catholic.

"Yeah, why not?" Kieran said, unruffled, maybe even considering the possibility.

The three Swedish SIMSers walking behind us burst out laughing at a joke Berndt made in Swedish. Translating, Gunilla said it probably wasn't Jesus because it wasn't "*Kristi-flygger dag*," that is, literally, the "day Christ flies," or Ascension Day.

When we got to the beach the truth turned out to be much more banal. Instead of Bob Dylan or Jesus Christ, it was just another wealthy businessman friend of Nancy's who owned a couple of helicopters and had proposed bringing them up to the ashram for the day to take Maharishi and the Beatles for a ride.

On the rocky shore a crowd consisting mostly of locals had already gathered to stare at this strange device that had alighted near the water, like some gigantic dragonfly. Despite its size, it seemed like a flimsy thing to have made so much noise. It sat there, engine idling, its long blades gradually slowing down above the little plastic cockpit.

Across the river the sadhus and sanyassis had gathered as well. None of them looked too happy and no wonder. First the fireworks, now this. It was probably the first time a helicopter had punctured the airspace above the Valley of the Saints. As if that weren't enough bad karma for the region, Colin, standing beside me, said he'd heard that morning about plans to build an airstrip somewhere up the river, providing easy access to the ashram. Apparently the plans had just been approved by the Indian government. Rumor had it that the business friend of Nancy's was in on the deal and another reason he'd flown up that day was to fly over the proposed site and show it to Maharishi. So Mike Love hadn't just been blowing off steam the night before.

While we all watched, Maharishi stood near the helicopter laughing, just out of range of the still revolving blades. Standing there with a big yellow dahlia in one hand and fingering his beads with the other, he looked like a child waiting for his first ride on a pony. Finally the blades came to a standstill and Maharishi started towards the cockpit, accompanied by two bramacharis. Despite his dangling dohti he managed to climb in unassisted on one side, while John Lennon climbed in on the other. As both of them settled down next to the businessman-pilot in the middle, a bunch of reporters surged forward to take pictures.

Once Maharishi and John were safely on board and everyone had cleared back out of range, the pilot stepped on the gas. Maharishi waved his dahlia through the open window at the cameras, the blades began to twirl, the sand to swirl, the dahlia lost all its petals, and the chopper gradually lifted skywards.

Soon after that, as the crowd began to disperse, a second helicopter arrived and then a third, and the three of them kept up a continuous racket well into the afternoon. Back up at the ashram, since meditation was out of the question, most of us spent the rest of the day writing letters or reading or just sitting in the sun.

That night at the lecture, when one of the SRMers dared to complain about the noise, Maharishi said it was good practice for us to learn to meditate no matter what loud noises or other disturbances were going on in the background. He said this in all seriousness, as if the Day of the Helicopters had been built into the course as part of our training, and apparently oblivious of having admonished Herr Schraff not all that long ago for going down to meditate by the river, where he said that meditation was impossible, because of "the great noise of the Ganges."

One of the people taking pictures that day was a French fashion photographer named Arnaud with whom I had exchanged a few words in French when he was allowed on the ashram grounds. When I returned to Paris a few months later it was Arnaud's fault that I didn't get my old job back at IBM.

About a month after the helicopter incident I got a letter from David. In the letter he described walking into a classroom and finding all the students crowded around a table poring over a magazine. The class was one he had taken over from me after I left abruptly the end of January, "to care for my dying grandmother." The magazine was the March 9 issue of Paris Match, in which there was a short article on the Beatles in India and a number of Arnaud's pictures, including some he took of the helicopters on the Ganges. One of these pictures clearly showed me standing on the beach next to Colin, while in the foreground John Lennon grinned back into the camera.

David said that as soon as he entered the classroom that morning, the students, all with wide smiles, asked him to come and point out my grandmother.

(Photograph by Arnaud de Rosnay.)

(Photograph by Arnaud de Rosnay.)

❋ ❋ ❋

The following day was George's birthday, and that night, instead of a lecture, another celebration—but again without the fireworks. When I got to the lecture hall all four Beatles were already sitting on the floor down on the stage, along with Pattie and Jenny and Cynthia and Jane. They sat in a semicircle around the back, with George sitting in the place of honor next to Maharishi in the middle. There was also an older man who someone said was another guru from a nearby ashram, but who frankly looked like an escapee from a nearby insane asylum. After the group meditation he got up and performed some sort of ceremony with a lot of brass implements and little bells and then he did some complicated chanting that people were supposed to join in on.

Maybe it was the chanting, or the mad hatter look of the guru trying to lead it, but whatever it was everyone started to get the giggles. I think it was Pattie and Jenny up on stage who started it, giggling helplessly among themselves as the guru performed the puja, but soon it spread throughout the audience and everyone was having trouble keeping a straight face, except for some of the more dour SRMers, who looked around in disapproval. Prone to outbursts of laughter himself, Maharishi didn't seem to mind, and as the evening wore on he often joined in, which eventually won over the reluctant SRMers.

While the chanting was still going on Edna got up and started passing around garlands of marigolds that we were supposed to go down later and drape around George's shoulders. As she passed out the flowers, Edna herself started to get the giggles, all the time telling us to "shush!"

After the chanting Maharishi gave a speech in praise of George, whose birthday he said was ushering in a whole new age of peace and happiness. This time, after the speech, there was no request for spontaneous expressions of joy. There was no need. But Maharishi did ask if anyone wanted to sing a song, which led to another outburst of laughter when Mike Love got up to recite a chant he had composed, a chant that sounded like it had been inspired by Allen Ginsberg. Mike started out saying something about how "Transcendental Meditation CAN… reform the MAN…" but he had trouble getting beyond that, either because he couldn't think of anything to rhyme with "man," or he couldn't concentrate because of all the laughing, which he finally joined in on.

After that it was time for everyone to go down and stand in line to bestow the garlands, which George stood down in front to receive one-by-one, each time leaning forward with joined hands and saying "Thank you," or "Namaste," or "Jai Guru Dev," and then standing back up to wait for the next one.

By the time all the sixty-or-so garlands had been laid on George's shoulders he was so topheavy with flowers that it looked as if anyone gave him a push he would topple over. Now the laughter in the auditorium was unanimous. Even the staffers and the bald bramachary joined in.

After the hall had quieted down and George had been relieved of his leis and had sat back down next to Maharishi, it was time for his gift, which two of the staffers brought down from the back of the auditorium. It was something light but bulky, covered with a piece of canvas. When the staffers handed it to Maharishi one of them pulled off the canvas, revealing a world globe. As Maharishi took the globe he turned it over, so that the North Pole pointed downwards. Leaning forward into the mike, holding the globe aloft in his right hand, Maharishi explained that for George Harrison the world was at his fingertips, there for the taking, but these days it was a world turned upside down, and something had to be done to set it right.

Obviously, it was a lead-in for George to say something like "All you need is… Transcendental Meditation," but instead, he took the globe from Maharishi's hands, promptly turned it right side up, and then, as if amazed at his accomplishment, turned to the rest of us and said "I did it!"

"Look!" he said, wide-eyed, pointing at the globe, while all of us burst into cheers and applause, "I did it!"

CHAPTER 23

The sound of music

※ ※ ※

For the next two weeks, despite the temptation to come out and socialize, the great majority of course participants actually did stay in their rooms most of the time, or down in the caves wrapped in blankets, to log in hour after hour of long meditation. Throughout this period I continued to meditate eight or nine hours a day, some days even longer. I would start as soon as I woke up in the morning and go right on through the day, ordering my meals in or just going hungry.

For me, deep meditation continued to be an altogether pleasant experience, neither boring nor fraught with the kind of scary or strange experiences people occasionally brought up at the lectures, although so far no one had described anything as scary and strange as what had happened to Jeremy. As I sat there hour after hour it sometimes occurred to me that as long as someone kept bringing me meals and I could keep taking walks down to the Ganges now and then for exercise I would be perfectly happy to continue sitting there until the end of the course, or for that matter forever. In one of the lectures Maharishi had said the majority of people were born as householders but a few were natural born recluses, meant to be monks, and I figured I must have been one of them—better suited to contemplate life than to live it. Or maybe I was just born lazy.

During the best, quietest moments I would again experience that very pleasurable sensation of weightlessness, along with the feeling that my hands were expanding way beyond normal proportions. Sometimes they lay there in my lap like huge, cottony clumps I couldn't imagine using to do anything. The feeling would just come over me, I could never call it up on command, and I never knew how long it was going to last, or how long it lasted. And sometimes it was accompanied by the distinct impression that someone or something was blowing cool air against my forehead in a steady stream.

Since this was unlike anything anyone else had talked about so far I finally decided to bring it up at one of the Q&As. It was one of the first afternoon lectures after they started up again in mid-March. Attendance was sparse, with only about thirty of us in the audience, and the lecture had been short and rather dull. In fact the high point seemed to be my question, causing people to turn and take note, including John Lennon, sitting two rows in front of me. It didn't seem to impress Maharishi though. After listening to what I had to say he sat there for a while, his head cocked to one side, not so much to think of an answer to my question—it occurred to me later—as to wonder why I of all people should be asking it. Then he said simply, "It is cosmic prana."

Afterwards, while I was standing in front of the lecture hall debating whether to go down for tea or return to my room for more meditation, John came up and offered me a cigarette. "He didn't give you much of an answer, did he?"

Until then I hadn't given Maharishi's response much thought, but John's comment made me realize I'd been slighted. "You're right," I said, "he didn't."

John was curious about the experience and asked me to describe it in more detail. He listened intently while I went over it again, asking me exactly where I felt the air on my forehead and what it felt like and if I was sure it wasn't just a draft in the room. While we were talking Paul came up and reminded John of a meeting they had with Maharishi.

"We wouldn't want to keep his Wunderbar waiting, would we?" he said with a smile.

Looking like he'd rather stick around and talk about cosmic prana, John nodded and crushed out his cigarette in a tin can full of sand on the cement ledge behind us. "See you later, mate," he said, and the two of them went off down the path towards Maharishi's cottage. I stood there for a while longer, foolishly happy at having been called "mate" by John Lennon. Even if I still had no idea what was going on during those moments of deep meditation, I was glad I'd asked the question.

✳ ✳ ✳

Around this time the weather turned decidedly warmer. Along with the change in the weather, storms would come rolling down from the Himalayas, suddenly engulfing the ashram in night-like darkness lit by flashes of lightening accompanied by simultaneous, deafening claps of thunder, knocking out electricity for hours. Soon these storms became a regular yet unpredictable part of ashram life, occurring any time of the day or night and lasting sometimes only minutes, sometimes as long as an hour or two, and more and more the cold wind they brought with them was a welcome change from the increasingly hot air moving up from the south.

It was during these days that everyone started coming out of long meditation, like butterflies emerging from cocoons, and accompanying the process, as if to help it along, was the constant sound of music.

Since the arrival of the Beatles, music had already been an important extra-curricular activity, but now it was everywhere, like the flowers popping up all over the ashram grounds. Up on the roof of the auditorium, in addition to George picking out tunes on his organ or his guitar, you might also find Mike Love or Donovan, who had also arrived during that time. As George sang and played, Donovan would strum along on his guitar and Mike would add a Beach Boys rhythm on a set of bonga drums, while anyone else who happened to be on hand would join in on the chorus. Down at the dining area, at all hours of the day and into the night, you were likely to find George or John or Paul or Mike or Donovan, alone or in various combinations, jamming away on new songs or old ones, singing anything from Hard Day's Night to Old Black Joe, while those of us sitting around would listen and clap and sing along.

One night, instead of a lecture, George arranged a concert of traditional Indian music with some friends of his who were visiting from Bombay. There were two sitars—one played by George—a couple of tablas, and several strange string instruments I'd never seen before. It was the first time I really listened to Indian music and I would have enjoyed it more if Maharishi hadn't kept giggling all the time. He too was sitting up on the stage, but his bench had been pushed to the side to make room for the musicians, and each time the Indian sitar player would go off on a riff—producing strange, exotic sounds—or one of the tabla players would burst into a vigorous solo, Maharishi would burst out laughing. People sitting around me either laughed along with Maharishi or pretended not to notice, but I'm sure all the Westerners in the audience, brought up to listen to live music in respectful silence, were secretly scandalized.

On the other hand, maybe this is what you did in India during a concert, to show your appreciation, like burping after an Arab meal. Whatever the reason, whether it was the thing to do or just bad manners, Maharishi's giggles and guffaws kept me from enjoying the music that night and going where it seemed to want to take me—a place that had a lot in common with where my mantra sometimes took me during meditation.

As it turned out, I soon got to hear more of that strange, ethereal music, and even to try playing it on my own.

Down along the cliff not far from Maharishi's bungalow was a small one-room house with lots of windows. Within a few days after his arrival George had converted it to a music room, or to be precise, an Indian music room. After lining the floor with thick carpets and placing a bunch of cushions and pillows around, George filled the room with various Indian instruments and invited people to come and listen to him or others practice and play, or even learn to play the instruments themselves.

Which is how I learned to play the sitar. Or at least to sit on the floor with one leg up to hold it steady while George guided me through the first few rudiments of fingering.

In the end though I decided to learn the veena. The room had only one sitar and it was George's and he was often practicing on it and anyway it looked much too difficult for someone who had flunked violin and piano.

Veena is a generic name for a wide variety of string instruments in India. The one at my disposal was a crude box with a stick sticking out of it and a couple of strings attached. One reason I decided to try learning that instrument was that it looked that I just might be able to. A better reason was that Pattie and Jenny said I should. Both of them were learning to play Indian instruments of their own. Pattie had in fact been taking lessons for some time on a sitar-like instrument called a dilrubha and was already pretty good at it. Jenny's instrument was another kind of veena that looked a little like a zither supported by two gourds that rested on the floor at either end. The plan was for me to become proficient enough on my little box with two strings so that at the end of the course the three of us could give a little concert to a select group of tone-deaf friends.

I also had a plan of my own. By now, ever since the conversation I'd had on the cliff with Viggie after the fireworks, or rather the conversation we didn't have, I found myself spending more and more time with Jenny. We had meditated together along the cliff a few times, shared some meals down in the outside dining area, and together we'd taken a couple of walks down to the Ganges. In addition to being attractive and fun to be with, Jenny was smart and thoughtful and a good listener. Whenever we talked I felt I could tell her anything, straight from the heart, and Jenny would understand. On the few occasions when I ventured to voice some of my reservations about Maharishi and some of the sillier goings on at the ashram, Jenny would respond right away by saying she knew exactly what I meant and then share similar thoughts of her own.

With someone I found it so easy to talk to, making music seemed a natural next step, and it was only natural to imagine other steps beyond those. With Jenny sitting next to me, showing me how to press my fingers to the throat of the veena, and how to stroke the bow, the primitive sounds I produced produced surprisingly detailed images in my mind of a warm and comfortable room somewhere in Paris or London where the lessons could continue.

But it didn't happen. Because of events that none of us could foresee, there was no amateur concert at the end of the course, nor did I have a rendez-vous with Jenny, romantic or otherwise, after the course was over. Still, the hours I spent in that little room filled with sunlight and music and laughter, with the roar of the Ganges down below like the constant drone running through a morning raga, were among the best I spent in India.

In addition to all the songs being played and sung, there were a lot being composed as well, many of which would come out in their finished form in *The White Album* nine months later.

One afternoon, while taking the path from my room down to the kitchen, I saw Paul coming the other way. Like George, Paul was affable and friendly and eager to talk with the rest of us who had been at the ashram from the beginning. But now, picking out chords on his guitar and obviously working on a tune, he just nodded and smiled as he went by, the words that trailed behind him having something to do with revolution, well, you know…

The next day at teatime I was sitting with Paul and John and a few other SIMSers at one of the tables lining the cliff. Paul sat directly across from me, with John to his left, at the end of the table, picking out notes on his guitar and every now and then jotting things down in a little notebook with blank pages. I too had brought along a notebook, one of the small ones they had a surplus of down at the printshop and gave out free for the asking. It was a little six-by-eight inch booklet with the words "NOTE BOOK" on the cover and above that a picture of a candle and superimposed over that the enigmatic word "Manjeet" in red letters. While humming along with John, Paul picked up my notebook and began to doodle on the cover. As Paul sketched, John's strumming started turning into the song I had heard Paul practicing the day before. There were a few more stops and starts, while John took time to jot down more words and cross out others, then they both ran through the entire first verse of "Revolution 1."

After the song John set down his guitar on the chair beside him and went back to jotting down notes. Paul put the finishing touches on whatever he'd been drawing on my notebook, gave it an approving nod, and leaned forward to hand it back. On one half of the cover was now a sketch of a man dressed as if he had just stepped out of the eighteenth century, wearing a lace collar and a long, unbuttoned coat. The man had a lot of hair and a full moustache and beard and looked a little like a cross between Paul and Maharishi, with sad eyes staring out through large round spectacles. From his right hand a bottle had just escaped, and his index finger was still pointing at it, on its way to the ground.

I studied the sketch, then looked up at Paul and said, "So you're an artist too." He gave a modest shrug. "And that song," I said. "Yesterday it was nothing. How can you guys just pull stuff out of the air like that?"

Still tuning his guitar, John peered over his glasses at me and then at Paul and said, "How do we do it, Paul?"

Paul smiled at me, the smile saying "Don't mind John, he's just that way." Then he shrugged and said, "I dunno John. How do we?"

"We just do, don't we?"

"I dare say we do."

At that point John started in on his guitar again and Paul picked up a couple of spoons and started clicking them together and they started putting to music what Paul had just said. Soon this turned into a kind of melodious chant, using as a singing mantra the name of a town up the river they had recently visited. "Do-do, Dare-a-dare-a-do, Dehra-Dehra Dun, Dehra Dun-Dun..."

The little ditty took hold and gathered momentum and must have gone on for a quarter of an hour, with John on guitar and Paul on spoons and the rest of us clapping and laughing and singing along.

(Sketch by Paul McCartney, photograph by David Davies.)

❋ ❋ ❋

One night during those days the evening lecture ended with one of the SRMers asking Maharishi to tell the story of his first encounter with Guru Dev. It was obviously a story many of them had heard before, but for me it was the first time. Acknowledging the question, Maharishi nodded and paused and looked down at the flower he held in both hands. It was as if someone had suddenly dimmed the lights in the lecture hall. Everyone leaned forward, not wanting to miss a word. Quietly, Maharishi began by saying that when he was young he was a seeker, like the rest of us. One day, with a group of like-minded friends, he went to look for this holy man that they had heard about. The pilgrimage took an entire day, and much of it was on foot. By the time they reached the end of their journey, and were approaching the house where they had been told Guru Dev was living, it was twilight and night was falling. In the gathering darkness they thought they could see someone sitting in a patio behind the house. Then, just for a second, a flash of headlights from a passing car fell on Guru Dev's face. From that moment on, Maharishi said, he knew there was no question. He had found his guru. This was the man he would follow and devote the rest of his life to.

In telling this story that night, with the Beatles sitting down in front, Maharishi emphasized how young he and his friends had been at the time—university students just our age, in fact. He also talked about how open and accommodating Guru Dev had been with him and his friends, ready and willing to spend time listening to their own ideas and aspirations, even though he was much older and had a busy schedule as the much solicited Shankaracharya, who as I understood it, was a kind of archbishop of that region of India.

A few nights later, after the group meditation, the Beatles announced they had a gift for Maharishi—a song they had composed—in return for all he'd done for them. Carrying their instruments, and joined by Mike Love, they trooped down to the stage and sat in a semi-circle facing the audience, next to Maharishi. After tuning their guitars and getting settled, Paul, John, and George started playing a short introduction, while Mike and Ringo, supplying percussion on a couple of tablas, and joined by a few others sitting down in the front row, started chanting, over and over, "Jai Guru Dev, Jai Guru Dev,…"

From the beginning, the chanting, chords, and rhythm sounded a lot more like the Beach Boys than the Beatles, and that sound came through even more clearly by what followed. After the third or fourth "Jai Guru Dev," Paul and George and John started singing,

> We wanna thank ya Guru Dev
> Just for bein' our kinda guy.
> (…Guru Dev, Jai Guru Dev…)
> You know we'll always follow you
> Until the day we have to say goodbye.
> (…Guru Dev, Jai Guru Dev…)

There were a couple more verses that I don't remember, because I didn't write them down, but the song ended with everyone singing, at the top of their lungs,

> A-B-C-D
> E-F-H-I
> JAI GURU DEV!

The song brought down the house, or at least half of it, as the SIMSers exploded into laughter. Many of the SRMers, on the other hand, were scandalized, but could do little but join in the applause. As for Maharishi, it looked like he didn't know what to do, whether to laugh along with the SIMSers, seeing the Beatles' little song as the good-natured homage that it was—or as blatant disrespect, which was obviously the way the SRMers saw it.

As for Mike Love, he didn't seem to understand that he had just participated in a parody of his own group, that prefigured "Back in the USSR." Or maybe he thought that thanks to his presence and influence at the ashram, the Beatles were beginning to change their tune and bring it into closer harmony with the Beach Boys' style of singing. Or maybe he was above all that and was just happy to be part of the fun, even if it was partly poking fun at him.

Another musician who joined the group around this time was Paul Horn, a jazz flute player from New York. Or rather re-joined. Paul had already put in an appearance down in New Delhi where he had been on hand to participate in Maharishi's World Peace Conference, and up at the ashram he had a room reserved for him in Block 4 whenever his schedule of gigs and concerts allowed him to make the trip to Rishikesh.

Paul had been with Maharishi for several years and had already attended the teacher-training course two years earlier, an experience he said changed his life. Although Paul belonged to the inner circle of Maharishi's movement, he had none of the obsequious officiousness of a Walter Kuhn, or the condescending flakiness of a Nancy Nixon, or the just plain weirdness of a Charlie Jackson. In fact he was a pleasure to be with and talk to. Totally unpretentious despite his fame as a musician, Paul had a ready, down-to-earth sense of humor, along with a street-wise savvy that probably came from growing up in New York City. Paul was also open and friendly to everyone on the course, although he seemed more at home with us SIMSers, despite the fact that he was approaching forty.

One day while Paul and I were having lunch together I mentioned the swimming hole I'd discovered with Jenny during one of our walks along the Ganges. Located right below the ashram, it was a place where the water along the edge of the river swirled around within a circle of half-submerged rocks. Paul said he not only knew the spot but had swum there himself two years ago. Since it one of the hottest days so far, he suggested we go down there for a dip after lunch.

We each returned to our rooms to put on trunks and grab a towel, then met at the gate outside Block 1. Down at the river we continued along the sandy beach until we came to the spot, just below the ashram kitchen, where the river curved away in a sharp elbow towards the town of Rishikesh. In the crook of that elbow was the circle of rocks, about thirty feet in diameter, where water eddied around in a slow whirlpool.

Paul was the first to go in, stripping off his white kurta and sandals and wading in up to his waist. Instead of actually taking a swim, Paul filled his lungs with air, took hold of a medium-sized rock, and immersed himself lengthwise behind it, head and all. Holding on to the rock with both hands, letting the current sweep him backwards, Paul looked like a flag in a breeze, or a big piece of seaweed.

After about twenty seconds he emerged from the water with a gasp and scrambled back up to the beach. "God! Does that feel good!" he said, grabbing his towel. "It really does something to your metabolism!"

I had already been in the water a few times, but only up to my waist and never for very long. Now I decided to go in all the way. Feeling my way on the submerged rocks I could just make out beneath the surface, I went in up to my chest, then took a dive and swam a few strokes, crossing the little swimming hole. After the first shock, instead of feeling cold, the water seemed to burn, burning its way into my bones. And then it actually started to feel good, as Paul said. Taking care to stay within the perimeter of the little pool and not get swept outside into the main flow of the river, I let the current in that little eddy swirl me around a few times, keeping my mind away from whatever eyeless monsters might be lurking in the deep invisible middle, and fixing my gaze on the cloudless sky and the tree-lined cliff above me.

When I clambered back out I was shivering all over and my teeth were chattering. But I too felt invigorated, renewed.

On the way back up to the ashram I told Paul about the feeling I'd had while leaping on the boulders lining the river, the first time I'd come down to the Ganges. Trying to put it into words, I said it felt like a spiritual hardon.

Paul laughed and said he'd never had that feeling himself, but the whole area was so charged with weird energy he wasn't surprised. He said he'd heard about some things happening there that nobody knew much about, not even Maharishi.

At tea that afternoon Paul and I shared our little exploit with the people sitting around us, and not without some bravado. "Yeah, it's cold, but just a few seconds is all it takes and then, wow! What a feeling!"

Paul repeated his conviction that it had a stimulating effect on one's metabolism and added that even a quick immersion into the world's holiest of rivers was bound to be good for one's spiritual evolvement as well. Both of us maintained that our post-swim, pre-tea meditations had been especially deep.

As word of our bathing expedition spread and the midday temperatures continued to rise, more and more people followed our example, going down to the Ganges in the heat of the afternoon for a quick bracing dip, if not to swim, at least to wade and splash and cool themselves off before returning to their rooms to meditate. Someone said even Nancy Nixon went in. Fully clothed, of course.

Not so for some of the female SIMSers. Combining a wish to accelerate their spiritual growth with getting a good tan, Sarah and Rosalyn and Gunilla and even Jenny and Pattie went down to bathe and afterwards lie on the rocks in their bikinis, bringing the sadhus and sanyassis out of their huts on the other side of the river to wash their robes, and wash them again, and again.

The skimpiest bikini belonged to Gunilla who, being Swedish, would have been perfectly happy to remove that last vestige of bourgeois restraints and lie their naked. But Berndt and others persuaded her not to, saying that Maharishi would not have approved.

In fact Maharishi did not approve of anybody going into the water, even to wade, much less to swim. In a lecture that I didn't attend, he virtually pleaded with everyone not to venture more than two or three feet into the Ganges, saying that the currents above Rishikesh were "wery wery dangerous" and could sweep us out into the middle where we would drown. He also reminded us of something he had said before, namely that washing removed from the surface of the skin the beneficial coating of "ojas" that was produced by long meditation. As with his attempts at the beginning of the course to discourage "socializing," Maharishi had the sense not to ban swimming outright, knowing that to do so would have driven people into open disobedience.

At any rate, people paid little or no attention to Maharishi's warnings and wishes and as the temperatures continued to rise they went down to the Ganges in increasing numbers to bathe, wade, swim, or just lie in the water and wallow, letting it wash away the ojas along with the sweat.

For me, this unwillingness to follow Maharishi's explicit instructions was a healthy sign, proof that we were still able to think for ourselves, despite the inclination of the SRMers to suspend all critical judgment in the presence of their guru, letting him make decisions for them. Once again I was certain this resistance to conform was thanks to the presence of the Beatles and to the healthy spirit of irreverence they brought with them.

One afternoon during tea, Maharishi's admonition not to go into the water, and virtually everyone's blithe disregard for it, led to another little off-the-cuff performance by John and Paul, at which I luckily happened to be present.

During a recent lecture, Maharishi had said that we were all swamis, at least potentially, since "swami" simply meant teacher, which was what we were all in training to become.

Paul and John's little ditty, that they performed standing at the end of the long outside table, was a variation on "Mama don't allow." Paul introduced it with with "A one, and a two, and a…"

> Maha don't allow no swamis swimmin' in here,
> Maha don't allow no swamis swimmin' in here,
> I don't care what Maha don't allow,
> Swami gonna swim here anyhow!

CHAPTER 24

Dear Prudence

※ ※ ※

Despite the music and the moments of lightness and laughter, running through this period were dark undercurrents of growing tension and dissension that I was only vaguely aware of, caught up as I was soon to become in a swirl of emotions of my own. This third phase of the course extended roughly from mid-March to mid-April—at which time we were to abandon the heat of Rishikesh for the cool of Kashmir—and it was supposed to entail a resumption of lectures three times a day and gradual reduction of the time we spent in meditation until we were back to just twice a day, morning and evening. It should have been a time of making plans and pulling together, and at first it was, but eventually all the plans and projects came to naught and instead of pulling together, at the end of this period the whole course started falling apart.

Maybe the heart of the problem was that the two branches of Maharishi's movement were at cross purposes. This four-week period was also a time of many things happening and a lot of people coming and going—one of the reasons we never really got down to a schedule of three lectures a day, or on some days even one.

Two of the people who showed up at the ashram towards the end of this time were Charlie Jackson, the head of SRM, and Jerry Jarvis, husband of Debbie and director of SIMS.

Like Paul Horn, Jerry Jarvis had been on hand for the World Peace Conference in Delhi and I had talked with him briefly there. Jerry was a soft-spoken man of thirty-five or forty who combed what was left of his reddish hair over a thoughtful head. Of medium build, not much taller than I, Jerry tended to laugh easily and often, and his unwavering good humor, no matter how much craziness was going on around him, was either a built-in part of his nature or due to all the hours he spent meditating. Despite his role as leader of the more dynamic branch of Maharishi's movement, which nowadays was attracting thousands of new members worldwide every day, Jerry was always calm, easily approachable, and when you talked to him he listened. Caring, sincere, attentive, Jerry Jarvis struck me as a kind and generous man who was convinced that the more people who took up Transcendental Meditation, the kinder and more generous the world would soon become. But perhaps Jerry's chief characteristic—surprisingly, considering his position of responsibility—was an almost self-effacing humility.

The chief characteristic of Charlie Jackson, on the other hand, was anything but. When they both arrived in Rishikesh I was more familiar with Charlie, having talked with him, or rather listened to him talk, several times, and seen him perform twice, once in the hotel room of the Continental while he strutted around in circles saying meditation was "a piece of cake," and once again while doing an impersonation of John Wayne during the explosive confrontation with the students at the University of Delhi.

Charlie loved to perform. He loved being the center of attention. Once while sitting around over tea with a bunch of us younger meditators, Charlie told the story of an automobile accident which he claimed nearly cost him his life and turned him into a Seeker of Truth. The way he told it, the story sounded like the conversion of Saul, but instead of going blind and falling off a camel, Charlie ran a red light and got smashed into by a truck that totalled his car and left him lying on the roadside with a cut finger and the sound of the wings of the Angel of Death getting closer and closer. The reason the Angel passed him by, he said, was that he'd been chosen to become Maharishi's disciple. That is, ahem, disciple numero uno, Worldwide President of the Spiritual Regeneration Movement.

By contrast, Jerry said the reason he decided to give up his job and devote his life to spreading Transcendental Meditation was that one day, after coming away from one of Maharishi's introductory lectures, it seemed like a good idea.

So on the one hand a dominant alpha male, autocratic, authoritarian, proud of his position as leader of the pack and determined to defend it at all costs, against all comers; on the other an unassuming, mild-mannered man with no interest in dominating anything or anyone but only in spreading this simple new technique of meditation as quickly as possible, to as many people as possible. In a way, these two men, so radically different in content and style, summed up and typified the differences between the two branches of Maharishi's movement, which were bound to come into conflict sooner or later. As it happened, that defining conflict, engineered by Charlie Jackson, with help from Nancy Nixon, was to take place at the end of this crucial four-week period, and it would have long-lasting consequences for the future of Transcendental Meditation, or "TM," as it was soon to be renamed.

One evening in late March I was sitting around outside after dinner talking with George and Prudence. We were sitting in armchairs that people had carried out and placed in the scraggly garden next to the path not far from Block 6. As we talked it soon became apparent that all was not well with Prudence. This seemed only normal in a way since she had just completed four or five weeks of nonstop, round-the-clock meditation, during which she had hardly seen the light of day. What was not normal was that instead of gradually warming up to the conversation Prudence seemed to get further and further away, and to become less and less coherent. It was as if she had trouble understanding what we were saying, and the more we talked the less she understood. Even stranger, and a little scary, were some of the things she said. At that time there was a rumor that as soon as Mia finished whatever she was up to in London she was going to come back and rejoin the course in Kashmir, this time staying on until the end. George asked Prudence if this was true and if so, wasn't it going to be nice to see her sister? Prudence listened, nodded, blinked, and then said "Oh, so she's coming too."

It was getting dark fast, the way it always did there as soon as the sun went down, and even though it was still warm—as yet no breeze was coming down off the mountains—Prudence shivered and pulled her gray shawl tighter around her shoulders. After a while I leaned forward and said, "Prudence, are you okay?"

There was a long pause while she looked down at her hands in her lap. The hands were clenched together and her knuckles were white. Finally she said quietly that she was afraid but she couldn't say of what. Even if she wanted to, she couldn't. There were no words for it.

We tried to tell her it was just a knot of stress she had encountered during long meditation. All she had to do was wait until it came undone and everything would be all right. She nodded, looking at us, her pale blue eyes wide open.

I had the uneasy feeling that if I stared too long into those eyes they would pull me over into wherever Prudence had gone. The place seemed vaguely familiar. I was pretty sure I'd been there on a few brief visits—most recently during a bad acid trip at Stanford—and I didn't want to go back. I knew the place well enough though to know that when you were there it was the only place there was. The rest was an illusion, maya, a fairy tale we all keep making up as we go along, to keep from seeing how absolutely, terrifyingly alone we all are really.

Prudence seemed to be teetering on the verge of falling even deeper. Not only was I afraid to look at her, I was also afraid of saying something that might push her over another precipice. I looked at George. He looked at me. Both of us were at a loss for what to do. We asked Prudence if she wanted us to get help, or take her to down to see Maharishi, but she shook her head. We asked her if she wanted us to leave her alone and she stared at something beyond and behind us and shook her head again and said, as if to herself, "Then I would be alone with all my fright."

On the roof of the auditorium a bunch of crows were calling in the night. After another uncomfortable silence, George leaned forward and touched Prudence on the knee. She jumped at the touch and looked at him, and then at me, and then down at her feet. And then she gave a terrible, hopeless little moan and she began to cry.

Each taking an arm, we helped Prudence out of her chair and started up the path towards Block 6. At the gate George put his arm around her and continued leading her the rest of the way to her room.

I went off down the road in the gathering darkness, glad that my room was at the other end of the ashram, glad that my own experience with deep meditation had been so benign. At least so far.

As I walked down the road the only light coming through windows was from flickering candles, so I figured the electricity must have gone out again. Lately it had been going out more often than usual and staying out for hours at a time—maybe because of storms up in the mountains that would suddenly rush down and engulf the ashram, changing the weather in a matter of seconds from dead calm to violent wind and rain and sometimes hail that would lash the trees and tear away at limbs and brush, rattling windows and doors and threatening to rip them off their hinges.

Back in my room I made sure my door was secure and lit a candle and bunched up the blankets and pillows in my bed to sit down and meditate, but every time I closed my eyes I just saw Prudence staring back at me.

Early the next morning I was sitting on the veranda in front of my open door, absorbing the sun slanting in beneath the roof. The remains of the breakfast that had been delivered to my room at seven now lay in the tray on the floor beside me and I was happily engaged in a combination of meditating, dozing, and digesting. There had been no storm the night before and the morning was bright with promise and full of songs of colorful birds I still didn't know the names of.

At the sound of approaching voices I opened my eyes and was surprised to see Maharishi coming down the road towards Block 1. He was accompanied by Tarzan-Devendra, who was carrying a furled umbrella, and the bald bramachary who held a large black ledger under one arm. At the upper entrance to Block 1 they turned in and started going around the path surrounding the little flower garden in the middle of our U-shaped row of rooms. In front of every door the little group would pause while Maharishi and the bramachary consulted the ledger in front of them.

For some reason, I was suddenly seized by panic. All I wanted to do was slip back inside my room unnoticed and quietly close the door. I waited until the three of them had reached the far corner of the little courtyard and were looking up at the two rooms in the corner occupied by Tony and Terry. But before I could make my move inside, Geoffrey burst out of his room, leaped down from the veranda onto the path, plucked a marigold from the garden, strode up to Maharishi and bowed, the flower wedged between his two joined hands.

"JAI GURU DEV Mahawshi!"

Maharishi turned around, took Geoffrey's flower, returned his greeting, and saw me. I scrambled to my feet, joined my hands, and repeated the invocation.

Maharishi seemed glad to see me. Followed by the two bramacharis, and now Geoffrey, he proceeded around the path until he was standing directly beneath me.

"You will pack up your belongings and move to another room, yes?"

It was one of those questions you could not say no to. Maharishi explained that Devendra would wait until I had finished packing then show me to my new lodgings.

The bald bramachary closed the ledger, stuck it back under his arm, pulled his shawl around his shoulders, and followed Maharishi back across the road and down the garden path.

It took me less than ten minutes to load everything back into my suitcase, zip it shut and drag it to the door of my room where Devendra stood waiting. With a huge smile he scooped up the suitcase as if it were a handbag, bounded down the steps of the veranda and started marching up the road.

Devendra led me as far as the top of Block 4, where he turned into a narrow, weedy space between Block 4 and 5. Behind the two rooms on that end of Block 4 was a low wall over which Devendra flung my suitcase and then himself and then reached down to take my hand. Instead I gave him the Olivetti and managed to clamber over the wall on my own.

We were standing in the washroom space servicing the two rooms at that end of Block 4. Except for the low wall, the layout was similar to the lavatory area behind Gunar's, Geoffrey's and my room in Block 1, with a sink in the middle and a shower stall to the left and an enclosed toilet next to that. In addition though, there was a small room off to the right, through a flimsy door that would not open all the way. The room had bare concrete walls, a low ceiling, a drain in the middle of the floor, and a narrow window that looked out onto the jungle beyond the ashram fence. Apparently the space had been intended as some sort of laundry room, but now it contained a narrow bed with a thin mattress, the standard issue wooden armchair with white plastic webbing, a stool, and a small table.

Devendra stood in the doorway, smiling.

"Nice and cozy," I said.

Devendra's smile grew even larger. We exchanged another Jai Guru Dev and then he leaped back over the wall and bounded back off towards Maharishi's cottage.

Ten minutes later, as I emerged from the shower that had the same hot water problems as the showers in Block 1, the door next to the door leading into my little room banged open, actually banged open into it, and out came Gunilla the Swedish SIMSer. She was wrapped in a light blue or green terrycloth robe that almost came down to the top of her thighs and had been washed so often you could almost see through it. In her hand she held a toothbrush and toothpaste and soap. A towel was draped over her left shoulder. In recent weeks, during midday breaks in long meditation, the two of us had swum together often enough down at the Ganges that we had gotten used to being nearly naked in each other's presence. Still, she seemed shocked to find me first thing in the morning standing five feet away from her back door wearing only a towel.

Momentarily at a loss for words—Jai Guru Dev seemed hardly appropriate—I gestured towards the laundry room and finally managed to convey that I was her new neighbor.

Gunilla laughed. Then she glanced into the little room and said, "My goodness! You're going to live here?"

I said it wasn't all that bad, at least there was a window and the window had glass and the glass wasn't broken. She then asked the obvious question that I hadn't even thought to ask myself.

"But why?"

Indeed. Why had I been moved out of my comfortable little room in Block 1 into this damp little hovel? Especially since the influx of visitors had recently fallen off and there was no need for extra rooms.

We found out the answer over lunch, while sitting next to Berndt, Geoffrey and Larry. Berndt said that during the night Prudence had completely flipped out and started shouting and screaming and throwing things around in her room, waking up everybody in Block 6 and a lot of people in Block 5 as well, including Berndt. After a while several people managed to take or carry Prudence down to Maharishi's bungalow. But Berndt said that even Maharishi could not do anything to calm her down, so finally Dr. Gertrude was called for and she came down and gave Prudence a strong shot of some sort of sedative. When Prudence regained consciousness, the plan was to move her into my old room, which Geoffrey said a group of staffers who arrived with tools and lumber shortly after I left that morning were now transforming into a padded cell. The plan included hiring a private nurse who would stay with Prudence round the clock. Apparently she had been so violent up in Block 6 that there was some fear she would do herself serious physical harm.

For the second time that day my new next door neighbor asked the obvious question. Why was Prudence staying at the ashram? Wouldn't she be better off at a proper hospital down in Delhi, or better yet, back in L.A.?

To this question, Berndt, ever the cynical realist, gave the obvious answer. Maharishi did not want the negative publicity. Tom, sitting across from Berndt, just shook his head and muttered something inaudible. Geoffrey, sitting to his right and directly across from me, looked ashen-faced. I wondered if he was remembering his admonition to the rest of us six weeks ago, that once you begin to doubt him, "everything starts to come apart."

※ ※ ※

Because of what had happened to Prudence there were more people down in the dining area for lunch that afternoon than usual. After lunch a bunch of us proposed to meet again down at the swimming hole. Since we were supposed to start easing out of long meditation that seemed like a good place to do it, especially since it was now starting to get blisteringly hot by mid-afternoon, even on days like today when there were more clouds than sun.

After returning to my new room to finish unpacking and change into trunks I stopped by Block 1 to get Larry, who had proposed walking down to the beach together. All of the furniture had been moved out of my old room and stacked up on the veranda in front of it, along with a pile of long bamboo poles, and through the door came the sound of hammering and sawing, making meditation impossible for anyone nearby.

On our way down to the river, Larry said he'd heard that two nurses were on their way up from Delhi and should be arriving at the ashram before nightfall. He himself was leaving the next day with Mike Love for a little jaunt to Japan. Mike wanted to buy some cameras and had asked Larry along to give him advice. Larry said he was glad to be splitting this scene and hoped that when he came back Prudence would be back to normal.

"Well," he said, "you know what I mean."

"Yeah," I said, knowing he meant Prudence's normal was not all that normal.

After a while Larry laughed and shook his head and said, "Blakely, you're so fucking lucky I can't believe it."

"You mean because I got moved out of Block 1?"

"I mean because you got moved within scoring range of the beautiful Gunilla. Your karma is so amazing it's unreal!"

I don't remember exactly what I said by way of a reply but I do know I had no designs on my new shower mate. First of all, I didn't think I could make it to square one with her, and second, I wasn't sure I wanted to. While I had grown increasingly friendly with Gunilla over the past ten weeks, I still considered her out of my league, or beyond my reach somehow. She was almost too beautiful, too sexy, too exotic, and there was something else I couldn't put my finger on. During conversations with the Scandanavian contingent over meals and down at the beach I had learned that while her mother was Swedish, her father had come from Czechoslovakia, which to me explained her high cheekbones and somewhat slanted eyes. Now when I looked at Gunilla I could imagine hordes of horsemen from the east thundering across the Steppes in the middle ages under Ghengis Khan or Taras Bulba. Not that I had anything against the descendants of Ghengis Khan or Taras Bulba, but that vaguely Oriental side of Gunilla's clashed with my own very western, Californian background and must have contributed to my sense that on some deep level we would not be a good match. As David would have said, and did say about someone I brought home one night to the apartment we'd briefly shared, she was not my kind of girl. Which did not prevent me from becoming friends with her. Maybe it even made it easier. For where there are no ulterior motives about sex, friendship can flourish.

When Larry and I got down to the bend in the river Berndt, Gunilla and Soren were already there. None of them had been in yet, all three Swedes preferring to soak up the sun until they were as hot as the rocks they were lying on and then leap into the water and sizzle, sauna-style.

Me, I stripped down to my trunks and went in right away, placing my feet on the yellowish-brown rocks that I had been using as steps since my first swim with Paul Horn a couple of weeks earlier. The water still seemed as cold as it had then, if not colder still, in contrast now to the hotter air, but within seconds my body had gotten used to it and I felt keenly alive. Because of the heavy rains of the past ten days, branches and logs and entire trees and God knows what else were racing downstream in the middle of the river. While swimming around the perimeter of the little pool I had to be careful not to be swept out among them through gaps in the rocks.

Despite the mostly cloudy sky, floating on my back and looking up I could see patches of blue that were bluer than any sky I'd ever seen. Up on the cliff that bordered the ashram I thought I could see people looking down at us among the trees and waving, but I couldn't be sure.

Shortly after I climbed out, Pattie and Jenny and Geoffrey and George also arrived at the little beach and started taking off garments and folding them and laying them on towels and testing the water. Geoffrey said it looked a lot more inviting from up above than when you were sitting right beside it and Pattie teased him about his cold English blood. It had been several days since my last veena lesson with Jenny and Pattie down in the music room, which had been converted to a bedroom for Donovan. A few days earlier I had been down there for an impromptu concert with George on the sitar and Donovan on guitar, the audience consisting only of Geoffrey, Jenny, Pattie, Cynthia and myself. After a while Maharishi had come to join us and sat down and listened too, this time without continually bursting into laughter. After George and Donovan had stopped playing and put away their instruments everybody went off with Maharishi to his bungalow for tea except for Cynthia and me, the two of us staying on in the little house full of open windows to chat and listen to the river below and watch the sun get lower in the sky. Like Pattie and Jenny, Cynthia was warm and friendly and easy to talk to, but she often seemed preoccupied and a little sad.

That afternoon on the beach, the good times spent in the music room seemed so innocent and far away. But that's because of what had happened to Prudence. Now there was a Before Prudence and an After Prudence.

There was very little talk of Prudence that afternoon. It was almost as if the topic were taboo. But there was talk of how little sleep people had gotten the night before, people up in Blocks 5 and 6, that is. Jenny said that Cynthia had been badly shaken by the whole incident and was now sleeping it off. Geoffrey seemed especially somber and hardly said anything the whole time, but that was understandable, given that he would be in closest proximity to Prudence from now on. To escape the noise, Gunar had moved in with Eva up in Block 4, but Geoffrey had nowhere else to go, except the caves, and I couldn't imagine him staying down in the caves at night. Geoffrey did confirm what Larry had said earlier, that two trained nurses were on their way up from Delhi, and he hoped they would be able to help Prudence get over this spot of "sticky karma."

As the afternoon progressed others came down to join us until there were at least fifteen people sitting or lying around in various states of undress, while fifty yards away on the opposite shore about the same number of sanyassis had gathered, some to do their laundry or ablutions, while others simply stood and stared. I had spread my towel on a mix of gravel and sand next to Gunilla and Berndt on one side and Larry and Jenny and Pattie on the other, and we were all carrying on a disjointed conversation in and out of slumber induced by swimming and sunbathing and ten weeks of indolence. Wearing her skimpy bikini, Gunilla was lying on her back on a long low rock whose uniform and lifeless flatness accentuated the living curves of her body. At one point, Larry picked up a smooth, oval stone about the size of his fist and laid it gently on Gunilla's stomach, just over the navel. No one asked why he did this, not even Gunilla. Maybe Gunilla was asleep and the weight of the warm stone on her belly had not awakened her. Everyone else was now wide awake though, especially the men, all of whose eyes were fixed on this smooth rock, gently rising and falling.

That afternoon I stayed down at the beach until most of the others had left, starting the climb back up to the ashram with Berndt and Gunilla and a few other diehards, after the heat of the day had begun to wane and the light had begun to fade. After we'd checked through the gate and were passing in front of Block 1 we stopped to look at the new construction that had gone on all afternoon. In front of my old room thick bamboo poles had been lashed together about two inches apart to form an enclosure resembling all too closely a jail. In the narrow doorway of the enclosure stood one of the staffers with his arms crossed. He was a sturdily built, older man with a turban. The last time I had seen him, just after the arrival of the Beatles, he'd been standing guard at the lower gate. Rumor had it that he was a Gurka warrior Maharishi had sent for specially, kind of like a Samurai, to deal with the pushier reporters. Standing now in that passage in front of my old room, not moving a muscle, it was as if he didn't see us staring at him twenty feet away.

An hour later over dinner word went around that the two female nurses had indeed arrived and would be taking turns staying in Prudence's room, in which an extra cot had been installed. Apparently Prudence's state had stabilized. Late that afternoon someone had seen her being escorted up from Maharishi's cottage with a couple of bramacharis and one of the nurses, and she had seemed docile enough.

That night in the lecture hall there was almost a full turnout. As soon as the group meditation was over, several hands went up at once, all belonging to people wanting to ask the same question: what had happened to Prudence?

Maharishi nodded and thought for a while, as if deciding how best to answer, as if the question had not been expected. He then explained that Prudence's state was due to all the drugs she had taken before learning to meditate. The drugs had done deep damage to her nervous system—damage in the form of "a huge iceberg" that she had encountered during the unstressing brought on by deep meditation. "It is good this happens now," Maharishi added, "so that we can speed the healing process."

"How long will this process take?" someone asked from down in front.

Maharishi wobbled his head. "Three, four days. Not long."

The next morning I went down to an early breakfast and found Geoffrey sitting by himself at the end of one of the outside tables. When I set my tray down next to his he greeted me with a weak smile. I asked him how the night had gone and he sighed and looked away and waited long enough for me to wonder if he'd heard my question. Then, looking down at his uneaten breakfast, he told me it wasn't the occasional screams that bothered him, or the whimpering. He had been expecting that and could deal with it. It was the long silent moments in between. He said at those times he kept wondering what she was thinking, what was going on. He said the worst of it was that he wanted to help her but didn't know how.

"But," he said, suddenly sitting up straighter, "this is just part of her karma, and when she works through it she'll come out better than before. Mahawshi knows what he is doing," he said, raising a finger in the air and turning to look me in the eye. "We can be sure of that."

When I pointed out that this was part of his karma too he gave a rueful little smile and said, "Yes, I know."

But Prudence did not get better. And as the days wore on she only got worse.

At one of the lectures soon after Prudence's breakdown Maharishi invited a yoga instructor up onto the little stage to show us how to do a simple set of asanas or hatha yoga exercises. He said that from now on we should all interrupt periods of long meditation, "every two-three hours," to do at least a few of these exercises, the ones we could easily manage. The idea was to supplement the long meditations with some non-strenuous physical activity that would "culture the body just as transcending cultures the mind." But plainly the idea was also to prevent what happened to Prudence from happening to anyone else. In future courses, this ten-minute series of asanas breaking up each hour of meditation was to become a built-in requirement and came to be known as "rounding."

During this time Maharishi also encouraged people to get a massage as often as once a day, for similar therapeutic reasons. To this end he had the couple who did massages set up their tables in a shady space along the road that fronted the blocks of housing, in clear view of my old room down in Block 1. One morning while getting a massage I happened to see Prudence escape from her room and run across the road. Seconds later the female nurse came running out after her and was joined by the guard on duty at the gate. Together they managed to corner Prudence behind a tree, then lead her back across the road and into her room.

It was like watching an animal trying to escape from a cage. And as the nurse and gate guard led her back to her room she had let out a plaintive, low-pitched moan that sounded more animal than human. Out of the corner of my eye I saw the wife of the man who was working on my back glance at her husband and almost imperceptibly shake her head.

During this whole time Prudence was being taken down to Maharishi's bungalow at least once a day for one-on-one sessions with her guru and medical checkups with Dr. Gertrude and probably other sorts of therapy as well, but nothing seemed to help. John Lennon even composed a song for her, which he went down to the courtyard to sing outside her door. But the whole time he sat there singing outside my old room the door remained closed and Prudence never even looked out the window.

If John couldn't lure Prudence out with his gentle song, who could?

CHAPTER 25

Coming apart

※ ※ ※

On Tuesday, March 26, Paul and Jane Asher left the ashram to return to London, although hardly anyone on the course knew it at the time, since they left without fanfare and most of us were still meditating a good portion of the day. According to the few who had seen them off, they left in an atmosphere of harmony and goodwill, Paul expressing his gratitude towards Maharishi and saying his five-week stay at the ashram had changed him for the better in ways he hadn't anticipated or thought possible. One would think that this parting comment, which within a few days had made the rounds of the ashram, would have laid to rest suspicions among the old guard SRMers that the Beatles were not serious about meditation. Unfortunately, this was not the case.

A few days after Paul left there was a meeting between Maharishi and George and John that I only learned the details of much later but which in retrospect sheds light on events that were soon to follow. The meeting started after dinner and was rumored to have lasted on into the night. The central topic was a film that George and John proposed to make, about Maharishi, Guru Dev, and the whole Transcendental Meditation movement. It would start with background information about Guru Dev, with running commentary by Maharishi, and include songs composed by the Beatles specifically for the film—many of which had already been written—along with other songs that Mike Love or Donovan or others might want to contribute. It would include shots of the lectures and interviews with people on the course.

Shooting would begin in Rishikesh, move on up to Kashmir, and end with a huge concert the Beatles would put on in Delhi.

The idea was to show what all of us were really doing at the ashram, in order to counter all the misinformation that had been disseminated by the press in recent months, to show people how good it was to meditate, how easy it was to do, and maybe persuade a few of them, especially the younger ones, to take up meditation too. George and John were proposing that the Beatles produce, direct and distribute the film through Apple Productions, kicking back a percentage to Maharishi. John and George said Paul and Ringo were ready and willing to return to Rishikesh to participate. If Maharishi agreed they said they would call Neil Aspinal back in London and have him put together a film crew and dispatch it to India on a chartered jet. Filming could start within days.

At the end of the meeting Maharishi gave the proposal his enthusiastic approval. How could he not? Apparently it included the Beatles setting up his own TV and radio station in Rishikesh or New Delhi.

The next day, as word went around about "the Guru Dev movie," all the SIMSers were ecstatic. To think that people all over the world would finally see what meditation was all about, while watching the sequel to *Help!* and *Hard Day's Night*! The very idea helped divert attention from what had happened to Prudence and dispel the gloomy atmosphere that had reigned over the ashram ever since. Unfortunately, it was only a *belle éclaircie*.

Also present at that long nighttime meeting between Maharishi and George and John was Nancy Nixon. By that time, although Nancy was still on speaking terms with John and George and friendly with the Beatles' wives, she had come to consider John as a kind of evil genius, and the antipathy was mutual. In recent weeks he and Nancy had had a number of run-ins during which John had not minced words—but John did not mince words with anybody. As a result Nancy had begun to side with the other SRMers who resented the Beatles' presence at the ashram, just as she had turned against Mia Farrow, and now she doubtless had grave misgivings about the Beatles sponsoring a movie in which Maharishi would be the costar, or maybe even the sidekick, about the Beatles in India.

And so around the same time George and John called Neil Aspinal in London, Nancy Nixon placed a call to Charlie Jackson in L.A. Which is why, a few days before the arrival of the film crew from Apple, Charlie arrived with a crew of his own. He also arrived with a signed contract with a Hollywood-based company called Four-Star Productions, stipulating that they had exclusive rights to film Maharishi for the next five years. Charlie claimed that Maharishi had already made such a commitment during an earlier visit to the States. Whether this was actually the case, or Charlie's maneuver was just a ploy to wrest the project out of the Beatles' hands and put it under the control of the SRM, is unclear. In any event, since Charlie had power of attorney for Maharishi in the U.S., he claimed the contract he'd signed was legally binding.

Naturally, the arrival of Charlie and his own film crew led to more cancelled lectures and long meetings down at Maharishi's bungalow, during which there were apparently vehement and sometimes violent verbal exchanges between the SIMSers on one hand, represented by the Beatles and their entourage, and the SRMers on the other, represented by Charlie Jackson, whom John Lennon now referred to openly as Captain Kundalini.

Although most of us were unaware of what exactly what was going on, it was obvious that something else was wrong and that the Beatles were not happy, all of which brought back the clouds of gloom, this time thicker and more threatening than before, and meant that George and John stopped showing up in the lecture hall, where Four Star Productions had set up lights and camera, while waiting for some action. Action that they had been led to believe would include the Beatles and their friends.

※　※　※

On April 4 Martin Luther King was assassinated. When the news hit the ashram it only added to the general desolation, especially among the American SIMSers. A few days later a delegation from *Ebony Magazine* showed up, no doubt in hopes of finding sympathy and perhaps some sort of solidarity from Maharishi, as a fellow human being with dark skin.

That afternoon Maharishi called a press conference and asked everyone to attend, especially the Americans. For once I sat down in front, hoping for the best. But the press conference turned into just another introductory lecture, and those of us who were hoping Maharishi was breaking away from his conservative politics were sadly disappointed. I remember feeling acutely embarrassed for the two black women and two black men whose polite but pointed questions went pointedly unanswered and who were most definitely not made to feel that they had something in common with Maharishi in particular and all Indians in general by virtue of the color of their skin. At one point one of the women asked Maharishi what he would do if he were told to move to the back of the bus, even though there were plenty of seats up in front.

Maharishi shrugged, fingering the petals of his flower, and said it was a question of pride and self esteem. What did it matter where one sat on a bus, as long as one's pride remained intact?

Once again I was reminded of the happy hungry man Maharishi had invoked at the Paris Hilton, only here no one dared stand up to protest.

After the press conference, to raise my spirits, I wandered down to the kitchen for tea and found Charlie holding forth with a bunch of younger people at an outside table. It was here that he talked about his close encounter with the Angel of Death, and I sat down to listen. After he finished the story of his conversion someone asked him what he'd thought of the press conference with the editors of Ebony.

Charlie shrugged. "Nigras can't meditate."

Nobody said anything, probably because we were all wondering if we'd heard correctly.

"He said so," Charlie added, gesturing vaguely towards Maharishi's cottage. "They have to wait at least a few more lives until their nervous systems are pure enough to transcend."

One evening during those hot dark days I went down to the cliff to watch the sun set and try to put things in perspective and make sense of it all. That day Larry had returned from his trip to Japan with Mike Love. Over lunch he'd told me about their return from Tokyo to Delhi. From the airport they had gone directly to the Oberoi to spend the night. When they were told there was no vacancy at the Oberoi, Mike flipped out and demanded to see the manager. When the manager arrived and said the same thing Larry said Mike threw a scene that soon threatened to turn into a brawl. Luckily, Nancy's friend Avi was among the onlookers and since Avi was either part owner of the hotel or knew someone who was, a room was soon found for Larry and Mike and the brawl narrowly averted. Unfortunately, also among the onlookers was a reporter who wrote an article on the whole scene that Larry said appeared the following morning in one of the Dehli dailies, concluding that such aggressive behavior by Western followers of Maharishi only confirmed earlier rumors about drunken orgies up in his ashram.

And then there was Nancy's son Rick. He had arrived at the ashram a few weeks before but instead of settling into long meditation he'd gone off on another safari with Nancy and Avi and had actually shot and killed a Bengal tiger (the inspiration for John Lennon's song "Bungalow Bill"). It was a story I would not have believed if I hadn't heard Rick himself bragging about it over lunch one day.

And then there was Prudence.

And now there was Charlie and his film crew.

While I was musing over these recent developments and trying to reconcile them with the dawn of Cosmic Consciousness Jenny Boyd came up behind me.

"You look absorbed in your thoughts," she said.

Glad to have a sympathetic listener, I poured those thoughts out while she listened. After I'd finished neither of us said anything for a while and then, off the top of my head, I asked Jenny if she knew how much it would cost to take a taxi down to New Delhi. She said she didn't, but could find out.

"You're thinking of leaving us?" she asked.

It was actually the first time the thought had crossed my mind, but now that I'd mentioned it it seemed like a good idea. Since I had an open return I figured I could show up at the airport and just wait for an empty seat on the next flight to Paris. The only thing holding me back was the money I would need to get down to Delhi—I had only a few hundred rupees left. I figured I would also have to go see Maharishi to tell him I was leaving.

"Somehow I don't think he'll mind though," I said. "He might even be glad to see me go."

Jenny thought for a while and said, "You never know about him though, do you? What he really thinks."

I let that sink in then asked her if she'd heard anything about the Guru Dev movie. She said she didn't know exactly, meetings had been going on pretty much nonstop since the film crew had arrived, but she was pretty sure the Beatles' movie was a dead issue and George and John and the others were not happy.

I nodded and said this confirmed rumors I had heard. Then I asked her if she'd heard the story about Mike at the Oberoi.

"Oh yes. He's been talking about it ever since he came back. He actually seems rather proud of the whole thing."

We both laughed.

The sun was now almost touching the horizon and had begun to turn blood red, its light filtered through all that Oriental dust.

"When you think of all that could have been," Jenny said.

I thought of our long talks up on the roof of the lecture hall, the plans to change the world, to sow the seeds for real change. All that seemed terribly naïve now, and very far away. "Yeah," I said, "and the worst is that now no one will ever know."

She turned to me and said she would miss me if I left and I said I would miss her too. But as it happened she would be the first to leave and this was the last time I would talk to her.

We exchanged addresses and promised to write and headed back up the path to our respective rooms to put in another hour of meditation before dinner.

CHAPTER 26

Coming together

It was probably that night, but I can't be sure, because I have no record of it—not in my lecture notebook, nor in the smaller notebook in which I kept track of my meditations, nor in the third notebook, now decorated with Paul's sketch, where I jotted down bits of poetry.

Why is it we never write about the most important things? If I had I would have seen it coming, would have known that it was bound to happen, ever since that day I saw the rock on her stomach, which I kept seeing again like a three-second film that kept playing over and over, during meditation or while waiting for sleep or sometimes when I was wide awake. The indelible image of that smooth black rock, just above the top of her bikini bottom—the elastic band stretched tight between her two hips to expose a quarter inch of darkened empty space between her bathing suit and her skin—while the rock kept rising with each intake of air into her lungs, and falling with each release.

I sometimes wondered if it would have made such a deep impression on me if I had been alone. Or if it needed the presence of other males sitting nearby, all of us concentrating fiercely on that eroded lump of igneous basalt, to turn it into the philosopher's stone that it became in my imagination.

I do remember the evening lecture had been cancelled again that night. I had had dinner with Berndt and Gunilla and the three of us walked back to the housing blocks together. When we got to the road, Berndt said goodnight and turned right to return to his room in Block 5. I was about to go around to the passage between block 4 and 5, to climb over the wall as usual, but Gunilla said I should go through her room. She said I should always go through her room from now on. It was silly. Her door was always unlocked. Even if she was meditating I could just knock softly and pass on through.

"You're sure?" I said. "But what if you're, you know, with somebody or something?"

She looked at me and laughed and said, "Come on!"

And so I followed her up on to the veranda and we came through the unlocked door into the room I'd only glimpsed until then through the half-open door in the back. She lit a match and held it to a candle by her bed and I saw the door leading out back and went towards it and put my hand on the doorknob but did not turn it and Gunilla turned around and looked at me and smiled and I let go of the doorknob and took a few steps back towards her.

I guess it was a case of "*reculer pour mieux sauter.*" All these thoughts of platonic friendship with no sex. At any rate, two hours later as I lay in Gunilla's bed with her beside me, not only was there no other place I wanted to be, there was no other place I could imagine being. I was home. This was what I had come to India for. This was why our guru had put us so close together. So that we would finally get the point, see? Despite appearances to the contrary and certain differences in our background—no, because of those appearances and those differences—we were made for each other. This was the girl for me. Now I just had to convince her that I was her man. Lying in her arms that night, anything was possible.

So this was why nothing had happened between Rosalyn and me, why my arm never quite made it around Viggie's waist, why Jenny never seemed to pick up the signals I kept sending out to her. This is why with Gunilla it had been so easy and so natural and so… When it finally happened it was like a bomb dropping on a dam, releasing all that pent up libido that came surging forth and pouring out and swirling around, sweeping everything along with it, all memories of Jill, all worries about where I was and what I was doing, all deep rooted phobias of vandal hordes galloping westward, even, and especially, all the old prejudice and grudges, built up over the centuries and passed on to me through my mother, that all Norwegians bear against all Swedes. In short, anything that got in the way of lying naked next to Gunilla and fully enjoying that moment and wanting it to last forever.

I was lying on my back and she lay on her left side, with her back facing me. Her head lay partly on the pillow and partly in the crook of my left arm, with my forearm passing up beneath her chin and my left hand resting on her shoulder. By the change in the rhythm of her breathing and the little jerks and twitches up and down her body I could tell she was going to sleep. Her long dark hair lay across my chest over the light cotton bedspread we had pulled up over us after making love. I reached over with my right hand and absently picked up a few strands of hair and rubbed them back and forth between my forefinger and thumb. Immediately that old familiar feeling swept over me, the sensation of fulness in my mouth and of my hands expanding and of my body becoming weightless, all of it all at once and extremely pleasurable. It was like my dance on the rocks the first time I went down to the Ganges, but now I had broken through to the other side. I was there.

The last time I had experienced that feeling so clearly was while driving my old MG in the coastal mountains above San Francisco Bay, the MG that had paid for my trip to Paris and eventually brought me here. Did I need further proof that I was where I belonged? That I had finally arrived at my destination? I closed my eyes and let that feeling take me, take us both. With my eyes closed, the bed started to rise up and float away. We were in a rocking cradle in the middle a river heading for the sea.

I was brought back by the sound of the candle spluttering on its little dish on the table just beside my head. The candle would soon have to be replaced. And I would soon have to do something about my left arm, pinned beneath Gunilla's head. It had long since ceased to tingle and my hand and fingers were numb.

In the corner of the ceiling directly above us two daddy-longlegs, their long legs apparently entwined, were doing something that caused them both to vibrate and shake back and forth. Were they fighting? Dancing? Making love? Trying to untangle their legs?

"Gunilla," I said softly.

"Mmm?"

"Do you like spiders?"

"Mm, I love them."

"Well then," I said, pointing to the ceiling with my right hand, "check this out."

She turned over, looked at me, then looked where I was pointing and gave a little shriek.

"SPIDERS!" she said.

"I thought you liked them," I said.

"I thought you said spices. Please take them away!"

Vaguely wondering why she thought I would have asked her a question about cuisine at such a time, I grabbed a Kleenex and stood up on tiptoe on the corner of her bed. Carefully, I tried to wrap the two daddy-longlegs in the tissue without damaging their fragile bodies. Then I took them out the back door and dropped them over the wall.

I stood there for a while looking up at the millions of brilliant stars, as many stars as there were names for God. As many stars as there were mantras. Straining my ears, I listened for sounds of animals in the jungle—the other day John Lennon said he'd actually seen a tiger, quite close to Maharishi's cottage—but that night I heard nothing. By then it was past midnight and it sounded like everyone at the ashram was fast asleep, even, I hoped, poor Prudence down in my old room.

When I went back into Gunilla's room the candle had gone out and she was fast asleep.

The following morning we each pretended nothing had happened, going down for breakfast at different times and sitting apart from each other at the morning lecture and during lunch. In place of the afternoon lecture organizational meetings had been planned, with Charlie Jackson in charge of the various SRM meetings, and running the SIMS meetings, Jerry Jarvis, who had arrived at the ashram a few days before. Rather than attend the meetings, both Gunilla and I had intended to play hooky and spend the afternoon down by the river, but instead we ended up once more in Gunilla's bed. We spent the afternoon and on into the night making love, meditating, meditating, making love, now and then doing asanas on the floor where there was just enough room between the bed and window for one of us to do them while the other sat cross-legged on the bed and pretended not to watch. We also took a lot of cold showers.

During the in-between times we told each other the stories of our lives. Gunilla told me how her father fled to Sweden from Czechoslovakia before the war, married her mother, and then got himself killed in an accident under a bridge in their big black Volvo as he was driving home from work one dark and stormy night when Gunilla was still too young to remember him clearly and her baby sister lay asleep in her crib. So we had that in common, the absence of a father, her from early childhood, me from early puberty.

She said her mother used to punish her for things she had not done by locking her in a closet under the stairs. So we had that in common too, a mother unhinged by the untimely death of her husband, and who gave us each a taste of terror, hers of being locked up in dark places, mine of being abandoned by the one I love.

She told me of her artist boyfriend Bertil back home in Sweden with whom she shared the apartment over her mother's flat in an upscale suburb of Stockholm called Ektorp and whose gold ring she wore on her wedding ring finger.

So we did not have that in common.

Late in the afternoon as we lay in bed without the bedspread over us because it was so hot there came a soft knock on the door. Gunilla put her finger to her lips and said nothing but the door opened anyway and Paul Horn came in, or started to, until he saw us lying there. Looking very surprised, he raised his eyebrows and apologized and left.

Paul was Gunilla's next door neighbor. Maybe he'd opened her door by mistake. But after a while Gunilla giggled and asked me if I knew what it meant to make love Spanish style. I didn't but I figured it out soon enough. I asked her why she wanted to know and she said Paul had once asked her if she would mind if he did that. It was a bad time of the month, she said, and neither of them had any... She glanced at the corner of the table.

"Rubbers," I said. "So did you, um..."

"No, because I didn't know what it meant, and we didn't have any..."

"No but I mean," I gestured at the two of us. "Did you, with Paul, like with me now? Some other time of the month perhaps?"

"Oh, I see what you mean. Yes, but only once. It was... how do you call it?"

There were numerous possibilities but Big Mistake was all that came to mind. Of course there was always Dark Betrayal, but that was before I knew her so she wasn't betraying anyone, was she, except Bertil but maybe she and Bertil had another name for it. And anyway, hadn't I wanted to make love any old style with Rosalyn and then Viggie and then Jenny, and would I not have done so gladly if the occasion had arisen? So what right did I have to get jealous? None of course. So when she asked if I was jealous I lied and told her no, of course not, and squirmed and lay there staring at the ceiling until I finally got up the nerve to ask her if there was anyone else on the course who, you know, and she said Tom and I said, oh no, my heart sinking, "You mean Tom the Actor?" and she said yes, but I shouldn't worry because that too was just a one night thing, or maybe two, a fling, not serious, and anyway it had happened a long time ago, at the very beginning of the course before he and Rosalyn, you know…

I propped my head up on my elbow and looked at her and picked up a few strands of her hair and rubbed them together between my thumb and forefinger and again that feeling came over me, not as strong as the night before but there it was and it seemed strange I could just call it up like that on command. For a long time neither of us said anything and then she turned and looked at me and sighed and said, "It's incredible how fast this is happening."

"Yeah, incredible!"

"Beautiful!"

"Beautiful."

She moved her head closer, resting it against my arm.

"When I was a kid learning English in school," she said, "'beautiful' was such a hard word for me to spell." She said she finally learned it by associating it with the word "ugly" in Swedish. She explained that the word for ugly was "ful," pronounced roughly like "fuel," and to learn to spell the word she had broken it up into its Swedish-sounding parts: bey-ah-ew-tee-fuel.

CHAPTER 27

Last days in Rishikesh

※ ※ ※

Afew days later the Beatles left, and left in a hurry. It was during the second week of April. I had gone down for break-fast, early as usual, and was assembling a tray to take back to Gunilla when George came running down from Block 6 out of breath and obviously upset. He ran around shaking hands and saying goodbye to the few of us who were down at the kitchen at that hour. He said something had happened. He couldn't explain what. There wasn't time. The taxis were waiting. He said he was sorry to go and he looked it. He also looked a little frantic and I wondered why. What could George Harrison be afraid of?

George said it had been a wonderful time and he hoped we would all keep in touch and that maybe somewhere, one day, well who knows. And then he ran back up the path and we heard the taxis start up one by one and chug off up the road and they were gone.

Word soon got around that not only had George and John left, along with the remainder of the Beatles contingent, thus virtually emptying out Block 6, but some of the other people on the course as well, including Rosalyn and Tom. To me, Tom's leaving came as no surprise, and I was frankly glad to see him go, given what I now knew, but I was sad and sorry to hear that Rosalyn had left too, she who had spent all her savings to come to India in order to become a better teacher when she returned to New York. As recently as a week ago I had talked with Rosalyn while having tea and she'd seemed perfectly happy with the course and with her experience in long meditation. She also seemed just as curious and excited to learn about the mantras and become an initiator as she had been while sitting next to me on the flight to Bombay. She told me about a private meeting she'd recently had with Maharishi, who had advised her to socialize less and meditate more, saying that when she came out of long meditation socializing would be even more enjoyable. And it was true, she said. Now that she was beginning to emerge from long meditation she felt more alive, more in tune with what was going on around her, more in touch. And in fact that day she had looked radiant. So why had she so suddenly dropped out? Certainly not just to follow Tom.

Nobody seemed to know exactly why the Beatles left, or why they left in such a hurry. But for whatever reason, they were gone, leaving many feeling bereft, especially the SIMSers. On the other hand, some of the old-time SRMers—Charlie, Nancy Nixon, Walter Kuhn—seemed to positively gloat. A takeover by the younger generation had been averted. The course was back on track, and once again Maharishi could give them his undivided attention.

As for me personally, although I was sorry to see Rosalyn go and would miss Jenny and Pattie and the others, I was not much affected by the new development, caught up as I was by the new development of my own, wrapped up as I was in the arms of my new neighbor—no longer just my neighbor, but nobody knew—or was supposed to.

During these days Gunilla and I continued to behave in public as if we were still just friends, but by night we turned back into lovers, either in her bed or in mine. Although the bed in my room was even narrower than hers, the room was cozier, less prone to unwelcome knocks on the door, and even though the window was smaller, the view outside was more interesting and exotic. When it was not raining we would keep the window open and the occasional noise from the jungle, even if it was only the cawing of crows or the mooing of a holy cow, would sharpen our pleasure and sometimes allow me to entertain the fantasy, or contemplate the fact, that the primal garden was maybe not so very far away.

"I'll be Adam, you be Eve," I said to her one day, but she just laughed.

Despite the fact that we continued to keep our romance under cover, and that I declined Gunilla's offer to use her front door—continuing to climb over the wall in the back, at least during daylight hours—word soon got around about the two of us.

One day I was standing in front of Block 4 with Reumah, waiting for Gunilla to come with us down to the kitchen for lunch. She was standing on the veranda in front of her room, talking with Sarah and Gunar's Eva. Finally the three of them stepped down from the veranda and started to walk single file across a foot-wide plank that had been laid across a puddle that had formed because of all the recent rain. When it was Gunilla's turn to walk the plank, seeing that it was springy she paused in the middle and started jumping up and down. Although Gunilla had a beautiful body, she did not always seem to have full control over it, giving her a natural clumsiness that only made her more endearing in my eyes. Now, after a few jumps, Gunilla landed in the puddle. When everyone had stopped laughing and Gunilla was once more on her way across the plank, Reumah turned to me and said, "Yes, we love our Gunilla, but Richard certainly you see that you could never be happy with such a girl."

Seeing my mouth fall open, Reumah just laughed and shrugged and added, "You are so different, the two of you!"

And then there was the time Gunilla was down at the beach and found herself talking with Charlie Jackson. I was not feeling well that afternoon and had stayed behind in Gunilla's room to meditate. Gunilla said that she told Charlie how before coming on this course she had never liked Americans, but now her opinion had changed, thanks to some Americans she had gotten to know. Like who, Charlie wanted to know, and Gunilla said well me, for example. Whereupon Charlie gave her a look and asked her if she didn't prefer bigger men, i.e., bigger men like him.

When Gunilla came back to her room she was livid. "It was so terrible!" she said. "Everything he said had a double meaning and the double meanings were so, so crude and vulgar!"

It was an occasion for me to teach her a bunch of new words: cad, heel, hypocrite (that one she knew), womanizer (that one she found very funny), creep, scumbucket, sleezebag,...

If Gunilla shared my opinion of the hardcore SRMers at the ashram, she had a deep, unwavering devotion for Maharishi, and in that respect, Reumah was right, we were different indeed. Given my own relative lack of devotion, the way she felt and talked and acted towards her guru sometimes made me uneasy.

One morning very early she woke up and said she was cold. We were sleeping in my room and the window was open. I got up and closed the window and got back into bed, but before I went back to sleep she suddenly sat up and said she had to go see Maharishi and give him a flower. Outside it was only just beginning to get light. I rolled over, thinking this was maybe happening in a dream, hers or mine, and went back to sleep.

Later when it was completely light I woke up and found her gone. The cover was thrown back on her side and there was a depression in the pillow where her head had been. I got up and looked into her room but she was not there either. Back in my own room I got into bed intending to meditate but instead just lay there feeling the void she'd left behind.

Then she was back, sitting on the edge of my bed. She was wearing a rose-pink long-sleeve silk shirt with tiny buttons halfway down the front made of pieces of sea shell, and white cotton pants she'd had made to order by the tailors down in the village. Instead of a belt, the pants were held up with a lightweight cotton cord inside a hem. While I tugged at one end of the knotted cord she told me she'd been to see Maharishi, and that they must have talked for an hour or more.

"Just the two of you?" I said.

"Ja, and it was so beautiful! I came away flying."

"Nice," I said. By then the knot had come undone. But Gunilla was hungry. "Starved!" she said. "Let's go have breakfast before the kitchen closes."

By that time we were no longer hiding the fact that we were together, showing up for meals and lectures together and even holding hands as we walked down the ashram paths. But that morning I wasn't hungry and wanted to stay in my room to meditate so she went down alone.

All that day I felt out of sorts and depressed. It was all the more surprising because of how consistently euphoric I'd been feeling up 'till then, ever since Gunilla and I first slept together. To me it had been a continuation or sequel to the way I'd felt on the plane between Paris and Bombay. To think this was happening, and happening to me! The most beautiful girl at the ashram was in love with _me_. The night before she'd even said so.

So why was I depressed and worried? I figured it was due to the rude awakening that morning. The desolation of waking up and finding her gone, calling up old fears of being abandoned. And then there was *post coitum* and all that, but since there hadn't even been any coitum to begin with there was even less reason to feel triste.

But it wasn't just triste, it was more than that. Much more. In fact, when you thought about it I had all kinds of reasons to worry.

First and foremost was the fact that Gunilla and I didn't see eye to eye on Maharishi. I knew that would have to change, one way or the other, if we were going to stay together.

And then there was her boyfriend Bertil. Gunilla had told me that even before leaving for India she had been thinking of splitting up with him and now she knew it was the first thing she had to do when she got back to Sweden. It would not be easy. They had been together for six years. He had no inkling of her change of heart and his letters to her were as ardent as ever, but the more she thought about it the more she was resolved, as soon as she got home, to tell him he would have to move out of the apartment they shared, and which belonged to her mother. After being away from him for three months, and with the new perspective on her life that she had gained through long meditation, she said she knew she had to be free.

Free. But what about me? What about us? Could we be free together? Or what if, as soon as she was back home, she discovered she was still in love with Bertil after all, or fell in love with him again? Or what if she found somebody else? She had told me about another meditator in Sweden, someone named Stig, with whom just before she left she'd had a brief but passionate affair, unbeknownst to Bertil.

And there was me, the way I was physically. Just a little taller than Gunilla when I stood up straight but probably weighing less. 120 pounds before I left for India and no doubt less than that now, after two-and-a-half months of the runs. Maybe Charlie Jackson was right. She needed someone bigger, stronger, someone her size. What if once she was back in Sweden she put her arms around somebody more substantial and realized I had been a will of the wisp? A figment of her imagination overheated by six weeks of meditation?

My deep, abiding fear was that when the course was over and I had gone back to Paris and she to Stockholm our little story would be just a little story that had ended, and now more than anything else I wanted that story to continue, as I was sure it was supposed to, had to, against all the odds.

And so we talked about her coming to visit me in Paris, or me going to visit her in Sweden, or both of us returning to California. But when? For how long? And to do what?

There were so many questions.

To seek answers we consulted oracles, all of which seemed only to reaffirm Reumah's bleak assessment of our future as a couple. All of which we readily discounted, as readily as we'd discounted Reumah's bleak assessment.

First there was the "Choosing a Mate" section of Gunilla's horoscope book that said a relationship between Aquarius and Capricorn was a bad idea, because of basic incompatibilities. But who really believes in astrology anyway?

Then there was the time Gunilla and I went up on the roof of Block 1 where Terry and Larry were lying on their stomachs doing the I Ching, with Jeremy sitting over them in an armchair, giving pointers. "Ask us a question," they said, as soon as we arrived, and Gunilla blurted out, "What's our future as a couple?" Larry gathered up the sticks and let them fall and Terry opened the book and found the right page and read the hexagram: "Take not a maiden who, when she sees a man of bronze, loses possession of herself. Nothing furthers."

Jeremy, his cane across his knees, looked up at me and leered. No, since his exorcism in the lecture hall he had not changed. Sitting there in the shade, grinning up at me, he looked like the devil himself.

Later, as we were walking down to the Ganges, Gunilla pointed out that they were only using forty-seven sticks, instead of the regulation fifty. Plus, they should have been sitting around a table and not lying on the ground.

"Yeah," I said, "and both the sticks and book belong to Jeremy."

And then there were the pendants.

"The what?"

"Pendants," Gunilla said. By then we were lying on the beach next to the swimming hole. We'd spread our towels next to the long flat rock Gunilla had been lying on a few weeks earlier when Larry had placed the stone on her stomach. Berndt was lying on his own towel a few feet away. "It's when you take a small object and hang it from a thread over two peoples' hands to see how they feel about each other."

"Why don't you just ask them?" I said.

Gunilla laughed. "Because people lie to each other, and to themselves. And sometimes they don't even know."

"Maybe you're right," I said. "So how does it work?"

Gunilla explained that if the people were neutral to each other the object at the end of the thread would go around in circles. If they were "in harmony" and good for each other it would swing to and fro between them. If they weren't good for each other it would go back and forth in the other direction, horizontally, cutting them off from each other.

"And who holds the string?" I said.

"Anybody. It doesn't matter."

"How about just hanging it from the limb of a tree or something?"

"No. It has to be a person. Someone who can pick up the vibrations between the two people and pass them on through his fingers."

"But don't you think it depends on who holds it, what the string does? I mean, depending on that person's feelings about the two people, he makes it go in circles or back and forth, even just a little bit, unconsciously."

"No. When Berndt does it he holds it absolutely still. He knows something about it too. Shall we try it?"

"Sure," I said. "Why not?"

Gunilla called Berndt over and took off her gold ring, the one with the inscription inside that read, "Bertil 4-2-'62." She plucked one of her long hairs, ran the hair through the ring and held it by the two ends, between her thumb and forefinger. We both knelt down on either side of the long flat rock, with Berndt standing over us at the end. Gunilla laid her right hand, palm down, fingers together, in the middle of the rock in front of me.

"Here, you put your hand down in front of mine, like that."

"Our fingers touching?"

"No, but almost. Like that. That's right."

The rock was warm. Slowly, Berndt lowered the thread of hair until the ring dangled just a few inches above and between our two hands. For a long while it just hung there, barely moving. Then it started going clockwise in small circles that gradually got larger and larger. Slowly the pattern changed to an ellipsoid, and then levelled out into a straight line, swinging to and fro between the two of us. Then it changed back to a circle, wider this time. Gradually the circle became another straight line, but now the line traced a wall between the two of us, as the ring swung left and right. After a while it seemed to want to form another circle, but instead it only made another sloppy elipsoid and then it stopped swinging altogether, spinning in the light breeze.

"Do you feel something in your fingers, Rikard?" Berndt asked.

"I dunno. Yeah, I suppose so."

"Yes. It is very tiring, doing this. It drains psychic energy."

"You feel tired?"

"Oh yes, I have a headache."

Berndt handed the ring back to Gunilla, who slipped it out of her strand of hair and put it back on her finger.

"Well," Berndt said, "you will get along for a while, but then you will have great difficulty. I advise you not to marry."

We all laughed.

"But it was Bertil's ring," I said.

⁂ ⁂ ⁂

That was the last full day we spent in Rishikesh. The following evening we were scheduled to leave the ashram to spend the last two weeks of the course in Kashmir. The plan was to have an early dinner then drive down to Delhi in taxis to avoid the heat of the day. As soon as we arrived in Delhi we would board a chartered plane to Srinagar. While everyone was excited about the trip and happy to escape the heat we were also worried about Prudence. Would she come with us or stay at the ashram, and if so who would take care of her?

It turned out we didn't need to worry.

The afternoon of the pendants, after Gunilla and I had come back up from the beach, we learned that Prudence had suddenly gotten better. It was Ian from Australia who told us the news, standing in the door of Gunilla's room which he'd found open while returning to his room, also in Block 4. He had just been down at the kitchen where Prudence had been sitting at one of the outside tables with some other people having tea. Ian said she looked completely normal, even better than normal, smiling, laughing, participating in the conversation. When Ian sat down to join them she'd greeted him by name and asked him how _he_ was.

For Ian it was nothing short of a miracle, especially since just a few days ago he'd seen Prudence being ushered down to Maharishi's bungalow with an escort of staffers and the full-time nurse, and "she'd looked like a zombie!"

For Ian to talk about miracles was in itself a bit of a miracle. Ian was one of the few people on the course I considered a hardcore sceptic. Like me he was a doubting Thomas—one reason I liked him—and after Prudence got sick and Maharishi had insisted on keeping her at the ashram, Ian's doubts had multiplied, making him wonder if Maharishi wasn't a fraud and coming to Rishikesh hadn't been a big mistake. But since then, because of some experiences of his own during long meditation, and now because of the transformation that had come over Prudence, all his doubts had melted away. Not only was coming to India well worth the time and money, he said, he was sure it was the best thing he'd ever done.

Sitting next to Gunilla that afternoon, with Ian silhouetted in her doorway, I too had no reservations about being there. It seemed unbelievable that only ten days before I had been standing on the cliff with Jenny talking about escaping in a taxi. Like Ian, I no longer had doubts about where I was and what I was doing. Or maybe those doubts no longer mattered. What mattered was the person next to me whose hand I was holding.

Ian said he had to go back to his room to pack. The departure for Kashmir wasn't scheduled until twenty-four hours later, "But you never know around here," he said, "things can change pretty fast."

Ian was one of the few people on the course who right away had accepted Gunilla and me as a couple, another reason I liked him. Now, when he leaned back into the room and said, "See you later, you two," I felt like getting up and giving him a hug.

That night I got sick. Gunilla woke up in the middle of the night to find me piping hot and trembling and mumbling things she didn't understand. All the next day she nursed me with tea and aspirin, which helped bring down the fever but did nothing to keep me from running for the toilet every ten minutes to eliminate more liquids, one way or the other. Gunilla kept asking me if I wanted her to go get Dr. Gertrude, with whom she was on friendly terms, but I kept saying I didn't need a doctor. Maybe in my weakened state Mary Baker Eddy had come back to take over, hovering in the shodows, waiting to claim the body when it did not die.

Luckily I had followed Ian's example and packed the night before, so when the time came to rendezvous at the upper gate where the taxis were going to pick us up, all I had to do was drag my suitcase up the hill.

But a few hours before the time came Gunilla didn't think I was going to be able to drag my suitcase anywhere, or myself for that matter, much less survive the six hour trip to Delhi. Despite the last dose of aspirin my fever seemed to be on the rise again and I kept asking for more blankets, even though it must have been 90° in the room.

Finally Gunilla went to get Dr. Gertrude up in Block 5, over my weak objections. Gertrude looked into my eyes, ears, nose, and throat, listened to my heartbeat and my breathing, thumped on my chest. Next she extracted a thermometer from her little black case and told me to take my temperature. The thermometer looked bigger than usual, maybe because I was delirious. Seeing my confusion, Gunilla leaned down and said quietly, "It's not for the mouth. You're supposed to put it in your, um…"

"Asshole," I mumbled, ever the diligent teacher of English.

Both Gunilla and Dr. Gertrude discreetly left the room while I inserted the thermometer for the required three minutes. When they returned I gave the thermometer back to Gertrude who looked at it, looked at it again, showed it with some surprise to Gunilla and then proclaimed that despite certain appearances to the contrary I was not sick, or at least not too sick to travel.

Which is why my return trip to Delhi was such a trip. Especially while driving through Hardwar, where Kumba Mela was in full swing. From that portion of the voyage I still retain a number of very vivid and very strange images which I'm still not sure are memories of things I actually saw and heard, or hallucinations.

Kumba Mela is a little like the Hindu equivalent of a Mardi Gras carnival, except that instead of thousands or hundreds of thousands of people there are millions, and the festival, if it's an important one, can last for several weeks and go on day and night. That year it was an especially important one—one reason George Harrison had been hoping to attend—and that night our little taxi made its way through the crowds of pilgrims like a lost boat bobbing through a hurricane. I don't know where the other taxis were. Probably lost in the crowd. Or maybe they'd taken another route, to avoid the hurricane. Or maybe they'd all sunk.

In the taxi I rode down in I was sitting in the back seat on the right and I'm pretty sure Gunilla was sitting next to me but I don't remember who sat up front next to the driver—I'm not even sure there was a driver—but through that window I do remember seeing more people than I'd ever seen in one place at one time, all of them all packed together, of all ages, dancing, singing, chanting, blowing on horns, beating on drums, in all states of dress and undress, in all states. There were gaudily painted, wildly decorated trucks and buses and carts crammed full of people, and camels and oxen and cows festooned with lights and flowers, and at one point, I am almost sure of it, a blue tiger riding on the back of a matching blue elephant.

I also saw the naked blue sadhu, I'm almost sure of that too, the one whose balls were tied to a piece of rope that was tied at the other end to a bunch of bricks. He saw the taxi from a distance as it was inching through the crowds, and came over and looked down at me through the open window and laughed and shouted out something over all the noise that I'm sure meant, "You see? I told you so!"

If I'd been able to, I would have opened the door and gotten out and hugged him too.

The next morning I was sitting on a plane next to Gunilla who had the window seat and kept looking out the window and looking back at me with this lovely smile, her mouth slightly open, her blue eyes shining. When she smiled and she was happy she held her tongue against the roof of her mouth, behind the top row of teeth. Gunilla still had two baby teeth that had never fallen out to make room for the two eye teeth that had never grown in. It gave her smile an innocent, childlike quality that was one more reason I loved her.

Outside, through the window, I could see Paul Horn and a few members of Charlie's film crew standing around a camera set up on a tripod, filming our departure and waving goodbye.

So we're leaving them behind, I thought. Hooray. And then I put my head on Gunilla's shoulder and slumped into a deep and dreamless sleep. We say dreamless, but how many dreams do we dream and where do they take us when we don't know we're dreaming?

My next occasion to use a rectal thermometer came a little over two years later, when I needed to check the temperature of my infant son. This time I realized the mistake I had made that night at the ashram and inserted the smaller end.

CHAPTER 28

Million Gold honeymoon

※ ※ ※

Cigarettes, saab? Fresh fruit? Chocolate candy, saab? Scotch whiskey? Million Gold?"

The boy squatting in the bottom of the flat-bottomed punt he had poled over next to the houseboat was not trying to sell me Swedish cars. "Saab," we soon figured out, was the Kashmiri equivalent of Sahib. He was offering to sell me all the other items though, and I would soon be in need of Million Golds. That was the brand name of a locally manufactured condom, and Berndt said that since our group had arrived in Kashmir and settled into houseboats on Dal Lake they had been selling like hotcakes.

Even with frugal usage, the supply of Prophyltex I'd brought along from Paris had finally run out and recently I'd been reduced to carefully washing, drying and re-rolling the last few for days we needed to be extra careful. But how many times could you use a recycled rubber before it sprang a leak? It was not a question we wanted to find out the answer to. So obviously it was time to restock my supply.

But there was a financial problem. A twelve-pack of Million Golds cost rupees 38 and my life savings, the money that was supposed to last until I got back to Paris, was down to just over rupees 150, about 20 dollars U.S. I had written David to ask if he could wire me a loan but that would arrive in Delhi and we weren't due back in Delhi for another ten days.

I suppose we could practice celibacy. And if that didn't work there was always Spanish style.

I leaned over the railing and called down to the boy in the little boat. "Those Million Golds…"

"Yes Saab?"

"Do you have packets of six?"

I didn't need to worry about being overheard. I was all alone on the houseboat, having been banished from the lecture currently in progress to go back to my room and practice the puja. It had been a kind of public flogging, set up by Charlie Jackson, of that I was sure. When Charlie found out that Gunilla and I had managed to wangle a room together, in spite of his efforts to keep us apart, he must have been really pissed and told Maharishi, which was why Maharishi had told me to stand up and recite the puja even though none of us had had time to learn it yet. Even so I did pretty well, getting all the way down to "*Shruti Smriti Purana-nam alayam*" before I stumbled and stood there tongue-tied.

We had arrived in Kashmir two days earlier, our plane landing just before noon in the little Srinagar airport. The night before, due to the usual delays, we'd ended up leaving Rishikesh at midnight rather than 6:00 pm, and since the trip down to Delhi had taken twice as long as expected, because of Kumba Mela, we'd arrived at Palam Airport in Delhi fifteen hours later than we were supposed to. For that reason we'd been told to board the little chartered Caravelle in a hurry, leaving behind our luggage which would be brought up by truck "in a day or so." An hour later, as we gathered on the runway outside Srinagar, shivering and yawning, a lot of people must have wondered why we hadn't also been told to bring along some heavy woolen clothing, along with our toothbrush and pyjamas. It was all too reminiscent of the night, two-and-a-half months earlier, we'd stood on the cliff listening to the roar of the Ganges fifty feet below, while waiting to cross the footbridge. Except this time the separation between us and our luggage was bound to last a lot longer. Luckily, in my delirium I had thought to bring along the Olivetti.

It was drizzly and cold, a sharp contrast to the sweltering heat in Delhi, but not a welcome one. We'd been expecting balmy, springlike weather in what was supposed to be one of the most beautiful places on earth, but this place looked like Goleta airport on a bad beach day, except there was no beach. On the flight over Gunilla had nudged me awake so I could look down through the window at an endless expanse of high mountains covered with snow, but now there was only fog and cold and the mountains, if there were any, were hidden behind low clouds.

Finally we were herded towards a couple of waiting buses, which we climbed onto, tired and hungry. The buses took us through the narrow, crowded streets of Srinagar, over bridges and along canals, finally coming to a stop alongside some stone steps leading down to some rickety wooden docks where thirty or forty shikaras were all tied up in a row waiting to take us on the next and last leg of our journey. A shikara is a narrow, flat-bottomed wooden boat, rising out of the water at both ends and wide enough in the middle for a cushioned sofa big enough to accommodate two people, and covered by a slanting roof held up by four poles. With the driver seated on the pointed stern, a few feet above the water, propelling the boat with a paddle or a pole, a shikara is a lot like a gondola, and Srinager, built on the edge of Dal Lake on a series of islands and peninsulas connected by canals and bridges, is not unlike Venice, but Venice as it must have been about eight hundred years ago, without the Piazza San Marco and the Doge's palace. Temples and palaces there were, but they were much more modest and built mostly of wood and crowded in around them were countless more humble looking structures, a jumble of tumble-down buildings housing stores and offices and apartments, ragged curtains hanging out of open windows, the buildings all patched together and delapidated, leaning this way and that, held up by timbers running from rooftop to rooftop or down to the ground. Catching glimpses of the city through the windows of the bus as it took us through the maze of narrow streets, and now gazing up at the three and four-story buildings lining the water, some obviously about to fall into it, the city of Srinagar had the feel of having been thrown up helter-skelter over night, but that night had been a long time ago. One had an impression of impermanence, but that impermanence had lasted for centuries and would likely last for centuries to come.

The shikaras were all painted wild colors and draped in vividly colorful fabrics and many of them had names painted on wide boards above the arched canopies: Lotus Rose, Srinagar Princesse, Silver Star, Happyness. One, with a broadly smiling, very skinny boy standing in front, holding its bowline, was called the Rock Hudson.

As people clambered out of the buses, made their way down the steep steps, and stood at the edge of the docks, spirits began to rise and so did the clouds. While our group divided into smaller groups and climbed into shikaras, Gunilla and I climbed into the Rock Hudson and the little boy handed the bowline to the man perched on the stern. By the time our little fleet was crossing the shallow lake on the way to its destination there was more blue than gray in the sky and the blue was bluer still in contrast to the brilliant white topping a dozen towering peaks that revealed themselves one by one as the clouds parted and disappeared like a veil being slowly lifted away. As people started taking in the spectacular beauty of the surroundings it began to appear that we were in Shangri-la after all and shouts of laughter echoed across the flat water, along with exclamations on the order of "Oh my God!" "Oh look at that!" "Oh wow!"

The Vale of Kashmir is a lush, lake-studded region that has always been fabled for its beauty. During the British occupation of India it became a favorite hill station for officers and their mem-saabs. Although the floor of the valley is 5,000 feet above sea level, surrounded by peaks that rise four or five times higher still, the climate in Kashmir is moderate enough and the soil rich enough to make it one of the most fertile farmlands in Asia, with fruit trees and flowers and vegetables growing in abundance, almost untended. By mid-April everything is bursting into bloom, which is why the day of our arrival there were flowers everywhere. As we made our way across the lake flower vendors rowed up next to us in roofless boats weighed down to the gunwales with piles of every kind of spring flower imaginable, and at our destination there were so many flowers in vases on every horizontal surface that the fragrance made you dizzy.

Our destination was a floating two-story dining room/dance hall on a barge which was tied up next to a little grassy island which was mostly taken up by a sprawling, two-story wooden structure painted green and white and ringed with balconies, called the New Green View Hotel. The hotel was where Maharishi and a few notable guests were going to stay throughout the duration of the course in Kashmir. The floating dining room was to be the lecture hall.

It was a wide, low-ceilinged, heavily timbered room with varnished wooden tables and benches and armchairs made of split logs scattered about. With a huge fireplace at one end and stuffed heads of tigers and leopards on the walls, the place looked a lot like a hunting lodge, and seemed an unlikely meeting place for future teachers of Transcendental Meditation, most of whom were vegetarian.

In front of the fireplace, in which no fire burned, Maharishi was sitting on his deerskin, laughing and making welcoming remarks and twirling a large pink rhododendron blossom on a stem. Sitting next to him was Charlie Jackson who ever since the Beatles had left had made it obvious that he was second in command.

As everyone climbed out of the shikaras and onto the barge and settled into benches and armchairs it was clear that the general mood had changed from the dejection and disappointment of an hour before to excited anticipation, tinged with hopes for a hot meal followed by a hot bath followed by a long nap.

After a welcoming Jai Guru Dev from Maharishi, Charlie stood up to make room assignments for the next ten days. Holding a list of everyone left on the course, Charlie would call out a name, ask that person to pick a roommate, then give the two of them the name of a houseboat. The houseboats, which we had seen as we approached in the shikaras, were all tied up in rows and connected to the Green View Hotel by a network of wooden bridges and passerelles. There were fifteen or twenty of them and they all looked like floating shoeboxes, decorated with a lot of lacy woodwork around the windows and balconies.

Instead of taking seats with the others in the dark interior of the barge, Gunilla and I had perched ourselves on the railing with the sun on our backs, so that the first time Charlie called out Gunilla's name he didn't see her. "Gunilla?" he repeated, peering out over his half-moon glasses.

"Here," she said, and raised her hand.

Finally locating her, Charlie asked whom she wanted to share a room with. Then seeing me sitting next to her, he added, "What girl do you want to room with, Gunilla?"

Sarah was sitting a few feet away. She looked at Gunilla and winked.

"Um, Sarah?" Gunilla said.

Which is why, a few minutes later as people went off to their various houseboats, Sarah went off with Berndt, who had told Charlie he would room with me, and Gunilla and I went off together.

The houseboats varied in length from thirty to fifty feet. Each came with its own cook and at least two houseboys, whose tasks included waiting table for all three meals plus tea, making beds, tending the wood stoves in every room and keeping the fire going under the hot water cistern on the roof so we could all take as many hot baths as we wanted, a feature that after the problematic plumbing at the ashram was deeply appreciated.

Like all the others, our houseboat was furnished and decorated in Anglo-Oriental opulence, with thick, locally made carpets on all the floors, and bookshelves full of old, unreadable books, to which, soon after we arrived, I added my copy of *Finnegan's Wake*. There were cupboards and drawers filled with real crystal and handpainted china and genuine silver-ware, and every room was full of musty, overstuffed sofas and armchairs with antimacassars. In short, the houseboats were exactly as their British occupants had left them twenty-one years earlier.

The houseboat Gunilla and I were on was one of the smaller ones, with only three bedrooms instead of four or five. Our bedroom was at one end, next to the kitchen. The two others, at the opposite end, were occupied by Geoffrey and Gunar in one, in the other an English woman named Dot and Annaliese, the healer from Germany.

Like many of the houseboats, ours had a deck on the roof with a spec-tacular view in all directions. That afternoon, when Gunilla and I climbed up to take a look around, we laughed out loud and fell into each other's arms. With water everywhere and mountains everywhere beyond that, Maharishi couldn't have chosen a better spot for a honeymoon between a Capricorn and an Aquarius.

That night at the lecture we were all given a long, narrow sheet of paper. On one side were forty-five lines of delicate, incomprehensible letter-ing. On the other was a transcription of the text in Roman letters, showing how it was to be pronounced by nonnative speakers of Sanskrit. This was the puja, the long chant mumbled by John, my initiator, in that smoke-filled room of the Paris Continental. It was also our homework for the next ten days, committing to memory those forty-five lines, so that when we returned to Delhi we could recite the whole thing, word by meaningless word, in front of Maharishi, who would then tell us whatever we needed to know and give us the mantras.

Not only would we have to recite the sanskrit text, we also had to per-form the ceremony that went with it, ringing little bells and lighting candles and pushing little brass bowls around on the table in front of you, beneath the stern gaze of Guru Dev, all at the proper time and in the right order.

For example, to begin the invocation, while repeating, "*Apavitrah pavitro wa sarwa wasthan gatopi wa*," you were supposed to break a flower off its stem, dip it into water and sprinkle it around the room. Twelve lines down was a list of items for which there were one-word translations, for example "*vastram* (cloth)." At that point you used both hands to pick up the new unused white handkerchief the person had brought, and moved it in a big circle, clockwise, in front of Guru Dev, while reciting "*Vastram samarpayami shri Guru charan kamalebhyo namah.*" Then came *Chandanam* (sandalpaste), of which you were supposed to have a ready supply on the table in front of you so you could smear a little dab on the handkerchief and repeat the clockwise circle while saying "*Chandanam samarpayami shri Guru charan etc.*" Then came *Akshatam* (rice), then *Dhupam* (incense), and so on. At the end of these various offerings came *Arartikyam*, at which point you took a candle, held it to a little lump of camphor you had previously placed on a little holder designed specifically for that purpose, and it burst into a bright, white flame, which you also moved in a circle in front of the gaze of Maharishi's guru, while the burning camphor was transformed into tiny threads of ash that hung in the air along with all the smoke from the incense and candles.

In other words, a pretty complicated little ceremony, all the more difficult to learn because none of us would know what any of the words meant while we rehearsed them. That night when someone asked Maharishi if we could have a translation, he wrinkled his nose and waggled his head and said, "Meaning does not matter."

It was the same thing with the mantras. Everybody knew they all meant something, were the names of gods which were the representation of essential elements or something, but Maharishi maintained that if people knew what these ancient sounds referred to while repeating them, their minds would remain on the level of meaning, which was always superficial, open to interpretation and debate, rather than letting the mind, thanks to the inherent virtues of those ancient sounds, transcend that level and dive deeper—letting the vibrations do their work.

To all of us, after two months of not worrying about making sense, this made perfect sense. And so we set about memorizing this long stream of meaningless sounds. At the same time we all chose to ignore the fact that what we were learning was a religious rite as integral and important to Hinduism as the mass was to Catholics—a fact we were all aware of, however, on the superficial layer of meaning.

But in fact, two weeks was plenty of time to learn the puja. Especially if you memorized it a few lines at a time, two lines in the morning, two lines in the evening, like dat like dat, as Maharishi advised, and spent the rest of the time sightseeing, enjoying the scenery, just taking it easy, so that when the time came for the "big push of energy" we would all need for the work of spreading Transcendental Meditation in our home countries, we would be ready.

So why, two days after we arrived, while we were all sitting around in the hunting lodge waiting for the lecture to begin, had Maharishi pointed at me sitting in the back with Gunilla and told me to stand up and recite the puja from beginning to end?

Yes, Charlie had most certainly been behind it. After hearing that Gunilla and I had disobeyed his orders and ended up sharing a room together, he had no doubt told Maharishi that the freeloading American who'd said he was a Frenchman had broken the moral code—now back in force since the Beatles had left—and was shacking up in one of the house-boats with the beautiful Gunilla.

Hence my public shaming. Walking back to the houseboat, I was surprised at how little it affected me. Maybe this was the beginning of cosmic consciousness. Being impervious to the slings and arrows slung by idiots like Charlie Jackson. It was also a powerful consolation to know that Charlie was writhing in jealousy every time he imagined Gunilla and me in bed together.

My only real worry was how the scene would have affected Gunilla. Lately we'd been making plans for her to visit me in Paris for a couple of weeks on her way back from India, as a prelude to spending the rest of our lives together. As I saw it, the only obstacle lay in the difference in our degree of commitment towards Maharishi—her absolute devotion vs. my relative lack thereof—which she sensed but we had never talked about openly. But I was pretty sure, for example, that if I did not become an initiator and Maharishi sent me back to France without my mantras Gunilla would not come to Paris and the end of the course would be the end of our little story.

And so, while walking alone back to the houseboat, I decided to learn the puja so well that when the time came for me to perform it in front of Maharishi, he would think I had taken private lessons from Guru Dev.

After seeing how well I did it he would have no choice but to make me an initiator, if not the head of SIMS Europe. At the same time I decided that between now and the end of the course I would make a suitable show of devotion whenever the occasion arose.

After all, having Gunilla come to Paris was well worth a puja.

It turns out I didn't need to worry. If Charlie had been hoping to drive a wedge between Gunilla and me by having Maharishi pillory me in public, his little plan backfired nicely. It also backfired on Maharishi. As soon as Gunilla returned from the lecture she came up onto the roof and took me in her arms. "That was so unfair!" she said. She seemed indignant, maybe even a little angry. She said that everyone else she'd talked to after the lecture felt the same way. "Why did he do that?" she said. "How could he do such a thing?" It was the first time I'd heard her be openly critical of her guru, and to me it was a step in the right direction. By way of celebration, we went back downstairs and closed ourselves up in our room and made love all afternoon until the houseboy knocked on our door to tell us dinner was ready.

After the free-for-all, chuck wagon atmosphere around the dining area at the ashram, meals on our houseboat were always a little strange, partly because they were so formal, but also because of the strange mix of people sitting around the table.

Because they were English, Geoffrey and Dot seemed more comfortable in that setting than the rest of us. In fact they seemed right at home. Watching them sip tonic without gin in the parlor, one could almost imagine that they came with the houseboat, along with the servants and the cook, in order to make non-British guests feel at ease and show them which fork to use with the first course, how to fold their napkins, and to keep the conversation going during the meal.

That night the conversation was all about shopping. In addition to the spectacular scenery, another reason tourists flocked to Kashmir in those days was for the deals that could be made on locally hand-woven shawls and rugs, handpainted statues and bowls and boxes made out of lacquered papier maché, not to mention gems and silver and furs. A rug that went for $5000 in Paris or London or New York cost $500 on the streets of Kashmir, and that was the asking price, before the haggling began—haggling being another amusing part of the tourist experience.

And since we had a lot of free time on our hands in Kashmir, that's what a lot of people on the course turned into, a bunch of blissed-out wide-eyed tourists, eager to haggle. That morning Dot said she and Mrs. Harrington had each bought two saris that were "absolutely ravishing" and cost a fraction of what they would have cost in Delhi. They had also seen a wide variety of puja sets, that they intended to go back and take a closer look at when they had more time.

As the name implied, a puja set consisted of everything you needed to do the puja, including dishes of various sizes to hold the fruit and flowers and sandalpaste and betel nuts and coconut, bowls for water and rice, a couple of incense burners, a couple of candle holders, and a little lamp to burn the camphor in—all of which were usually made of brass or tin. We'd been told that when we performed the puja for Maharishi down in Delhi we'd be able to use the implements already in the room where he would be sitting. But when we performed initiations back in our home countries we would need one of our own, and "a puja set in London or Frankfurt, my dear," said Dot to Annaliese while the houseboy took away our plates, "will cost you ten times what it will cost you here."

That night for dessert the cook had made what Geoffrey identified as a genuine "old Yorkshire apple cake," complete with clotted cream. While serving us each a slice and a dollop, Gunilla proposed a little shopping tour the following morning in the streets of Srinagar. Since before leaving Sweden, Gunilla said she had been hoping to buy a Kashmir shawl with money she'd put aside for that purpose. She'd heard that they were warmer than any other kind of woollen shawl and yet so finely woven you could pull them through a wedding ring.

I knew she knew about Kashmir shawls because she'd told me Stig, her one-night Stockholm lover, had one, which he'd bought during his own trip to India the year before. I wondered if she'd pulled it through the same ring that had told us she and I were basically incompatible. We were not incompatible now. While watching her scoop cream onto slices of cake I marvelled at how beautiful her hands were and she was, my exotic, erotic Oriental princess whose ancestors, I imagined, might have come from not too far away from here.

As the chatter continued I zoned out and imagined that all the others seated around the table in that cluttered room were members of Gunilla's family in that old world, whom she had brought me here to meet. While

I made polite sounds and pretended to be interested in the conversation, all I wanted was for that conversation to cease and dinner to be over so we could go back to our little room and use up the rest of the recycled rubbers.

※ ※ ※

Every houseboat had its own shikara, and some of the bigger ones had two. The next morning, after breakfast and meditation, Geoffrey and Annaliese and Gunilla and I climbed down the wooden gangway into ours—Dot having decided to stay home and practice the puja, and Gunar having made plans with Eva who lived a few houseboats over. As Gunilla and I settled into the cushioned sofa and Geoffrey and Anna-Liese sat down on the little bench facing us, Geoffrey asked me why I was bringing along my portable typewriter. I told him what I had told Gunilla, that since I didn't intend to do any shopping (since I didn't have any money to do any shopping with) I would find a tea house or café somewhere and write a few letters while they were busy buying souvenirs.

Our driver poled us across the water and dropped us off at a place where a set of ancient stone steps rose up out of the lake. Pointing towards a small street that led away from the street that lined the water, the driver said if we continued in that direction we would soon find a large souk or bazaar. He then reached down inside his many-layered shawls to pull out a large silver watch on a leather thong and said he'd be back at the same spot in exctly two hours, in time to take us back to the houseboat for lunch. Our shikara driver was a tall, wiry man who looked fifty but could have been thirty and who always had about three days growth of beard. He also had a gentle smile full of teeth stained by the hookah he smoked in the stern whenever he wasn't pushing or paddling, and sometimes when he was. I had deduced that he was in some way related to our cook and the two house-boys, but in that country you had the feeling that everybody was closely related to everybody else, all of them, according to a local legend, descendants of Noah. One big happy family, until religion came along to fuck things up, as usual.

I knew vaguely that Kashmir was disputed territory and we'd all heard that tension was brewing because of some sheikh somewhere who had just gotten out of or been thrown back into jail, which was why at the airport there had been squads of machine-gun toting soldiers standing around everywhere, and now in a muddy little park on our way to the sidestreet there was another small group of soldiers with weapons slung over their shoulders. Unlike everybody else in Srinagar, they did not smile as we walked by.

The sidestreet, actually a narrow, unpaved alley, was lined on both sides with little ramshackle shops, each one displaying an array of carpets, fabrics, flowers, spices, clothing, footwear, flatware, hardware, and just about anything else that could be grown, raised, made, dug up or discovered within a radius of 500 miles. The shops were actually little more than open stalls made of unpainted, weather-beaten boards, with the owners standing around in front waiting to lure you inside. Adding to the noise and confusion were bands of undernourished ragamuffins shouting as loud as they could, either asking for handouts or trying to drag or push you towards the shops of their parents or other relatives or whoever else was paying them a bounty for every Westerner they managed to drag in.

About fifty yards down the lane, where another road branched off to the right, we came to a rudimentary café with wooden steps leading up to a narrow terrace about three feet off the ground and fifteen feet long and a yellow sign on the railing that proclaimed in peeling black letters, "Srinagar Bar and Grille." On the terrace were a few tables and at one of them at the far end a man wearing a cylindrical fur cap sat in front of a cup of something reading a newspaper. I told Gunilla and Geoffrey and Annaliese that's where they could find me when they'd finished shopping. They continued on down the road while I pretended to scrutinize the menu tacked up to the railing next to the sign.

After my houseboatmates were out of sight I approached the man in the fur cap sitting at the end of the terrace. "Excuse me." I said. Then pointing to myself I added, "Tailor? Men's clothes? Suits?"

The man put down his paper, looked at me over his glasses and said, "If you're looking for a haberdasher, just continue down this street." He pointed down the alley that branched off to the right. "Savile Row," he said. "Fifty metres on your left. You can't miss it."

I thanked the man and continued down the sidestreet, quickly attracting in my wake a pack of about a dozen children, all of whom were curious to know what was in the light blue leatherette case I carried in my right hand.

I had decided that if I really wanted to impress Maharishi when I performed the puja I should be wearing a suit. The only suit I owned was one I'd had made by a tailor when I got the job at the New York Times. It was fashionably cut out of dark worsted wool, totally unsuitable for Delhi in May. And anyway I'd left the jacket back in Paris.

Savile Row turned out to be a relatively large, well kept shop with awnings out in front and in the back several people sitting on the floor around low tables on thick carpets busily at work in front of sewing machines. The proprietor, who was standing out in front smoking a cigarette, literally saw me coming. He flipped his cigarette out into the muddy street, shooed away all the children, and ushered me inside.

"I would like to buy a suit," I said.

"Yes, sahib," he said (not "saab"). "God has led you to the right place."

"But I have no money."

"Ah."

"Instead I have this," I said, holding up the case.

"Ah."

Wherever I went in India, the Olivetti had always attracted attention, and whenever I used it in public someone would invariably come up and offer to buy it. Since I'd never dreamed of selling it, I'd never asked how much they were willing to pay.

The tailor and I were standing next to a counter draped in different colored fabrics. He pushed the fabric to one side, I set the Olivetti on the counter and unzipped the case. Out of my shirt pocket I took a piece of paper I had brought along for the occasion, a blank page I had torn out of my meditation notebook. I slid the sheet behind the roller, gave the roller a few turns, then typed out, "What a good typewriter this is! Don't you agree?"

The tailor made a slight smile.

I punched the tab key, sending the carriage back to the left, ringing the little bell. Then I cranked the roller up a few more spaces and asked the tailor if he wanted to give it a try.

"That will not be necessary," he said, still smiling. He turned to look at me, sizing me up, and asked what kind of fabric I would like. I pointed to a bolt of light blue linen on the counter that almost matched the case of the Olivetti. He nodded and said my suit would be ready the following morning. When I returned with the typewriter he would give me the new suit plus 500 rupees.

"Eight hundred," I said.

"Five hundred," he said.

"Seven-fifty," I said.

"Five hundred," he repeated.

I looked at him, wondering what I was doing wrong. "Okay," I said, "five hundred."

That night I woke up from a dream in a cold sweat. I'd been trying to scream but couldn't. Gunilla thought I was sick again.

"No," I said. "It's just a dream."

She went back to sleep almost at once while I lay there watching the play of light on the ceiling reflecting off the water through an opening in the curtain. In the corner of the room next to the door the wood stove was making little clicking noises as it cooled down. There was the smell of smoke in the room. Both had figured in my dream.

It was nighttime. I was driving my old '55 Chevy through the roads around Portola Valley. My mother was sitting beside me on the passenger's seat, next to the door. She was crying softly, dabbing a wadded-up Kleenex to her eyes and nose.

We came to a sharp turn in the road where a car just ahead of us had skidded and rolled over. It lay upside down in the middle of the pavement. As soon as she saw it, mom started quoting Mary Baker Eddy. "Accidents are unknown to God… All is infinite Mind and its infinite manif…"

I got out of the Chevy and ran to the overturned car, knowing there was someone pinned beneath it. The car was my old MG. The right front tire was still spinning. The car was making little clicking noises and there was the smell of smoke and burnt rubber. At my feet a puddle of oil and gas was spreading quickly across the pavement. I knew the car would burst into flames at any minute. As I leaned down to look under the car I realized the puddle was not oil but blood. The person pinned beneath the steering wheel was Jill. She hung upside down, her head an inch above the pavement. She turned and looked at me, her eyes full of reproach.

"You told me this would never happen," she said. "You promised."

The next day there was a field trip to a nearby mountain resort called Gulmarg. Contrary to my impression while sitting on the plane in Delhi, the film crew had not stayed behind when the course moved up to Kashmir. In fact they were still very much with us, constantly looking for occasions to use up all the film they had brought along to shoot the Beatles, and this excursion was no doubt one of those occasions. It seemed to me that the person the film crew was most anxious to use up their film on was Gunilla, who, it also seemed to me, was a little too eager to oblige them and ignore me whenever they were around, even when Paul Horn was not there with them. And so that night at dinner, when the subject of the next day's trip to Gulmarg came up, I announced that I would be staying home to practice the puja, only too glad to spare myself the agony of watching everyone on the fucking film crew fall all over themselves while setting up scenic shots with Gunilla center frame. Besides, I had an errand to run.

The next morning, after our shikara driver had come back from taking everyone but me to where the buses were waiting to take them off to the mountains, I asked if he would mind making another trip to the same place he had taken us the day before, and wait for me while I ran my errand. He nodded once, removed the hookah stem from his mouth and told me with gestures to untie the bowline as I climbed on board.

At that hour the lake was an endless mirror, reflecting a perfect image of everything above it, everything above as unbelievably beautiful as everything below. Some people said Kashmir was heaven on earth and at times like this, when heaven and earth were one, you could see why. I tried to focus my attention on that heavenly beauty—the other shikaras on the lake, the white birds skimming over the surface, the majestic mountains—anything to keep my mind off the images of my nightmare that kept coming back in flashes, or the sight of the Olivetti on the seat beside me.

An hour later, on the way back to the houseboat, the bundle next to me in the shikara contained my new summer suit, a brand new shiny brass puja set, and a paper maché jewel box for Gunilla. On the ring finger of my left hand I was also wearing a big fat ring depicting Ganesh the elephant god. The vendor had sworn up and down that the ring was solid silver but he let me walk away with it for less than a dollar.

In my wallet I figured I had enough rupees left for a generous tip to the driver, a night on the town in Delhi, and two twelve packs of Million Golds.

CHAPTER 29

The lowdown at the Lodhi

❋ ❋ ❋

Back down in Delhi we were put up not at the YMCA
but at the Lodhi Hotel. It was the same kind of place in the
same part of town, except at the Lodhi the waiters in the dining
room wore white turbans with peacock feathers sticking out of them, and
some of the rooms had air conditioning.

Not ours. The room Gunilla and I shared did have a ceiling fan though,
that we kept running night and day, even after Gunilla got sick. She got
sick halfway through our second day back in Delhi, going back to bed after
lunch and staying there. It must have been something she'd eaten, she said,
that gave her an upset stomach and a low fever. She also said I should go
out and do things, see sights, take advantage of my last days in India, but all
I wanted to do was sit and watch her and be with her since these last four
days might be our last four days together.

It was Sunday morning, April 28. I was flying back to France on
Wednesday. Gunilla was going to travel around India and Nepal with Berndt
for two weeks after that, before taking their flight back to Stockholm. She
still hadn't decided if she could or would make a stopover to see me in Paris,
and I was certain that if she still hadn't decided by the time we parted company early Wednesday morning that would be it between us and we would
never see each other again.

In a way that was all right with me. But if it was going to end like that
I wanted to make the most of it while it lasted, and now making the most

of it came down to me sitting there watching her while the ceiling fan went round and round.

The room had two twin beds which we had pushed together into a corner. I had moved the table in the room to the end of the beds and now I sat there with my feet up on the foot of the bed and my hand resting on the stack of blank sheets of onionskin paper to keep them from being blown away by the intermittent breeze from the fan. I had bought the paper in the little store in the ashram village to type letters on and notes for my journal, but the paper was too lightweight for writing on by hand and too slick for the crappy ballpoint pen I had also bought at the ashram store.

Gunilla lay under the sheet on the bed next to the wall with her back turned towards the room. She was sleeping lightly, softly breathing. It reminded me of when mom got sick after dad died, and in those days she would get sick a lot. I would go to her room and push open the door and stand there for hours, watching as she lay under her electric blanket, checking for signs of life, making sure she was still breathing. Sometimes it was hard to tell.

Gunilla was not anything like my mother. If anything, she was the exact opposite.

Her fever had lasted all night, but when she finally woke up and turned over and saw me sitting at the end of the bed she said she felt better. Not good enough to go to breakfast though, she still felt tired and weak and not at all hungry. So I went to breakfast alone.

Breakfast at the Lodhi was served between 7:00 and 9:30 and when I got to the dining room waiters were starting to remove place settings from empty tables. I sat down at a table where Ian, Geoffrey, Sarah and Larry were in the middle of breakfast and invited me to join them. At the Lodhi, in addition to typical Indian items like pakoras and chapatis and curd and fruit, they also served western fare, so I ordered bacon and fried eggs sunny side up and hash brown potatoes. My choice raised the eyebrows of everyone at the table.

"It's my first American breakfast since I left America," I said. I thought for a minute, then added, "Almost two years ago exactly."

"Mazel tov," said Larry, who himself was sitting on the other side of a plateful of pancakes and ham.

Sarah asked how Gunilla was and I said she was better and would probably be fine by lunchtime.

"Good," said Geoffrey. "You'll both be there tomorrow then."

Tomorrow, Monday, was the day Maharishi was seeing the SIMSers for their one-on-one meetings. He was seeing most of the SRMers today. The meetings were being held in the house of some wealthy supporter in a residential neighborhood outside the center of town, so people would have to get there by pedicab or taxi. Specific appointments had not been made but people were supposed to show up roughly in alphabetical order between eight in the morning and five in the afternoon. For some unexplained reason the alphabetical order had been reversed, which meant that if your last name began with x y or z you showed up first thing in the morning, and if it began with a b or c you planned to get there later in the afternoon. This was fine with me except that late afternoon would probably end up being more like late at night and the more time I sat around waiting to see Maharishi, in a brand new suit that I discovered did not fit me all that well, would be that much less time I could spend alone with Gunilla. Since Gunilla's last name began with G we were planning to go out there together tomorrow right after lunch. We had set aside Tuesday to spend the whole day together, but who knows what would happen between now and Tuesday?

The waiter returned with two fresh pots of coffee and tea. After he'd refilled our cups and left I asked if anyone knew how long these meetings were supposed to last. Ian answered by saying when you figured in the course members who had already left and whom Maharishi had seen up in Kashmir, that left approximately forty people he was supposed to see in two days. "Eight to five," he said, "that's nine hours if he doesn't take a break for lunch, so that means less than half an hour."

Sarah said she thought it took a lot less time than that. Up in Kashmir she'd been sitting in the lobby of the New Green View Hotel when Lali had shown up for her one-on-one meeting with Maharishi and the whole thing couldn't have lasted more than fifteen minutes.

"More like ten, now that I think about it."

Lali was a pudgy young woman from Sri Lanka whom I must have exchanged five words with the whole time we were in Rishikesh.

"So did she become an initiator?" I asked.

"Well," Sarah said, "she came out with a big smile on her face and holding a flower so I guess so."

"I think anyone who's lasted this long is going to become an initiator," Larry said.

"Provided they can do the puja," Sarah said.

Larry shrugged. "Of course."

As the conversation continued in this vein I could see Geoffrey getting more and more uncomfortable. Ever since the early days in Rishikesh, whenever anyone asked Maharishi about the number of mantras initiators would have to learn and how he would choose who would become initiators and who would not, he would always answer by saying this was not something we should worry about, or even talk or think about. When the time came those of us who were ready would be able to receive the instructions. At the same time he made it clear that those instructions would be private—secret teachings he would be passing on from his guru to each new initiator. Even though becoming an initiator was the stated goal of the course, all of Maharishi's comments on the actual process—the initiator's initiation, so to speak—were always cloaked in mystery, clearly intended to discourage speculation, to make us understand that talking about it beforehand was not only a waste of time, but counterproductive, if not downright taboo. It was a taboo that everyone sitting around the table that morning was blithely breaking, except Geoffrey.

To Geoffrey's obvious relief, Sarah said she had to go back to her room and practice the puja. Ian immediately followed suit, leaving Geoffrey and Larry and me alone at the table.

The waiter brought my breakfast and set it down in front of me and I dug in, noting Geoffrey's hungry gaze, even though he had just finished eating. Geoffrey was a vegetarian and had been for many years.

"When's the last time you had bacon?" I asked.

He watched me pick up a strip with my fingers and bite into it. "I'd say more than five years now, since I started meditating."

"Mmm," I said. "Sure tastes good!"

"Oh come on, Geoffrey," Larry said. "Order yourself a plateful. You know what Maharishi says. 'If it tastes good eat it.'"

Larry was referring to Maharishi's laissez-faire philosophy that one's taste for "bad" habits, such as smoking and drinking and presumably eating meat, would diminish gradually and naturally the more one practiced meditation and the nervous system became refined. He also said that giving up those habits prematurely, before one lost one's desire for them, was often not a good idea and could even be harmful, because it would drive them underground, possibly causing stress. It was an argument we had tried to raise with Maharishi regarding drugs, when we went down to see him with George Harrison, but on that issue Maharishi had remained adamant, no doubt under the influence of the SRMers.

While Larry and I were trying to talk Geoffrey into a side order of bacon for himself, or at least having some of mine, Gunar approached the table. Gunar always looked a little dazed, but now he looked completely lost. His eyes and nose were redder than usual, and his shirt looked like he'd slept in it, after wadding it up and leaving it in the bottom of his suitcase for three months.

"Gunar," Larry said. "Join us."

"Yeah, please do," I said, pulling out the chair Sarah had been sitting in.

"Oh," Gunar said, "thank you." He sat down and put his hands in his lap and stared at them. "I am feeling not so good this morning."

"Why's that?" I asked.

"Well, Eva has left, and I feel so alone without her."

"Oh," I said, suddenly sympathetic. "When did she leave?"

"This morning at seven. I went with her to the airport."

"Where'd she go?" said Larry.

"Back to Norway."

"But that's where you're going too, right?"

"Yes. But first I travel around India for a while."

"How long?" I asked.

"Two weeks."

"And then you're going back to Norway too, to be with Eva, right?"

"Yes, but maybe something will happen. Maybe she will change her mind. Maybe her family will not like me. Maybe she will get into an accident. You never know."

I no longer felt sympathetic. Even though Gunar was my soulmate, born on the same day, with the same ancestral roots, I now wanted to reach over and strangle him. He thought he had problems!

The waiter came up and started clearing away the remains of Sarah's breakfast. Even though the kitchen had officially closed ten minutes ago, he put a clean napkin in front of Gunar and handed him a menu. I thought Gunar was going to burst into tears of gratitude.

After the waiter took his order and left, Gunar pulled himself closer to the table and said, "I suppose you have heard the rumor?"

"What rumor?" Geoffrey and I both said at the same time. Larry shrugged and bit into a piece of toast.

"I suppose people will say anything," Gunar said. "But it's so terrible!"

After some more coaxing Gunar said the rumor had to do with the reason John and George had left the course. "The 'real' reason," he said. "Or that's what they are saying."

"Who?" I said. "For God's sake, Gunar, come to the point."

The point, that Gunar had heard from Eva who had heard it from friends in Oslo she had called to tell them when she would be arriving, was that the Beatles left the ashram because they had found out Maharishi had been fooling around with one of the girls on the course. They hadn't seen it themselves, Gunar said, but someone they were travelling with had and had told them about it. Gunar said that Eva's friends had read the story in an article somewhere that also contained an interview John Lennon gave shortly after he arrived back in London.

Geoffrey's face turned purple. "How preposterous!" he blurted out. "What utter nonsense!"

"Yes, that's what I think also," said Gunar. "But that's what people are saying. And not only in Norway. Eva's friend said the story first started in England, but now it is spreading everywhere."

"What are people saying exactly?" Larry said. "Do you know any details?"

"Well only what Eva told me. That this person who saw it happen, his name was Allen or Andy or something. I am sure I never met him."

"Alex," Larry said.

"Ja, Alex. That's it. He went down to Maharishi's house late at night or early in the morning, not to see Maharishi, but to stand outside his bedroom and spy. And he says he saw them, how do you say it? With red hands."

"Saw who?"

"Maharishi and the girl."

"What girl?"

"An American, they said. Blond."

Larry and I looked at each other.

"And then this Alex, he went and told the Beatles and John got very angry and they ordered taxis and left right away that morning."

"How ridiculous!" Geoffrey said.

"Ja. It is quite silly, really." Gunar actually laughed. "According to this Alex, Maharishi had invited this girl to come and eat chicken and then to have sex with him. First chicken, then sex. It's funny, no?"

"It's not funny," Geoffrey said. "It's despicable! Disgusting!" Geoffrey stood up and threw his napkin on the table. "It just goes to show how they will stop at nothing to descredit him and everything he stands for. Well," he said, shoving his chair back under the table, "now at least we know what we're up against when we go home!"

Geoffrey marched off. The waiter brought Gunar a fresh pot of tea, filled his cup and left. Gunar added two spoonfuls of sugar, stirred, and asked me about Gunilla. I said she was feeling better.

"Ah, good," he said. "But after the course is over? Won't you be sad?"

I told him about our plans for her to join me in Paris, without telling him they were tentative.

"But then she must go back to Sweden. Won't you be sorry when she leaves?"

"The point is not to separate for too long," I said. "Maybe she'll come back to see me in Paris. Maybe I'll go see her in Sweden. Who knows?"

"But when you're apart, won't you be sad?"

Instead of stabbing Gunar with my fork, I told him that during the night I had gained cosmic consciousness and from now on I would never be sad again because all adversity would be like ripples on the surface of a lake.

Larry laughed and said it was time for him to go practice the puja. Not wanting to be left alone with Gunar, I got up to leave as well. Besides, I wanted to talk to Larry. We left Gunar as the waiter brought him a bowl of steaming porridge and placed it in front of him.

"Oh, thank you!"

I followed Larry out of the dining room, down a hallway and into the lobby.

"What do you think?" I said, when we were standing alone.

He shrugged. "He's only human. He never said he was a god."

"So you think it's true?"

Larry said he was sure it was true, at least as sure as he could be. He said he'd talked to Tom the morning they all left. Even though he and Rosalyn were no longer sleeping together by then, Larry said Tom was "really pissed!"

"Poor Rosalyn!" I said.

"Yeah." Larry sighed and shook his head. Then he gave a short laugh. "But you gotta admit she got what she came for."

"What do you mean?"

"Well, she wanted to feel Maharishi's vibrations from up close, remember? How much closer could she get?"

Larry slapped me on the shoulder and laughed out loud. His laughter echoed off the bare white walls as he went off down another hallway.

When I got back to our room Gunilla had gone back to sleep and lay once again with her face to the wall. It was not yet 10:30 and it must have been more than ninety degrees in the room. I crossed over to the sliding glass window behind a plastic curtain and closed it slowly so as not to wake her up, hoping to keep the even hotter air outside. The window looked out onto a barren passageway or courtyard with what looked like another one-story wing of rooms of the hotel, all of them with windows closed and curtains drawn. Sticking high above the roof of the wing of rooms was a street light whose neon glare had kept me awake the night before, along with the pulsing rhythm of the fan.

I sat down again at the desk I had set up at the foot of the two twin beds and looked at Gunilla softly breathing beneath the light sheet. In the other corner of the room, beneath the window, was another, smaller table where we'd laid out the puja set. By now I knew the puja so well I could have done it in my sleep and actually had the night before, waking up from a dream where I'd been performing the puja not in front of a portrait of Guru Dev, but in front of Guru Dev. He sat there motionless and looking as stern as ever but, as I realized with a sudden stab of anguish, quite alive.

Finally I picked up the crappy ashram pen and began to write, bearing down on the flimsy paper. I wanted to jot down the conversation I had just been a part of while it was fresh in my mind. I wondered if Larry was right and the rumor was true. Like Gunar, I had never met this guy called Alex but Jenny had mentioned him once or twice and now thinking back on that time it seemed to me I might have seen him down in the dining area having lunch with Rosalyn and Mike Love. But there were so many new faces in those days, with the film crew showing up along with a lot of other people, and the only face I was interested in getting close to was Gunilla's.

In a way it would make sense if that was why the Beatles left, on the spur of the moment like that. If it had just been a dispute over who had the rights to make and distribute the film, they wouldn't have left so suddenly and in such a huff. Underneath that wild, irreverent and provocative exterior, John Lennon could be a bit of a prude after all. And that would also explain what happened to Rosalyn.

While I was writing, trying to remember exactly what people had said, Gunilla rolled over on her back and looked down at me.

"Oh, Rikard?"

"Mhm?"

"I meant to ask you, what kind of bread do you prefer?"

"What kind of bread?"

"Yes. I don't know why I… But I want to know."

I anchored the loose sheets of paper beneath my plastic briefcase, got up and walked to the bed and sat down horizontally across it, leaning on my left arm stretching over her waist. She put her right hand on my shoulder. Her skin was warmer than mine.

"What kind of bread?" I said.

"Yes. Light or dark? Or French bread, what you get in Paris?"

I told her I couldn't imagine any better bread than a crisp, warm baguette, but you couldn't get a good baguette just anywhere any more, not even in Paris. "I also like dark bread," I said. "Whole wheat, you know?"

"Yes, yes." She laughed, her eyes sparkled. "Don't ask me why I asked."

She rolled back over on her side, facing the wall, her eyes slowly opening and closing and on her face the same smile she'd given me on the plane the morning we flew to Kashmir. The smile of a happy child.

"I was just thinking," she said, "for lunch I should have only toast and tea and then I thought of the dark bread they gave me to eat when I was sick in Austria and how good it was. And the dark Finnish bread you can get in Sweden,with good Swedish butter. Very thin and dark and made with whole…"

"Whole wheat."

"Ja. You like that too?"

"Yeah, it's good," I said.

"Oh, I'm so glad."

"When you come to Paris," I said, "I'll take you to a place where they make the best baguette in town. Once you've tasted it that'll be your favorite bread in the world, I promise."

"Mm," she said. "I'd like that."

I was thinking of a little boulangerie in the rue Saint Louis en l'Ile where David and I used to go get croissants for breakfast. Thinking about it, I wanted badly to be back there, with her.

"And a few stores down the street there's another place where they make their own ice cream."

"Mmm, ice cream!"

"I think you're getting better."

"I think that too," she said.

With the palm of my hand I brushed the hair back from her forehead, pushing it over her ear.

"Gunilla?"

"What?" She turned and looked at me, noticing the change in tone.

"Nothing," I said, and shook my head. "Nevermind."

I started to get up from the bed but she held on to my arm.

"What is it? What are you thinking? Tell me."

I settled myself back down on the bed again, with my arm stretching over her waist. I wondered if this was the right time, while she was sick and all. But would there ever be a right time?

"You remember that morning you went down to see Maharishi?"

She looked at me.

"In Rishikesh. We had spent the night in my room and you woke up very early one morning and had to go see Maharishi and give him a flower."

"So?"

"So what happened?"

"I told you. I gave him the flower and we talked and then he gave me a flower and I came back to you."

"He gave you a flower?"

"Ja. I told you. You don't remember?"

"You didn't come back with a flower."

"Well maybe I didn't. Maybe I threw it away. Who cares? What difference does it make anyway?" There was a rasp in her voice I'd never heard before. "Why is this so important all of a sudden, Rikard? What's the matter with you anyway?"

She threw off the sheet and pushed me away and grabbed the shawl that was bunched up behind her pillow and wrapped it around her shoulders and got up and went off to the bathroom and slammed the door.

I got up and paced back and forth a few times in that small room then sat down at the improvised desk and read over what I'd written, but now it made no sense.

After a long while Gunilla came out of the bathroom. She had exchanged the dark brown Kashmir shawl for the light blue cotton shift I'd seen her wearing for the first time when she came out of the back door of her bedroom and found me standing there with a towel around my waist. That time she'd burst out laughing. Now she looked very grave. She came over to the little table where I was sitting and pushed it towards me and sat down facing me on the edge of the bed, our knees almost touching.

"If I tell you this you must promise never, never to tell anyone else."

"Okay," I said, and nodded.

"Promise me you will never repeat this to anyone, ever," she said, "as long as you live."

Again I nodded and told her I promised and that she could trust me.

She started by telling me that in Rishikesh she had gone down early in the morning like that many times, to see Maharishi, whenever the spirit moved her. It was a habit she had gotten into, right from the beginning, she said, when he said anyone on the course should feel free to come down and see him any time. Gunilla said when she went down there sometimes he was with people and sometimes he was alone but he was always happy to see her. If he was alone and sometimes even if there were people with him he would send them away and have her sit down on the floor in front of him and ask her if she had any questions or if there was anything she wanted to know. I had seen the room only once when I went down with George and Terry and others to talk to Maharishi about drugs and I remember there was a low bed against the wall and mats on the floor for people to sit on and a big open window off to the right looking out onto the jungle garden.

Gunilla said when she first started going down there in the early morning she would always make a mental list beforehand of questions to ask him about the lectures or from her readings of the Bhagavad Gita, but after a while, as she began to feel more comfortable and secure in his presence, she started to feel like she could tell him anything she wanted, anything that came into her head, and he would always listen carefully and nod and ask her questions. She said sometimes she would fall silent and neither of them would say anything and she would just sit there and feel this, this strength and love coming off of him. She said she began to feel that Maharishi was a kind of father to her, the father she had lost, but better, because she knew that no matter what she told him he would understand everything and forgive anything and accept her completely for what she was, both good and bad, it didn't matter. When she was with him that was it, she said, nothing mattered, and she felt only this absolute trust and devotion that was so overpowering it would almost make her weep for joy and sometimes on her way back to her room that's what she did.

She said these early morning meetings with Maharishi usually lasted only ten or fifteen minutes but sometimes they lasted as long as half an hour or even longer and when they were over he would always give her a flower and send her on her way.

"But on that morning," she said, "you were right. There was no flower."

That morning started out like all the others, with her talking and him listening and sometimes asking questions but then there was a long silence, and after a while Maharishi asked Gunilla to get up and shut the door behind her. He had never asked her to do that before, but she didn't think much about it except that maybe he had something confidential to tell her and he wanted to make sure no one would overhear. So she got up and shut the door and sat back down in front of him and after she was settled comfortably on the mat he asked her if she would do something for him. Gunilla said the question took her by surprise because she'd never thought of her being able to do anything for him, it was always the other way around, so she said sure she would love to do something for him for a change and what could it be and he said take off her shirt. He said he would like to see her naked—well, from the waist up at least. She said she hesitated for a few seconds and then said of course, why not, one should never feel ashamed of one's body.

"Especially you," I said.

Gunilla blushed and looked down at her hands in her lap.

"And so?"

"Well of course, what do you expect? I took off my shirt."

"And your bra."

"I was not wearing one."

"That's right. I remember. And so?"

"And so I sat there like that, and at first he just laughed and waved his head, you know? And said I was so beautiful."

"How did you feel?"

She was still looking down at her hands. For a while she aid nothing but then she bit her lower lip and said, "Honestly, I felt… well, I would say I felt both excited and… ashamed."

"Ashamed. Why?"

"I don't know. It's strange, I never felt that before, but I felt like I wanted to cover myself, with my arms. You know?"

"Yeah," I said.

It suddenly seemed to me that this was none of my business. I had no right to know what happened next, and was not sure I wanted to.

"Do you want to go on?" I asked.

"Of course. I don't mind. I want you to know this." She shifted her position, bringing her legs up underneath her on the bed and tucking them in and pulling the little robe around her shoulders. I thought the robe must have been something her mother had given her when she was very young. It was that old.

"After a while he asked me to move closer," she said. "And then closer still. And then…" she shook her head and smiled, "Rikard it was so funny."

"What?"

"With both his hands he reached forward and held my, my…"

"Your boobs."

"Yes. And then he shook them. Just shook them back and forth. No one has ever done this to me and it felt so strange and so silly that I almost burst out laughing."

"And then?"

"Then he stopped and leaned back again and said he was tired."

"Tired."

"Yes. I guess the psychic energy."

"Uh huh. And then?"

"And then he well, kind of pulled his shawl off his sholders and lay down on his back."

"On the bed. With you just sitting there."

"Ja."

"Yeah, well, so did he, was he…?"

"Ja. I think so. He was,… how do you say?"

"He had a hard on."

She giggled. "Well, at least I think so."

"You don't know?"

"I couldn't tell for sure. His dhoti was all around him, and I didn't really want to… to look, you know?"

"Yeah, right. But then you…"

"No."

"No what?"

"You think I did him a blow job?"

It was an expression I had taught her. One of the first.

"Well didn't you?"

"No!"

"So what did you do?"

"I just… After a while I just put on my shirt again and said goodbye and left."

I felt like saying come on Gunilla, tell me what really happened, tell me the truth. But if that was the truth I didn't want to know it. It was not a truth that would make me free. Or if that was freedom, give me slavery.

And besides, what difference would it make?

And besides, I had my own emotions to deal with.

It could have been worse. I could have been seething with jealousy and anger and disappointment and outrage, but I just felt tired and weak and dispirited and disgusted and sorry. Sorry for *him*!

I looked at my watch. I had taken it off and set it on the little table. Unbelievably it said it was already almost one-thirty, the time the dining room stopped serving lunch.

"You want to go have lunch?"

"Oh ja!" she said. "Now I'm really hungry!"

CHAPTER 30

The secret of the secret

※ ※ ※

The next day, we went to lunch as soon as the dining room opened, then Gunilla and I returned to our room for one last cold shower, our fourth so far that day—outside the temperature was 104 and rising—then I put on my new suit and Gunilla draped herself in the light blue sari she had bought in Delhi when she'd first arrived.

It was easier to put on a suit than a sari. While Gunilla stood in front of the mirror in the bathroom, adjusting, tugging, unwrapping, yanking, re-adjusting, swearing, I sat fully dressed on the edge of the bed staring at the puja set on the little table in the corner of the room with the black and white picture of Guru Dev propped up behind it. The picture was the standard portrait that one could find on one the front page of Maharishi's commentary on the Bhagavad Gita. Gunilla had taken her copy and wedged it open to that page, leaning it against the wall behind the brass bowls and other paraphernalia.

I wondered what Guru Dev would think if he knew Maharishi was feeling up his female followers, especially the young and pretty ones. No doubt only the young and pretty ones. Feeling them up and maybe moving on from there, if he could. No doubt moving on from there, if he could.

I was pretty sure Gunilla was telling me the truth when she said that in her case he had not moved on from there. I was also pretty sure that if she had not just spent the previous night with me, had not been in the early stages of falling in love with me, he would have, and she would have let him.

As far as I could tell, that incident had done nothing to change Gunilla's feelings towards her guru. In her eyes he was then and still was now a wise man, a kind of saint, almost a demi-god, and if a demi-god wanted you to make love to him, or at least to give him a blowjob, and you had nothing against it a priori, why not? *Quoi de plus naturel?* What could have been more natural or more normal? All that meant was that this wise and saintly man found you attractive. And what could be more flattering? It might even speed up your spiritual evolvement.

Whenever Maharishi said evolvement or evolved, the word got all hung up in w's. "Ewolwed."

Why wasn't I angry at him? Why didn't I want to walk into that face-to-face meeting this afternoon and instead of performing the puja, punch him in the nose? For someone angry enough that nose would be a tempting target.

First, because I didn't want to spend time in an Indian jail. But second, and more important, I didn't feel like it. I harbored no resentment against the man, who to me had never been anything else. A human being like the rest of us, just as capable of making bad decisions and doing stupid things. Look at the mess he'd gotten into with the Beatles. Look at the way he trusted fools like Charlie Jackson.

Just as Gunilla's feelings towards Maharishi hadn't changed because of what had happened between them, neither had mine. Since I'd never put Maharishi on a pedestal, there was nothing for him to fall off of. As Larry said, he was only human and had never claimed to be otherwise. And while he had talked about the virtues of practicing bramacharya and storing up ojas, whatever that was, he'd never forced celibacy on anyone, as anyone selling Million Golds on Dal Lake would have readily testified. Besides, practicing celibacy was something a bramachary or disciple was supposed to do. Once you attained guruhood maybe the same rules no longer applied.

So no, I didn't hold it against Maharishi that he found Gunilla attractive. How could I? She was. If he had tried to come on to her as Charlie Jackson had, through hypocrisy and innuendo, that I would have found offensive. But Maharishi had just asked Gunilla to take off her shirt, if she didn't mind. And Gunilla had more or less willingly obliged.

If my feelings towards Maharishi had changed at all, it was that I now felt a kind of pity for him, because what he'd done in an attempt to seduce Gunilla—playing boobies, for God's sake!—had been so inept and pathetic.

On the other hand I also felt nervous and wary. And as I sat there staring at the portrait of Guru Dev I realized that nervousness in the pit of my stomach had nothing to do with the risk of screwing up the puja. It had to do with jealousy. What if Maharishi tried to make another pass at Gunilla before the course was over? If I were him that's what I'd do. The incident up in Rishikesh could only have whetted his appetite. He would want to strike again while he still had the chance, while this beautiful young woman was still within his reach on his home turf. The question was, would Gunilla resist this time? Would she want to and be able to? Especially if he increased the pressure somehow. She still hadn't told me if she was coming to Paris or not.

I undid the knot of the tie Berndt had loaned me, pulled it through the button-down collar, folded it up and put it in my coat pocket. It was too hot to wear a tie. I would wait until we got where we were going.

"I think I'm ready," Gunilla said from the bathroom. She came over and stood in front of me.

"How do I look?"

Even though I didn't like saris on Western women, Gunilla looked stunning.

"You're beautiful," I said. "Bey-ah-ew-tee-fuel."

As soon as I gave the address to the driver of the taxi he said "Atcha!" He said he had already driven out there and back several times that morning. "Many people!" he said. "Big celebration!"

"Yeah," I said, "It's graduation day."

"Atcha!"

The driver steered south and west until we were driving through a residential section where embassies and government buildings were mixed in with huge sprawling mansions separated from one another by high walls and wide straight streets kept clean by bands of sweepers and where the chaos and squalor of the rest of the city was no more than a vague and guilty memory.

The house where Maharishi was staying was owned by a wealthy industrialist who was said to have close ties with the government of Indira Gandhi. A turbaned butler met us at the door, bowed, and led us to a living room that was as big as a small barn. One side of the room was a wall of glass with sliding glass doors that opened onto a flagstoned patio and a well-tended garden with huge tropical plants that extended out to the walls on all sides and almost hid them.

In the large room there must have been thirty or forty people, most of whom Gunilla and I recognized from the course and with whom we exchanged nods and smiles and Jai Guru Devs as we walked in. Those whose eyes were open, that is. About half of them were sitting around on chairs or sofas or on the floor with their eyes closed, either meditating or mentally rehearsing the puja. Although most of the people were SIMSers I noticed a few SRMers as well, including Edna from Australia and Mrs. Ostrovsky from Brazil. I figured they were leftovers from the day before, people Maharishi had not been able to see. Or maybe they had messed up the puja and were back for a second try. Neither of them looked particularly nervous or upset. Mrs. Ostrovsky sat with her eyes closed in an armchair in a corner beneath a towering rubber plant and Edna was sitting at one end of a sofa chatting away with Ian who was sitting next to her.

At the far left end of the room, next to the chair where Mrs. Ostrovsky sat, was an arched entrance into a dark hallway where Jerry Jarvis stood talking to a guy about my age I didn't recognize. At the opposite end of the room, next to a wide doorway that led into another room and beyond that a kitchen, was a long table with platters of spicy food and fruit and sweets and pitchers of juice and lemonade. The room smelled strongly of incense and marigolds, the incense probably coming from the hallway and getting blown around by electric fans placed here and there. The marigolds were hanging in garlands from the edge of the table and other pieces of furniture and scattered loosely on shelves and tables all around the room. While standing there I realized I hated marigolds. I had seen enough of them up in Rishikesh where they grew like weeds, even out of cracks in walls, and to me their acrid smell was slightly vomitlike.

But there were also lots of vases of many other kinds of flowers everywhere, making the room look like a crowded flower shop or nursery, or for that matter, with everybody standing around in suits and saris, an Indian funeral parlor.

I noticed that some of the people were holding flowers and smiling broadly and it occurred to me that these were new initiators who now knew the secret of the mantras. Two such people were Berndt and Gert, the portly German I had shared a hotel room with on my first night in India almost three months ago to the day. Gunilla and I walked up to where they were standing in the middle of the room.

"Hej Berndt," Gunilla said.

"Hej Gunilla, hej Rikard."

"So," Gunilla asked, "are you both initiators now?"

"Oh ja," said Berndt, looking more amused than proud of himself. As for Gert, he nodded happily, holding up his flower as if it were a diploma.

"Piece of cake?" I said to Berndt, who knew the story of Charlie in the Continental. He gave me his wry, lopsided grin and said, "You will see."

While we were talking, Terry emerged from the hallway at the end of the room holding a flower of his own. He was wearing a tan suit and a dark narrow tie and dark brown wingtip oxfords that struck me as totally inappropriate footwear for a forest ranger. As soon as he saw us he gave a wide grin and a thumbs up with his free hand.

Shortly afterwards Jerry Jarvis re-emerged from the hallway and walked right up to where the four of us were standing.

"Gunilla," he said, "Maharishi will see you now."

"What?" she said. "Me? Already? Oh my goodness! Wish me luck everyone."

Before anyone could wish her anything she'd turned and left with Jerry, following him back across the room and into the dark passage.

Gunilla was gone exactly twenty-five minutes by my watch. When she re-emerged from the hallway I was standing at the other end of the room, next to the table of refreshments. While she stood there looking around, looking for me I presumed, there was an expression on her face I'd never seen before. She seemed stunned in a way, as if she had been in the dark and was trying to readjust to the light, or as if she were dizzy and trying to get her bearings. As I moved towards her the thought hit me that Maharishi had not made her an initiator. But then she would have looked crestfallen, ashamed, close to tears, whereas now she looked simply lost. For a split second I saw her as an abandoned child and my heart went out to her.

As soon as she saw me her face brightened.

"There you are!" she said.

I took her hand and we walked out into the garden. When we were out of earshot of the others I asked her if she was all right.

"Yes," she said. "It's just that… I'll tell you later."

"So are you… did you pass?"

"Oh yes." She held up a flower I hadn't seen before because she'd been holding it down at her side in the folds of her sari. It was a large rose bud, deep red and fragrant, on a ten-inch stem.

"Congratulations."

She smiled but it was not the smile of a child.

"Gunilla, what happened? What's the matter? Did he do something?"

"No," she said. "Oh no," she added with a short dry laugh when she realized what I was thinking. "No, he wouldn't dare. But I guess I'm… How do you say? All this build up and suspense."

"Let down."

"That's it," she said. "I am let down. And it's so hot!"

It's true that the temperature outside was several degrees higher than in the house. It was as if we had walked into a steamy jungle. Or an oven.

"Yeah," I said. "You must be stifling in that sari."

"Stifling?"

"Suffocating."

"Yes, I am. Let's go back inside where there are fans at least."

Back inside, while Gunilla stood at the refreshment table gulping down a glass of lemonade, Terry came up to say that he and Berndt and Ian were going to share a taxi back to the Lodhi and did Gunilla want a ride?

"Rikard," she said, "would you mind?"

It was not yet 3:00. I would probably be there until six at least. I told Gunilla she should go back to our room and take a cold shower and wait for me.

I walked with her and Terry back through the house and out the front door and watched her climb into the waiting taxi with the others. As they drove away another car drove up, a long black Cadillac limousine with smoked windows. The chauffeur got out and opened the back door and a well-dressed middle-aged couple got out, both of them wearing dark glasses, both of them obviously American. They walked past me and on into the house. Two more people who would see Maharishi before I would, further delaying my own meeting, keeping me away from Gunilla that much longer.

Back in the crowded living room that was not quite as crowded as it had been an hour before when we'd arrived I looked for a place to sit and finally found an empty armchair in the room next door, through the doorway next to the refreshment table where I saw the American couple engaged in earnest conversation with a tall, good-looking, dark-skinned man in a dark suit and a maroon turban—probably our host.

I sat down in the chair and closed my eyes, ready for a long wait. The nervousness was still grinding away in the pit of my stomach, making food unthinkable, making me sorry I'd eaten lunch. I didn't know whether it was due to my upcoming meeting with Maharishi, or to the look I'd glimpsed for a moment on Gunilla's face, or to the fact that she still hadn't told me if she was coming to Paris, or that I still didn't know, and maybe never would, if she loved me as much as I loved her, if she wanted to spend the rest of our lives together as I did, come what may, no matter what, that's all that mattered to me now.

Yes, that was it, the deep down source of nervousness. Wanting something so badly and not knowing if it was to be, wanting someone so badly and not knowing if she wanted me. Wanting. Not knowing.

Seeing Gert and talking to him again—up in Rishikesh we'd hardly spoken to each other—brought back that first night in Bombay and the long first day of waiting in the airport. The cancelled flight, the cancelled plans to take the train. Talking with Mia and Prudence, talking with Debbie and Nadine. The feeling of being someplace I recognized and halfway around the world from any place I'd ever been. Being a foreigner yet feeling I was home.

All that was so far away.

I remembered thinking on the flight from Paris how Rosalyn reminded me of Jill and how I'd entertained the thought, the possibility, the hope, that while I was in India I would both forget all that and at the same time regain whatever I had lost when my mother drove off down the street and into the night, showing me that in this world you could not even trust your mother, or when Jill told me she had slept with somebody else, showing me that in this world love, the dream of two becoming one, was only that, a dream, a false hope, a promise broken before it was made, an illusion, the opposite of absolute, that which is not, maya, poof.

I knew now that what I'd wanted to regain had nothing to do with them—Jill or my mother—or that time, then, but everything to do with me, now. I wanted to be reborn and give it another try, once more trusting, faithful, full of hope and promises that this time would never be broken and that I would never break.

What I wanted in fact was to go find a big tree, climb to the top, as far as I could, and fly away.

And here I sat, huddled next to a potted rubber plant, my eyes closed, full of anguish and desire. If it hadn't been tragic—if it hadn't been me, my life—it would have been funny. Comic Consciousness. He goes to India to meditate for three months and maybe find truth and freedom and ends up lost in a labyrinth of longing and despair.

It's true that in three months a lot of what I'd taken for solid and true had been swept away. Like one of those storms that would come screaming down from the Himalayas, unpredictable and unexpected, those three months had completely changed the landscape of my life so that I could in fact start over again. In fact I had no choice.

And this time I wanted to do it right. Doing it right, I'd decided, first meant doing right by the man who had brought me here and paid my way, even if he'd brought me here under false pretenses, even if he was my rival, even if he was a fraud—none of which really mattered. If Maharishi made me an initiator—and as Larry said, it didn't look like he was turning anyone away at this point—I had decided to tell him I was ready to go back to France and set up a SIMS center in Paris. I would start by holding an organizational meeting with all the Paris meditators, most of whom had learned to meditate when I did, and ask for their help and advice. Then I would give lectures, perform initiations, devoting myself entirely to spreading Transcendental Meditation throughout France.

I'd decided I would give it at least six months, and to look at it as a sort of personal contribution to peace in the world, a kind of penance for having gotten out of the draft. For even if I didn't believe in Maharishi, I did believe in meditation. Look what it had done for me.

I had also decided that, without telling anyone, I would put into effect some of the reforms we had talked about up on the roof of the lecture hall. I would not insist on a week's salary, for example, if people could not afford it. I would only take what they could afford, just as Eileen had done for me. And I would keep the mumbo jumbo to a minimum.

I found that I was actually looking forward to this and even excited about it. The only problem was Gunilla. Would she come to Paris or not? And if she didn't, would I stay there? I couldn't say. I couldn't imagine her not coming to Paris. Her not coming to Paris was unthinkable.

After a while I fell asleep, exhausted by all these thoughts and plans and by the unthinkable. By three months of destruction and re-construction. By having slept only two hours the night before. Even while Gunilla slept I'd stayed awake watching her, lit by the street light outside our window, listening to the fan go round and round. It turned into a kind of prayer wheel, that fan, the prayers as trite as the refrains of sappy love songs. Make this different. Make it last. Make her love me. Come to Paris. Come to Paris. Come to Paris.

I woke to someone touching my knee. It was Jerry Jarvis leaning over me. "Richard," he said, and laughed his gentle laugh. "It's time. Are you ready?"

"Ready or not," I said, "here I come."

The room was down the hallway through a door to the right that Jerry knocked on twice then opened.

Maharishi was sitting on his deerskin which had been spread on top of a low daybed. Despite the number of people he had already seen that day, he seemed wide awake and alert, sitting up straight, his white shirt loose over his rounded shoulders, his hands folded in the bowl formed by his crossed legs. There was the smell of candle smoke and incense in the room but it was not overpowering, since this room too opened out onto a garden, no doubt the same garden Gunilla and I had wandered in before the heat had driven us back inside.

By now the heat was subsiding. Once again I was struck by how fast the night descended there and with it the temperature, as soon as shadows began to gather.

To Maharishi's right, between the daybed and the full length sliding glass doors that led outside, was a table pushed against the wall where things had been set up for the puja. Without giving me time to pause in front of him, he nodded, pointed to the table and told me to proceed.

I performed the puja flawlessly, as I had performed it countless times those past ten days to myself and in my dreams. I recited every line smoothly and distinctly, without stumbling once, speaking not too loud but loud enough so he could make out every syllable. Without overdoing it, I even imitated an Indian accent now and then, letting my tongue roll back to pronounce the retroflex r's and l's and d's. It was all I could do to keep my head from wobbling. I myself was impressed by the graceful mastery of my movements, to which I added from time to time just the hint of a dramatic flourish.

I had been afraid that I might want to laugh, uncontrollably, as I had wanted to laugh in the hotel room of the Continental, especially knowing what I knew now. But as I recited those foreign words that meant nothing to me I found instead I had to fight an urge to cry.

I finished the puja and bowed to Guru Dev and turned to Maharishi.

He was not looking at me. He was not looking at anything. His eyes were closed. He opened them and nodded and motioned me towards him. There was lots of room next to him on the daybed but this time I sat cross-legged on the floor in front of him. He asked me what my plans were and I said I was ready to go back to Paris to lecture and teach meditation, if that was what he wanted. He asked how I would make a living and I told him about the job teaching English. When I'd arrived in Delhi there had been a letter from David at American Express, along with a money order for $100. David said he'd talked to Donahue, who was ready to offer me my old job back and even give me a promotion, making me his assistant manager. The money would be good, as good as IBM or better.

Maharishi nodded and thought for a while.

"And when you are leaving?" he said.

"Day after tomorrow," I said. "At nine in the morning."

"Alone?"

"Yes."

He closed his eyes and sat there motionless for what seemed a long time, maybe as long as two or three minutes. Outside in the failing light some sort of bird kept calling, maybe a toucan or a cuckatoo. Maharishi opened his eyes and reached for a half-size pad of paper and a ballpoint pen on a low table to his left. He tore a sheet off the pad, folded it in half and sat there for a moment, pen poised, looking not at me but maybe through me. In the upper left hand corner of the folded sheet he wrote something quickly then circled it several times. He jotted down a few more notes, underlined something a few times, then re-folded the piece of paper and handed it back to me.

I opened it and read. I was struck by how western his writing looked. It was the penmanship of an American school teacher. In the upper left hand corner was the word "Ing," circled in blue ink. Next to that on the right side

of the sheet he had written "Children up to 13." Beneath the circled "Ing,"
was the underlined word "Iying," and next to that, "Students above 13."

It was my mantra, the special sound designed specifically for me. I sat
there looking at it, seeing it written for the first time. We had been told not
to assign a meaning to our mantra, or to visualize how it would be written,
but I would have written it "Eyeing."

"My mantra is a word," someone had said up in Rishikesh, and I
realized this was his word too. This was everybody's word.

"When I'm back in France," I said, "am I supposed to initiate only
children and students?"

"No." He shook his head. "Anyone."

"Anyone, no matter what age. No matter what…"

"Anyone, yes."

"And I give them this second…"

"Yes, yes."

I sat there staring at the folded piece of paper. I looked up at Maharishi.
There was only one mantra. For everyone. Not millions. Not thousands.
One.

"You have other questions?" he asked. "Anything else you want to
know?"

I shook my head. I was dumbfounded. "No."

From a pile of flowers on the table next to him he selected a fat little
yellow marigold with the stem broken off and held it out to me.

"Jai Guru Dev."

I got to my feet, bowed my head over my joined hands, took the flower
and left the room.

When I got back to the Lodhi Hotel it was completely dark outside
and street lights were on and multi-colored neon signs were lighting up
the front of stores. There was no light on inside our room, but enough
light was coming through the open window so that I could soon make out
Gunilla sitting up in bed in the corner.

"Hej Rikard," she said softly.

I put my coat over the back of a chair, slipped off my black Italian shoes
that were still too tight, got out of my pants and laid them too on the chair,
then climbed up on to the bed beside her. In her left hand that lay open on

her lap she held the long-stemmed rose. It was beginning to droop. I picked it up and placed it on the nightstand next to my side of the bed.

"No fair," I said. "All he gave me was a marigold."

She gave a short, pathetic little laugh. More like a puff of air. Something between a laugh and a sigh.

"He wants me to stay on after the course is over," she said. "After all the others leave."

She looked at me. Even in the dark I could tell she had been crying.

"What shall I do?" she said in a little voice. Then she lowered her face to her hands and cried.

To me what she should do was obvious. But I couldn't tell her. It had to come from her.

"What did you tell him?" I asked, after she'd calmed down again. "What did he say exactly?"

"He..." She took a deep breath and blew it out. "Oh! This is so... dramatic!" She wiped her face on her sleeve. "He wanted to know when I was going back to Sweden." She was wearing the pink silk shirt with the tiny mother of pearl buttons halfway down the front. I grabbed a couple Kleenexes from the box on the nightstand and gave them to her.

"Tak," she said, and blew her nose.

"And so I told him... I told him in two weeks. But first I was going to travel around with Berndt." She gulped down tears and blew her nose again. "And he said, why don't I stay with him instead? Go back with him to Rishikesh? It was one of those questions, you know..."

"Yes, I know. Not a question. A command."

"Exactly."

Even though she was looking down I thought I saw a flash of anger in her eyes.

"As if he could just..."

"Just what?"

"Oh Rikard," she said and shook her head. "It was so awful! I could see he was embarrassed. I could tell what he was really asking me. People have asked me that before. But he didn't have the nerve. He didn't dare say it right out because..." She clenched both her fists and brought them down hard on her knees. "Because he's such a coward!"

She looked at me again and again there was that lost look in her eyes.

"Rikard," she said, her voice loud, almost a shout. "I don't want to sleep with a fat, fifty-year old man, even if he is the greatest guru in the world!"

I got up on my knees and moved towards her as she fell into my arms and once again burst into tears, this time sobbing, her body shaking. I held her and stroked her hair, brushing it away from her forehead and over her head and down her back. After she'd calmed back down again I put my mouth to her ear and kissed her and said, "How about if we go out to dinner you and I? How about if we go out on the town."

We went to a restaurant recommended by the man at the desk who said it was a good place to go for people who were in love. It was called the Mohti Mahal and it was located in the middle of Old Delhi and it had a large outside dining room with lots of tables and noise and other people having a memorable evening. Gunilla and I had tandoori chicken. Except for the bacon I'd had for breakfast at the Lodhi the previous morning, it was the first meat either of us had eaten in three months. We also ordered a bottle of Kingfisher beer for each of us and finished those and ordered two more.

As we were leaving the restaurant a man selling bracelets of jasmine on white thread sold us several and helped me tie them on Gunilla's wrists, so that as we rode back in the pedicab, with Gunilla's head against my shoulder, we were enveloped in the the scent of jasmine. As we wheeled slowly around Connaught Square black cars full of young people kept driving up close and slowing down and then they would speed away again, the young people hanging out the windows shouting and laughing and making obscene gestures as we kissed and kissed again in this land where statues make love in broad daylight and people only kiss in the dark.

"Wait 'till we get to Paris," I whispered.

The next morning we went back to Connaught Square where there was a travel agency where Gunilla changed her return ticket so that she would spend two weeks with me in Paris before going back to Stockholm, cutting short her trip to Nepal.

We had intended to spend the rest of the day sightseeing and shopping but instead we spent it in bed or under the shower.

The following morning Gunilla and Berndt left the hotel at 5:00 a.m. to catch a train to the Taj Mahal. When I woke up two hours later I packed quickly so as not to think about or feel her absence.

I lugged the suitcase to the front desk to check out and pay what we owed and the same man who had been there the night before said he hoped I had enjoyed my stay in India.

I arrived back in Paris late in the morning on that same day. Walking down the rue du Faubourg Poissonière on my way to meet David for lunch, I saw butchers standing out in front of the shops that they were closing for the day, their long white aprons smeared with blood. It was a holiday and everyone looked happy. There was a feeling of celebration in the air.

It was May 1, 1968.

Afterwards

The first meeting of the Paris meditators took place on a Monday evening a few days after I arrived. It was held in the Montparnasse apartment of a blind man who taught music and played the piano. I remembered him from the checking session at the Continental because when Maharishi asked people to describe experiences they'd had during meditation he was the only one besides myself with something positive to say. He'd said that sometimes while meditating the mantra would disappear and in its place he heard celestial music. "*De la musique céleste.*"

By Paris standards the blind man's apartment was quite large but with thirty people crammed into the living room and overflowing into the entrance hall it seemed a little cramped and cluttered, even with the grand piano pushed against the wall. I had been seated on a small sofa pushed against the opposite wall and after everyone was settled more or less comfortably in front of me on the floor or on various pieces of furniture I proposed we begin with "*une vingtaine de minutes de méditation.*"

I had come to that meeting prepared to talk about organizing introductory lectures and setting up a Paris center, but after the group meditation the only thing people wanted to hear about was my three months in India—what the ashram was like, what it was like to meditate for such long periods, and of course, since this was France, the food.

And so I told them about opening my door one evening after meditating for ten hours and finding a tray waiting for me on the veranda. I told them about bringing the tray inside and setting it on the little table and unwrapping the two chapatis and lifting the plate off the tin bowl of vegetables and rice that were still steaming and how it smelled and tasted better than any meal I'd ever eaten anywhere. And then I told them about standing on the cliff and watching the white temples of Rishikesh in the distance slowly take on color as the sun set behind the foothills in the west, and then about the hush of early morning as orange-robed sanyas-sis knee-deep in the Ganges just below us chanted prayers to Saraswati. I left out the bit about how we attacked those same sanyassis and the distant town of Rishikesh with a barrage of fireworks late one night or how Maharishi shattered the peace of the Valley of the Gods one afternoon with an invasion of helicopters. I just focused on the good stuff and as I talked, turning my experience into something far better than I remembered it, the way we tend to do with words, or the way words do with us when we let them have their way, my fellow Paris meditators listened more and more intently. Rose DaSouza, one of the two sisters David had written about in his first letter, was sitting on the floor just a few feet in front of me—later I learned that she had gone to London to learn meditation a month after I had—and as I described the physical setting of the ashram and what went on there she seemed more and more enthralled, leaning closer and closer, until she was hanging on every word, her eyes gleaming. I too could feel myself getting caught up and carried away, realizing in the telling what an extraordinary time it had been after all, maybe more momentous than I had thought, not only for me, but for everyone who had been there.

From there we went on to talk about long meditation and I described some of the experiences people had had, including my own little encounter with cosmic prana. I did not tell them about what happened to Prudence because it would have been so long and complicated and brought up issues I hadn't yet worked out in my own mind. Nor did I tell them there was only one mantra, or to be exact, three, as Gunilla later informed me. (Despite my masterful performance of the puja, Maharishi had apparently not wanted to entrust me with the full set.) The fact that instead of millions of mantras or thousands or hundreds, there were only three—or one—seemed to me unimportant, beside the point, as long as that was all it took to take us down inside ourselves, and bring us out again.

Next I asked them to talk about their own meditation, since that had been the main reason for the meeting in the first place—a kind of three-month check-up to make sure they were still meditating morning and evening and to discuss any problems they might be having and encourge them to continue. Predictably, a number of people expressed concern about sitting there while nothing happened, except for all these thoughts that crowded in and pushed away the mantra. I told them what Maharishi had told us, that during meditation all thoughts were useful and that, as a general rule, as soon as we realized we were dwelling on thoughts instead of the mantra, "we just put the mind back on the mantra." It was something Maharishi had said during the checking session at the Continental, but everyone seemed happy to hear it again. I also said that if they were still meditating regularly that was maybe proof enough that something was happening and it was not time wasted. I explained that to me what was important in meditating twice a day was re-establishing more or less conscious contact with a part of ourselves that we usually ignored, and even if stupendous things did not happen during that time, what was important was that contact was established and maintained. I also said that I thought the quality of contact during meditation was different from and perhaps more beneficial than what happened when we slept and dreamed. About cosmic consciousness I said nothing, but then nobody asked.

During this part of the discussion one woman raised her hand and told about an experience she had begun to have during meditation just after her initiation. It happened regularly for the first two weeks and then stopped, but lately it had started up again. She said she would be sitting comfortably repeating the mantra when suddenly for no reason she would feel her eyes fill with tears and the tears would well up and start running down her cheeks. She said when this happened she felt no emotion, good or bad, and she didn't know what other thoughts she might have been having at the time. As far as she could tell they were not tears of joy or sorrow. They were just tears and there were lots of them.

The woman was sitting on a straight-backed chair that had been pushed against the piano where it curved inward. She was in her late thirties/early forties, well dressed, well educated, attractive. The thought occurred to me that this was the woman who had stood up in the Hilton during the introductory lecture to tell Maharishi that one percent of the world's population was fifty million people and how absurd to think that he could teach them all to meditate. Now she asked if I could tell her why the tears were running down her cheeks.

No one at the ashram had ever talked about such a thing. I didn't know what to say, but with all thirty people staring at me I knew I had to say something.

And then the most astonishing thing happened. I realized how Maharishi did it. It was so easy!

To see if anyone else had picked up on it I formed my left hand into a loose fist and drummed the fingers of my right hand, one after the other, into the knuckles of my left. Ploppety-plop. Apparently nobody had, because nobody laughed.

I could have told the woman it was the cosmos weeping, and gone on from there. I could have become a real follower of Maharishi, *version française*, the skinny blond American just back from the Himalayas with a secret of his own.

You take a roomful of trusting, sincere people of all ages, doing all sorts of things in life, but all with a common interest in developing their inner lives, in focusing for a while at least on spiritual rather than material concerns, whatever those concerns might be, and at one end of that room you put someone who might just know—by virtue of three months in India or three years in a Himalayan cave, or a lifetime in the desert or a PhD in divinity school or a propensity to dream outlandish dreams—and at some point a charge of energy can pass from everyone sitting in that room to the person sitting at the other end of it and that person can become much bigger than he really is. While looking at those people gathered in front of me, all of them waiting to hear what I would say, it was amazing to feel the power that was flowing from them into me. Or could. All I had to do was let it, then tap into it, put it to use.

I asked the woman how often this happened and how long it lasted. She said that lately it happened not every time she meditated but almost, and almost always in the evening. She also said it lasted long enough for her to use up between three to five Kleenexes. Everybody laughed.

I told her I had never heard of such a thing happening and had no idea what it was or what it meant, if anything, but that it sounded good to me, especially since there were no negative side effects. I told her I hoped she would continue to meditate and come to the meetings and tell us more about this experience if it continued because we would all be interested in hearing more. I also told her that after the meeting I would give her a number where she could reach me—I had moved back into my old room in Eugene's apartment—and she should feel free to call me anytime until 10:00 p.m. The woman nodded thoughtfully and smiled and said thank you.

I had told everyone that the meeting would last an hour and a half at most. It had started at 8:30. Now I checked my watch and saw with a shock that it was past 11:00. With the consent of the blind musician and his wife

I proposed that we all meet again the following week at the same time and place and that next time we talk about organizing introductory lectures and setting up a Paris center.

※ ※ ※

As it turned out the next meeting would be attended only by people who lived close enough to walk there. By then the student strikes at the Sorbonne had spread to factories throughout France and had become a nationwide protest that threatened to shut down the whole country. In Paris the metro and buses had stopped running, gas stations had no more gas, and taxis, when they weren't also on strike, were hard if not impossible to find. There was no mail, telephone service was sporadic at best, and wildcat strikes at *Eléctricité de France* were starting to make Paris feel like Rishikesh. Luckily for me, since I'd returned from India with a negative balance in my bank account, throughout this whole crazy time the Institute for the Study of the English Language kept giving classes. Not at the occupied factories outside of town of course, but at some of the banks on the right bank where Donahue had been giving courses for years and the chief executives who still could not speak English preferred to ignore events occurring just across the river and maintain the illusion of business as usual, including weekly English classes. But most of my teaching those days took place in the little classroom just off the Carrefour de l'Odéon, where intensive classes were still being offered and students were still showing up to attend them, probably because they had nothing else to do.

One of those students who had lots of other things to do, especially at night, was a young doctor named Jean-Pierre Clauvel who after class one evening offered to take me around the corner to the *Faculté de Médecine* to sit in on a meeting of the faculty-student strike committee of which he was a member. After a tour of the occupied facilities and listening to a couple of speeches in the main hall given by students standing on statues, Jean-Pierre suggested we move on to the rue Gay-Lussac where barricades had been thrown up the night before and a number of cars overturned and burned. This was just before Gunilla was supposed to arrive on her stopover from India and rather than sitting in a French jail somewhere or on a one-way flight of my own back to the US I was hoping to be at the airport to meet her, so I declined Jean-Pierre's offer, but not without mixed feelings.

Those were heady days in Paris, especially in the Latin Quarter, where the air was laced not only with the sting of tear gas but also with the effervescence of unheard of new ideas—or maybe ideas that were not so new but this time might take hold and usher in a new world order. Walking through those streets you had the impression this time it just might happen, they just might pull it off, this youthful youth-driven dream of a world without hierarchy, prejudice, or injustice, where workers sat on the board of trustees, women took charge of their lives, racism was unthinkable, and it was forbidden to forbid.

But in those streets there was also a skin-tightening fear, especially if you were under thirty and walking past a long line of parked dark blue armored vehicles full of beefy CRS police who peered down through their barred windows as you sauntered by, pretending not to be a foreigner without a visa, work permit or *carte de séjour*, all of which I'd turned down when IBM offered them to me four months earlier and instead gone off to India with Maharishi.

One day when I had an afternoon class to teach I got to the Carrefour de l'Odéon and found it jammed with people. From my room in the 16th near the occupied ORTF building I had walked the two-and-a-half miles along the Seine, cutting in to the Latin Quarter at the Institut de France. But already in the rue Mazarine the going started getting slow because of all the people, most of them heading in the same direction, some carrying placards or rolled up banners. A lot of the marchers were wearing scarves that could be pulled up over their noses. It was a precaution that had become common since the police had started using tear gas. I even noticed a couple of people carrying old war surplus gas masks.

By the time I got to the Carrefour de l'Odéon it was so densely packed that I had trouble making my way across the street. Wearing my light blue Srinagar suit and a tie and carrying my plastic briefcase with Lado and Fries stuffed into it, I also felt a little out of place, although as I soon realized, the feeling itself was out of place. I could have been stark naked or wearing a space suit. The people swarming around me couldn't have cared less or been more welcoming. Most of them were my age or thereabouts but there were quite a few older people as well and even a few guys in suits like me.

I've never been comfortable in crowds but that crowd I was happy to be a part of and felt part of it in almost a physical sense. Somewhere off towards the statue of Danton, now adorned with six or seven students waving flags, someone was beating on drums and everyone around me was gyrating more or less in time to the beat, jumping up and down and dancing. Everyone was also chanting something I finally understood and started chanting too after a pretty dark-skinned girl with her long black hair bound in a red bandana said it slowly, shouting into my ear: "*Nous sommes tous des juifs allemands!*" Daniel Cohn-Bendit had gone off to Germany for a few days and his student visa had just been revoked by the French government, making him *persona non grata* if he tried to return.

Through occasional gaps off to my right, looking down the street towards Saint Germain des Près, I could see a line of CRS blocking the way. With sunlight glinting off their helmets, they stood elbow-to-elbow, truncheons at the ready. Behind that line I saw another and behind that one another line still. At some point I realized that the crowd I was threading my way through was not standing still but ever so slowly moving towards them, with a few of the demonstrators out in front shouting at the cops—not taunting or insulting them, it seemed, but actually trying to engage them in dialog. "Allez! Come on! Lay down your swords and shields!" From that distance I couldn't make out the expressions on the faces of the CRS, but it didn't look like anyone was about to lay down his hard rubber club and join the party.

When I finally made it to the other side of the street and stood looking back from the top of the Carrefour, I could see that the no man's land separating the demonstrators from the cops was about twenty-five yards wide and getting smaller second by second, inch by inch. Behind the three rows of CRS were several armored vans and trucks and men in army uniforms were setting up some kind of equipment that looked from where I stood like small artillery. For the time being the cops weren't budging, but if they charged it was going to be a massacre. I was already ten minutes late for my class and couldn't stay to watch, but I didn't want to watch anyway.

Donahue's classroom was in the courtyard of a building at the end of the short rue Antoine Dubois where it abutted into a stone stairway leading up to the rue Monsieur-le-Prince. As I continued up Monsieur-le-Prince and down the stairs I was surprised at how few people there were and how quiet it had suddenly become. It got even quieter as I pushed open the *porte cochère* at the bottom of the stairs and entered the cobblestone courtyard, the heavy door closing behind me. Three of my five students were already waiting in front of the door to the classroom, among them

Dr. Clauvel who lived close by in the 15th. As I unlocked and opened the classroom door he asked me in a sentence he had obviously been rehearsing if I had seen the "*manifestation*" in the Boulevard St. Germain. I said I'd not only seen it but had briefly been a part of it. This led to our first impromptu lesson of the day, on riots and police and demonstrations, during which they learned all kinds of useful new vocabulary. We ended with a pattern drill based on the expression "all hell breaks loose" using various tenses and modal auxiliaries: "All hell is breaking loose, is going to break loose, might break loose, has broken loose,…"

Three hours later, when all five students were taking a break for drinks and "free conversation" and I had been relieved by "Miss Palavacini" (despite the spirit of the times, Donahue still insisted that his teachers address the students and each other by our last names and the proper title) I let myself out the classroom door and crossed back through the courtyard. This time when I left the building I turned left towards the rue de l'Ecole de Médecine, taking the more direct route back to the Carrefour de l'Odéon. When I rounded the corner for a full view of the Boulevard St. Germain, I had to stop and take a second look. A hundred feet in front of me, in the street where three hours before there had been—according to conservative estimates later circulated by the government—250,000 people, there was now dead calm, no one, nothing.

Except for the debris. The main item littering the street was paving stones, thousands of them, that must have been pried up to hurl at the police after they charged and things turned ugly. There were also lots of shoes—mainly women's shoes, most of them high-heeled—along with scarves and other pieces of clothing. I even saw what looked like a few purses and pocketbooks strewn around here and there, but I didn't stop to pick them up and take a closer look. I just wanted to get out of there. As I sprinted across the street in the direction of the river the only noise was coming from a *garçon* in a white apron setting up tables and chairs in front of the café on the corner. The look he gave me as I went by was full of hatred or mistrust, thinking I was one of them.

For me May '68 ended on June 5 with the assassination of Bobby Kennedy and Gunilla's departure for Stockholm three days later. I actually learned of the assassination on the sixth when the news reached France. Gunilla and I had gone to Etretat for a few days—by then the trains were running again—and I was ordering oysters at the bar of a café near the water where they had a TV and the news was on and I saw the horrible footage of Bobby getting shot in that LA hotel. Seeing I was about to get sick the *patron* asked me what was wrong and I said I was American. He took my arm and led me outside to a place where I could sit down on a bench facing the sea. Gunilla joined me and after a while we returned to the café and sat at a table on the *terrasse* and the *patron* brought us the two dozen oysters and said they were on the house, along with a bottle of wine.

During the previous two weeks I had taken Gunilla on a lot of lengthy walking tours of Paris, sometimes interrupted by my having to teach a class while she waited at a nearby café or went window shopping in front of stores that still had windows. One afternoon I took her to the *boulangerie* on the Ile St Louis to buy us a perfect baguette but it was closed because of the strikes. The place where they made their own ice cream was also closed. One of the few places still open was the Alsatian tavern on the tip of the island where one night we had a beer with Clauvel.

When my classes lasted longer than an hour Gunilla usually stayed in my room to meditate and then go down to the Seine to find a place to sunbathe in her bikini because she needed to work on her tan before she went back to Sweden. Her favorite spot was right at the end of the downriver side of the long slender island, just a short walk from the rue Paul Dupuy, where she would spread herself out on a towel at the foot of the original Statue of Liberty. I would join her there after work, inevitably scattering the flock of men who had gathered to gawk, a few of whom would at some point have sat down next to her and tried to strike up a conversation. I told her just to ignore them, and wished I could just ignore them.

No matter how philosophical I always tried to be on those occasions, no matter how often Gunilla had told me not to worry, that she loved me and me only, every time I would start across the Pont de Grenelle and see her in the distance lying nearly naked at the bottom of the statue with a loose circle of hungry males standing nearby trying to look nonchalant, like some sort of unwanted body guard, I would always get this knot in the pit of my stomach. For some reason, at those times I would think of the naked blue sadhu and wish he were there.

When I wasn't teaching and we weren't sunbathing on the banks of the Seine or in the Bois de Boulogne or strolling through Paris or meeting friends for dinner and a movie, Gunilla and I would stay holed up in my little room and make love and talk about getting married. We decided she would come back to visit me in October, before her classes started up in Stockholm, and in December I would go visit her in Sweden.

Which was exactly what happened. Except that when I went to Sweden I stayed there. During the next six months I learned Swedish and Gunilla and I went on a lecture tour to spread Transcendental Meditation throughout Northern Sweden. We got as far as the little ski village of Åre, where we were put up in a luxury hotel in exchange for lessons in yoga and meditation. One day when we had the afternoon off we drove Gunilla and Bertil's old Volvo over the mountains into Norway and down the other side to the tiny fishing village that my mother's father had abandoned in the 1890s to escape a short hard life of poverty and seek his fortune in the promised land across the sea.

And in April in the little coastal town of Västervik south of Stockholm Gunilla and I had a hippie wedding with all our friends from SIMS-Sverige in attendance, including Bertil and his new girlfriend and Berndt who had warned us never to get married.

And in June I returned to the States with my new bride to introduce her to my mother who, to celebrate the occasion, overcooked a roast beef which neither of us took a bite of because by then we were strict vegetarians.

After a few days with my mother in her new house in La Crescenta we escaped up to Santa Barbara where I walked through the door of the French Department at UCSB and they offered me a job as a TA if I enrolled in their graduate program.

And so I set out again on a career that I was not made for, with a woman who was not made for me, was not even in my style, and none of it made any sense until I finally sat down to write about it.

After I left India that feeling of fullness and expansion that used to come over me while driving the MG or gazing at the back of Notre Dame or fingering a few strands of Gunilla's hair gradually became fainter and fainter, occurring less and less often until it finally stopped happening altogether and became a distant memory that in its turn began to fade.

And then forty years later, after I'd completed the first draft of this book and brought it back from the shop where I'd had it copied and printed in order to send it off to an agent who read only hard copy, I reached into the bag and pulled out the box and opened it and took out the printed manuscript and held it in both hands, feeling its heft and substance, and there it was again, that tantalizing sense of fullness—a momentary, ever so subtle shift into another dimension, or at least the awareness that another dimension existed—a shadowy recollection of something that I thought I'd lost. As I flipped through the pages, all 400 of them, I felt my hands grow bigger and my body grow lighter, as if I were being lifted up towards the something that has always been there, leading me towards the someone I've been waiting to become.

22316681R00188

Made in the USA
Charleston, SC
16 September 2013